Strategic Management During a Pandemic

The COVID-19 pandemic changed world dynamics, working scenarios, as well as professional and emotional dimensions. The virus has emerged as a significant threat for the continuity of business. Keeping the gravity of the problem in mind, companies must understand the need for change and must now update their strategy to account for pandemics.

The next pandemic may be more severe than the current one, meaning that organizations need to devise mechanisms and business models to fight with these situations and maintain business continuity. They should not only look forward to saving plants, machinery and infrastructure, but also concentrate on employee welfare, customer engagement and satisfaction during this crisis time. The book will not only present the evidence of various effective solutions to run a business in the time of a pandemic, but also put forward the new models and practices of business being followed by people at the time of crisis. It aims to create a bridge between existing business models and proposed business solutions, focusing on existing theories and most importantly case studies from the recent happenings.

This rich collection of chapters will provide insights regarding the business challenges, opportunities and practices during pandemic situations like COVID-19, making it particularly valuable to researchers, academics and students in the fields of strategic management, leadership and disaster management.

Vikas Kumar is a professor at Chaudhary Bansi Lal University, Bhiwani, India.

Gaurav Gupta is an assistant professor of Marketing at CHRIST (Deemed to be University), NCR, India.

Routledge Research in Strategic Management

This series explores, develops and critiques the numerous models and frameworks designed to assist in strategic decision-making in internal and external environments. It publishes scholarly research in all methodologies and perspectives that comprise the discipline, and welcomes diverse multi-disciplinary research methods, including qualitative and quantitative studies, and conceptual and computational models. It also welcomes the practical application of the strategic management process to a business world inspired by new economic paradigms.

Strategic Analysis
Processes and Tools
Andrea Beretta Zanoni

Strategic Management and the Circular Economy
Marcello Tonelli and Nicoló Cristoni

Strategic and Innovative Pricing
Price Models for a Digital Economy
Mathias Cöster, Einar Iveroth, Nils-Göran Olve, Carl-Johan Petri and Alf Westelius

Competitive International Strategy
Key Implementation Issues
Edited by Anders Pehrsson

Ambidextrous Strategy
Antecedents, Strategic Choices, and Performance
Agnieszka Zakrzewska-Bielawska

Strategic Management During a Pandemic
Edited by Vikas Kumar and Gaurav Gupta

Strategic Management During a Pandemic

Edited by
Vikas Kumar and Gaurav Gupta

Routledge
Taylor & Francis Group
NEW YORK AND LONDON

First published 2022
by Routledge
605 Third Avenue, New York, NY 10158

and by Routledge
2 Park Square, Milton Park, Abingdon, Oxon OX14 4RN

Routledge is an imprint of the Taylor & Francis Group, an informa business

Library of Congress Cataloging-in-Publication Data
Names: Kumar, Vikas (Writer on industrial management), editor. |
Gupta, Gaurav, 1986-editor.
Title: Strategic management during a pandemic / edited by Vikas Kumar
and Gaurav Gupta.
Description: New York, NY : Routledge, 2022. |
Series: Routledge research in strategic management ; 6 |
Includes bibliographical references and index.
Identifiers: LCCN 2021009828 (print) | LCCN 2021009829 (ebook) |
ISBN 9780367646479 (hardback) | ISBN 9780367646509 (paperback) |
ISBN 9781003125648 (ebook)
Subjects: LCSH: Strategic planning. | Organizational change. |
Crisis management. | COVID-19 (Disease)–Economic aspects.
Classification: LCC HD30.28 .S73956 2022 (print) |
LCC HD30.28 (ebook) | DDC 658.4/012–dc23
LC record available at https://lccn.loc.gov/2021009828
LC ebook record available at https://lccn.loc.gov/2021009829

ISBN: 978-0-367-64647-9 (hbk)
ISBN: 978-0-367-64650-9 (pbk)
ISBN: 978-1-003-12564-8 (ebk)

DOI: 10.4324/9781003125648

Typeset in Sabon
by Newgen Publishing UK

Contents

Figures

Tables

About the Contributors

Faisal Ahmed is an associate professor of International Business at FORE School of Management, New Delhi, India. He holds PhD and master's degrees from India and an executive certification in geopolitical analysis from Geneva. His research and consulting areas include Indo-Pacific/China trade and geopolitics, economic integration, South-South Cooperation, and, ocean diplomacy. He held the position of consultant to the United Nations and other organizations. He has led projects supported by the Ministry of Commerce and Industry, Government of India. Dr. Ahmed has published research papers in journals indexed in Scopus, Clarivate and ABDC. He has published one textbook, two edited books, several research papers as well as articles in leading newspapers including *The Hindu Business Line*, *The Economic Times*, *South China Morning Post* and *The Straits Times*, among others. He is frequently interviewed as an expert by national and international media including Rajya Sabha TV, Vietnam TV and the BBC.

Subrata Chattopadhyay is an MSc, MBA and PhD from IIT-ISM Dhanbad, and is currently a professor at the University of Engineering and Management, Kolkata. He has contributed to more than 40 international journals and published more than 23 papers in conferences. Besides, he has authored three books on Computations in Estate Management, Transport Management and Values and Ethics for Engineers and Managers and was editor of the book published at the Sustainable Development Conference, MDI Murshidabad, 2018. He has also published three cases in Scopus-indexed journals. He is on the editorial board of five international journals and has been conferred the prestigious Certified Management Teacher by MTC-Global for his innovative and dedicated teaching. He has successfully chaired and been invited as keynote speaker in several conferences in South Asia. He was conferred the prestigious MTC Global Top Thinkers award in 2015. In 2019 he was awarded Mentor of the Year by HRD India.

Manoj Gour Chintaluri is a management professional with over 25 years of experience at various levels of leadership in industries across

India and the Middle East. His core area has been Sales, Service and Marketing operations. The larger part of his experience is in Telecom, Alcobev, and the building materials industry. He has been associated with well-known brands in his career, namely McDowell, Knorr, Wheel, Brown & Polson, Haywards, Airtel, Docomo, Dulux, Racold and Ariston to name a few. In October 2020 he joined MDI on their Murshidabad campus faculty in the area of Marketing. He is an Alumni of NMIMS, Mumbai batch of 1998, and has been awarded PhD in 2020 from Gitam University, Visakhapatnam.

Varun Chotia is currently working as an assistant professor, Economics and Program Chair at Jaipuria Institute of Management, Jaipur Campus, Jaipur, Rajasthan, India. Prior to this, he has worked at LM Thapar School of Management, Thapar Institute of Engineering and Technology (Deemed to be a University). He has completed his PhD in Economics from the Department of Economics and Finance, Birla Institute of Technology and Science, Pilani. Before coming into research, he had almost two years of corporate experience working as a business analyst in corporate firms like IMS Health and Accenture Management Consulting. He has authored a number of research papers in international and national journals.

Archana Choudhary did her MBA at L.N. Mishra Institute of Social Sciences, Patna, and her PhD at KIIT University, Bhubaneswar. She is a faculty in the area of OB and HR at Birla Global University, Bhubaneswar. She has held the responsibility of FDP and National Seminar Coordinator for conducting a number of AICTE sponsored Faculty Development Programs and National Seminars and has a number of publications to her credit. She has conducted a number of MDPs and FDPs. She has been invited to chair sessions on HR and OB conferences. She has also attended a few workshops at Cornell University, New York, USA. Her research interests are in the area of turnaround management, entrepreneurship, learning and its implications, organizational change and career management.

Arunava Dalal is a BE from NIT Durgapur and PGDM from Symbiosis, Pune. He has over 16 years of industry experience in the marketing of products, new product development and leading and managing channel sales in the service sector. He has organized market studies, analyzed competitive moves and developed counters, reformed product packaging based on market needs, campaigned and enhanced brand visibility, resulting in enhanced market share, and handled product management. He is currently pursuing his PhD and has joined academe for his passion for teaching. His interest areas are service marketing, consumer behavior and areas related to sustainable marketing.

Ajay Kumar Ganguly has worked at Syamaprasad College, Kolkata, since November 2003. From 2011 to 2014, he was the Convener of Routine

Committee of Syamaprasad College. Academically, Prof. Ganguly has successfully completed MPhil, MCom and MBA and he has also qualified UGC NET. He is a doctoral student under University of Engineering and Management, Kolkata, and his doctoral research is on the impact of technological adoption in the service industry. His research interest lies in the domain of Service Marketing, particularly in the financial sector. He has published five articles in ISSN journals and presented a paper in the conference at the University of Pune in 2014.

Anu Gupta received BTech in Chemical Engineering from Punjab Technical University, India, and then MTech in Polymers from the Punjab University, Chandigarh, India. She has worked in the area of sustainable materials for her doctoral thesis at Indira Gandhi National Open University, New Delhi, India. She has been a recipient of the prestigious NFP (Government of the Netherlands) and DAAD (Government of Germany) fellowships. She was given an Early Career Award in the International Chemical Congress of Pacific Basin Societies (Pacifichem 2015), Honolulu, USA, in 2015 by the American Chemical Society. She has completed a research project sponsored by the department of Science & Technology, Government of India, under the Fast Track Young Scientist Scheme. She has also received grants from CSIR (India), Author Aid (UK), Education Strategy Center (Ethiopia), Society for Education and Research Development (India), Sandia Laboratories (USA) and the Indian National Science Academy. Dr. Gupta has been an active member of the International Union of Pure and Applied Chemistry, Indian Society for Technical Education, Society for Education & Research Development, Electrochemical Society (USA) and the International Association of Engineers. At present, Dr. Anu Gupta is working as assistant professor in the Department of Environmental Science and Engineering at Guru Jambheshwar University of Science and Technology, Hisar, India.

Gaurav Gupta has earned a doctorate in the area of Marketing from Punjabi University, Patiala. He has also studied marketing at the prestigious Wilkes University, Pennsylvania, USA, and teaching methodologies at IIM-Kozhikode. He has presented his research paper at IIM-Ahmedabad, IIM-Indore, IIM-Bangalore and has been included in the paper review panel of many Scopus-indexed journals. His papers have been published in ABDC listed/Scopus-indexed journals. He is a recipient of various fellowships awarded by the European Union and IIM-Bangalore. He got an offer of a doctoral fellowship from ICSSR (Ministry of HRD, India) and has been appointed as a member of Advisory Board for Cleveland Professional University, USA. At present Dr. Gupta is associated with Christ University, NCR Campus and has worked with Sharda University and Lovely Professional University. His teaching, training, researching and consulting interests include Brand

Management, Marketing Research, Mythology and Management and Case writing. He has published about half a dozen research papers in leading journals and has made presentations at several international/national seminars and conferences.

Hardik Gupta is an independent researcher working on business policy. He received his Postgraduate Diploma in Management (International Business) from FORE School of Management, New Delhi. His specialization is in international business and finance. He holds a BA (Hons) in Business Economics from SGND Khalsa College, University of Delhi. His research focuses on business environment, global business negotiations and trade and integration issues. He also has a keen research interest in global financial markets and financial systems. He has published articles in print and online media on contemporary issues including those related to pandemics and digital currency.

Akanksha Jain is a PhD scholar in the area of finance at the Department of Management Studies, IIT Delhi. Her areas of interest include mergers and acquisitions, corporate finance and banking.

Vranda Jain is currently working as Assistant Professor (Economics) at Jaipuria Institute of Management, Noida, India. She has more than a decade of experience in teaching postgraduate students of Management. She has participated in various conferences and has to her credit publications in journals of repute. Her research interest includes international trade, sustainable development and socio-economic policy analysis.

Vibha Kalra is a research scholar at Haryana School of Business (HSB), Guru Jambheshwar University of Science and Technology, Hisar, Haryana (India). She received her Master of Business Administration from ITM Business School, Navi Mumbai, Maharashtra, and her Bachelor of Business Administration from Bharati Vidyapeeth University Institute of Management and Research, New Delhi. She worked as freelance research analyst before joining a state university as a lecturer. Her areas of interest for research are Financial Reporting and Entrepreneurship. Her PhD research is focused on the topic Audit Quality and the expectation gap. She has contributed papers in various national and international conferences.

Smita Kashiramka is an associate professor in the area of Finance at the Department of Management Studies, IIT Delhi. She holds a PhD from Birla Institute of Technology and Science, Pilani, Pilani Campus, in the area of Mergers and Acquisitions. She has more than nine years of academic experience along with a brief corporate experience in the insurance industry. Her areas of interest include Accounting, the Indian financial system, Corporate Restructuring and Financial Management. She has published papers in international and national journals of repute. She has also presented papers in international peer-reviewed conferences.

Pravin Kumar is working as an associate professor in the Department of Mechanical Engineering, Delhi Technological University, Bawana Road, Delhi, India. He has more than 20 years of teaching and research experience. He obtained his PhD degree in Supply Chain Management from IIT Delhi and MTech in Industrial Management from IIT (Banaras Hindu University), Varanasi. His research area is supply chain and operations management. He has authored a book on engineering economics (Wiley India Pvt. Ltd.) and a book on industrial engineering and management (Pearson Learning, India). He has also published more than 50 research papers in international journals and conferences. His research articles have been published in journals such as *Applied Soft Computing*; *Annals of Operations Research*; *Resource, Conservation, and Recycling, Clean Technology and Environmental Policy*; *Environment, Development and Sustainability*; *International Journal of System Assurance Engineering and Management*; *Journal of Modelling in Management*; *International Journal of Mobile Communications*; *International Journal of Business Excellence* etc.

Vikas Kumar received his MSc in Electronics from Kurukshetra University, Haryana, India. This was followed by an MSc in Computer Science and a further PhD from the same university. He also did his MBA in the area of Information Systems and Operations Management. His PhD work was in collaboration with CEERI, Pilani, and he has worked in a number of ISRO sponsored projects. He is a life member of the Indian Science Congress Association, Computer Society of India, IETE, ICEIE, IPA, VEDA and IVS. Dr. Kumar has designed and conducted a number of training programs for the corporate sector and is a trainer for a number of Government of India departments. Along with 11 books, he has more than 100 research papers to his credit in various national and international conferences and journals, of which 55 are with the Scopus-indexed journals. He was the editor of international quarterly refereed journal *Asia-Pacific Business Review* during June 2007–June 2009. He is a regular reviewer for a number of international journals and on the panel of examiners on a number of government universities for UG/PG and doctoral programs. He has visited Sweden, France, Hungary, Austria, the Netherlands, Germany, China, Japan, Thailand, Indonesia, Malaysia, Algeria, Uganda, USA, Ethiopia, Slovenia, UAE and Jordan on sponsored research projects. Currently, Dr. Kumar is serving as a professor at the Chaudhary Bansi Lal University, Bhiwani, India, and is a visiting professor at the Indian Institute of Management, Indore, and the University of Northern Iowa, USA. Dr. Kumar is also the president of "Society For Education and Research Development". The specific areas of his interest include

Business Intelligence, e-Business, Social Media Analytics and Web Analytics.

Ravindra Hewa Kuruppuge is a senior lecturer attached to the Department of Operations Management, Faculty of Management, University of Peradeniya, Sri Lanka. He completed his BCom degree from the University of Peradeniya and MBA Degree from University of Colombo, Sri Lanka. He received his PhD from the Department of Management and Marketing, Tomas Bata University in Zlin, Czech Republic. He is an author or coauthor of more than 30 articles in scientific journals and presenter of several research conferences. His areas of research are Operations Management, Human Capital, Knowledge Management, Family Businesses and Tourism Management. He is currently teaching subjects such as Operations Management, Research Methodology and Tourism Management.

Eko Liao graduated from the University of Hong Kong with a PhD degree in Management. Her research interests include optimizing employees' personal thriving and work experiences in the workplace, and how leaders and organizations facilitate building a contemporary work environment to enhance such experiences. Dr. Eko Liao teaches management-related subjects at undergraduate and postgraduate levels (e.g., MBA, MSc, PhD) and for executive training programs.

Mikko Mäntyneva holds a PhD degree in Strategic Management from Tampere University of Technology, Finland. Currently he is working as a principal research scientist at Häme University of Applied Sciences (HAMK). He is lecturing on various graduate courses on management. His research focuses on customer relationship management, smart services, innovation management, circular economy, and knowledge management. He has participated in many international conferences and authored several scientific articles as well as six books on various management topics.

Ifeanyi Mbukanma received his PhD in Business Management with specialty in Personal Finance and Business Economics. Currently he is a postdoctoral research fellow (Economic Sciences), NWU Business School, North West University, South Africa. Prior to this he worked in the banking sector for many years.

Priyam Mendiratta is a PhD scholar in the area of finance at the Department of Management Studies, IIT Delhi. Her areas of interest include corporate finance, intellectual capital and corporate governance.

Prabhat Pankaj is a postgraduate in Economics and a PhD in applied economics. He obtained his first position in the university on graduation and a University Gold Medal on postgraduation. He has been teaching Economics at postgraduate and undergraduate level for about 30 years, in the universities and B-Schools in India and abroad. He has won prestigious fellowships of the Indian government and undertaken research assignments in Europe, Thailand, Bangladesh, Bhutan and Sri Lanka. Dr. Prabhat obtained an Executive Education in "Management and Leadership in Higher Education" at Harvard University, Boston, USA. Dr. Prabhat is also an expert on Bhutan's economic and social development and he is well networked in Bhutan throughout the country and worked extensively with the Center of Bhutan Studies, Thimphu. He is a keen researcher and a resource person on the subject of economics of happiness. He writes in the *Times of India* and *Economic Times*. He has four books and more than 30 papers to his credit. Dr. Prabhat is currently serving as the Director of Jaipuria Institute of Management, Jaipur.

Ravinder Rena is a profound academician and distinguished scholar in economics, writer, editor and adviser with over 28 years of teaching and research experience in the Asia-Pacific, African and European continents. Professor Rena is currently working as Professor of Economics and Internationalization Project Leader at the NWU Business School, North-West University, South Africa. He also serves as an Adjunct Professor at Monarch Business School, Monarch University, Switzerland. He has published books and more than 120 articles in reputed national and international peer-reviewed journals around the globe and presented over 50 papers in national and international conferences and seminars. He is founding Editor-In-Chief of the *International Journal of Education Economics and Development*. He has been a keynote speaker for various national and international conferences in Europe, North America, Africa and Asia. He has widely written in the areas of Economics of Education, Development Economics and Inclusive growth, Globalization and Higher Education, Microfinance, Rural Entrepreneurship, WTO, Sustainable development, FDIs and development aid. He supervised PhD theses and Masters dissertations across the globe.

Mohit Rewari has earned a Bachelor of Engineering in Electronics & Communication from BRCM College of Engineering & Technology (MDU Rohtak) and Masters in Business Administration degree with specialization in Finance from Haryana School of Business, Guru Jambheshwar University of Science & Technology, Hisar (Haryana). Mohit Rewari is the author of two books, *Project Management and Infrastructure Finance* and *Business Management and Social innovations*, and has published papers in international journals and presented a number of research papers in national and international conferences. He has 10 years of experience in academia and is at present associated with Chaudhary Bansi Lal University, Bhiwani (a state government university). His teaching, training, researching and consulting interests include Financial Management, Security Analysis, Project Management and ICT in Business. Also, he has published about half a dozen research papers in leading journals and has made presentations at several international/national seminars and conferences.

Shameem Shagirbasha is currently assistant professor in the area of OB/HRM. Prior to joining Great Lakes, she worked at National Oxygen Limited, as HR officer, the Institute for financial management and research (IFMR) as a faculty and the University of Gottingen, Germany, as Guest Scientist. She holds a PhD in Management specializing in HRM/OB from the Department of Management Studies, DoMS, Indian Institute of Technology (IIT – Chennai). She has an MSc in Applied Psychology specializing in Industrial Psychology from Pondicherry University and a BSc in Medical technology from JIPMER. She has been awarded gold medals for being University first in her UG and PG. Her thesis has been awarded “Best Thesis” by NAOP. She has presented papers in international conferences and won awards for best papers. She has published articles in international peer-reviewed journals and reputed media outlets. She has also authored a book titled *Emotional labour: Comprehensive review* and authored book chapters.

Hotniar Siringoringo is a professor in Gunadarma University, Jakarta, Indonesia. She teaches undergraduate students of the Industrial Engineering and Management (IE&M) department, the master’s degree in Information Systems (IS) and the doctoral program of Economic Science. She advises students on their theses for master’s degrees and doctoral programs. She also teaches abroad as visiting professor at West Pomeranian University of Technology in Szczecin, Poland, and Slovak University of Agriculture in Nitra, Slovak. She visited Ecuador as visiting researcher for the Ministerio de Telecomunicaciones y Sociedad de la Información, Quito, Ecuador, on the Prometeo project, April–July 2014. She has written papers on business, information systems, marketing and consumer behavior topics in international journals published by Inderscience, Elsevier and Emerald.

Tavishi Tewary has over 11 years of experience in policy research and trade impact assessment. She has published various research papers in international journals of high repute. She has also conducted FDPs on Data Analysis using SPSS. She has an academic experience of teaching postgraduate business school students for the past 11 years. She also has experience of providing scientific leadership to high-profile strategic sustainability and conservation initiatives with several years of research experience. She has managed cross-sectoral and interdisciplinary teams of professionals to deliver on complex research projects.

Amy Yamei Wang obtained her PhD in Management and Masters of Economics from the University of Hong Kong. She also holds a Bachelor of Commerce (Marketing) from the University of British Columbia. She has taught previously at the University of Hong

Kong and the Community College of City University. In addition to teaching, Dr. Wang's research interests include social exclusion, prosocial behaviors, group dynamics and social information processing. Her teaching interests include management-related subjects at both the undergraduate and graduate level such as Business Policy and Strategy, International Business, Asian Family Business, China Business and Principles of Management.

Cheryl Qianru Zhang is currently an assistant professor at the School of Business in Macau University of Science and Technology, located in Macau SAR China. She has earned a PhD in Law from Macau University of Science and Technology. She has the Legal Professional Qualification Certificate in People's Republic of China. Cheryl's teaching areas include commercial law, corporate governance and legal environment of business. She is the coauthor of the book chapter "Part II Complications, Groups, and Firms – Section VI Complexity and Culture: Negotiation Styles Inspired by Chinese Wisdom" in *Negotiation Essentials for Lawyers* (American Bar Association, Dispute Resolution Section. USA: ABA Book Publishing).

Foreword

Pandemic is the new buzzword in everyone's life. It has created the world of uncertainty and fear, where humankind has seen a lot of disruption. Not only in day-to-day life, but also the whole business world has been shaken up to the maximum. It has become a well-accepted notion that "corona virus" is a part of life now and the world has to adapt to the "new normal". With this advent, business houses are looking for combative strategies to come out of this messy situation.

The book *Strategic Management During Pandemic* by Dr. Vikas Kumar and Dr. Gaurav Gupta provides a hands-on approach to business models and strategies that would help corporations in handling the pandemic. The 12 chapters which form the body of this book have been authored by a group of industry practitioners and academicians, thereby bringing a variety of thoughts and perspectives to the table. The book comes across as a comprehensive cross-sectional study of the impact of the biggest global disaster of recent times. The book is going to be a very good resource for Business Management students and academicians who wish to understand the scope of business strategies.

I congratulate the chapter contributors and editors of the book for this excellent work. I hope the readers will benefit from this compilation of insightful articles.

Professor K.K. Aggarwal
Chairman, National Board of Accreditation (NBA)
India

Foreword

We have been living through unprecedented times during the past year, when the world as we knew it changed while surviving a global pandemic. It affected all phases of our life and has altered the way business transactions happen from local to a global scale. It is imperative at this moment for us to rethink our ways of life and design sustainable and reliable ways to coexist as human race on our planet. It is important for the world of business to recalibrate their methods and strategies in order to adapt themselves to and rebuild business to meet the changing needs. Both organizations and individuals went through drastic economic and psychological changes while coping and readjusting to the aftermath of COVID-19. While the resources and infrastructure of businesses are important, what is much more valuable in keeping businesses thriving is the welfare of the employees and the customers. A thorough analysis of the situation from the point of view of the business world is the need of the hour and this volume, *Strategic Management During a Pandemic*, will be an apt addition to take stock of the situation effectively. I congratulate Dr. Vikas Kumar and Dr. Gaurav Gupta for their strenuous effort in bringing out this timely work.

This volume, in my opinion, contributes to offering genuine solutions to a lot of problems we faced during the pandemic. The chapters in this volume, written by experts in the variegated fields of researching the business world, explore themes as varied as business strategies to supply chain management during the pandemic. We will get a brief introduction to the lockdown economies and business diplomacy and lobbying during the pandemic. Another important aspect expertly handled in the book is how the entire world went into a virtual mode of dealing with a lot of aspects of everyday life. Chapters in this volume provide an extensive overview into themes such as managing virtual teams and online learning and knowledge management in the changed circumstances where almost everyone had to learn to adapt to a virtual world to conduct their normal everyday transactions. The book also offers valuable insights into the challenges of the business world while they cope with the complex equations of manufacturing and offering customer service solutions in contexts that were unheard of before. The volume discusses the national and international perspectives of government policies and the effects of such policies on the overall functioning of the business world. The book promises to create a much-needed bridge between the existing theories of business and proposed business solutions in the light of the case studies that emerge from our learnings from the pandemic.

This book seeks to deal with the central problematic that revolves around the question, what is a successful and sustainable business model in a post-pandemic world? This well researched intervention efficiently curated by Dr. Vikas Kumar and Dr. Gaurav Gupta will give the readers a thorough introduction and nudge to think about new ways to fashion business models. This volume, in my reading, will provide a much-needed interface to the researchers who are thinking about global business transformations and will act as a valuable contribution to the academic community by offering a fresh and deep understanding of the pandemic and post-pandemic world of business. This book will also provide a roadmap to the effective strategies for the business leaders, consultants and coaches to reimagine and rebuild the post-pandemic business world.

Dr. (Fr.) Viju P. Devassy
Director
CHRIST (Deemed to be University), Delhi NCR Campus

Preface

Uncertainty is the catchword that the world has witnessed in recent times. Uncertain cough and fever, uncertain deaths, uncertain causes of disease, uncertain travel plans, uncertain work cultures, uncertain financial plans, uncertain government policies as well as the uncertain business opportunities have shadowed the year 2020. Beyond this certainly, COVID-19 also pumped fear into the mind of society. A combination of uncertainty and fear gave birth to the deadly panic that spread like a blitzkrieg and devastated the world, more than the virus itself. Social media has played a key role in this pandemic.

The pandemic has shaken the governments, policymakers, corporates and NGOs and compelled the human race to accept the "New Normal". COVID-19 has emerged as the single greatest threat for the continuity of business as most leaders are having a view to go for lockdown and save humanity, without worrying too much about the economy. Keeping the gravity of the problem in mind, companies have to understand the "need for change", where they have to be ready for pandemics, which are not isolated events like floods or earthquakes, having a limited geographical impact, instead being situations with worldwide impact. Many experts are taking a viewpoint that pandemics will reoccur again and the next pandemic may be more severe than the current one. Hence, organizations need to devise mechanisms and business models to fight in these situations and maintain business continuity. Businesses should not only look forward to saving plants, machinery and infrastructure but also concentrate on employee welfare, customer engagement and satisfaction during this crisis time.

Hence, there is a big need to look for effective solutions to run a business during a pandemic. At a time when several countries have announced lockdown, the viewpoint of every individual has changed, whether toward life or business. This book offers to make the nuts and bolts of strategic management to run a business during a pandemic. The book will not only present the evidence of various solutions, but will also put forward the new models and practices of business being followed by people at the time of crisis.

The first chapter, "Precursor to Lockdown Economies", focuses on the economic aspects of the pandemic and covers both the microeconomic and macroeconomic perspectives of the lockdown economy. It covers the economic aspects of individuals and organizations and then relates these to the business management aspects, including the policy perspectives. The chapter also examines the impact of the pandemic on micro, small and medium enterprises and suggests a viable plan for long-term sustainability in the post-pandemic scenario. Measures like developing a smart industrial village policy, ensuring access to information technology-enabled services at an affordable rate and providing financial assistance are presented by the authors.

The second chapter, "Global Economy and Business Strategies During Pandemic: A Multi-Country Analysis", explores the different models and approaches to business strategy, which needs attention at the time of pandemic. It discusses the negative impact of COVID-19 on the world economy and finds that there is a need for every nation to identify, sponsor and promote some unique sectors of the economy that have the potential to salvage the worrisome level of economic contraction. The authors consider the pandemic disturbance in the social-economic, political, religious and financial structure of the entire world. A multi-country analysis is presented considering the topmost economies: United State of America, China, Germany, United Kingdom, France, Italy etc. The authors recommend the need for coherent strategic policies to control and manage the pandemic to produce the least disruption to economic activities.

The chapter on "Business Diplomacy and Lobbying" by Ahmad and Gupta examines the influence of business diplomacy on pertinent global business issues including 5G technology, supply chain disruptions and opportunistic takeovers. The chapter reviews the thematic literature to investigate the nature and direction of discourse on business diplomacy. It also outlines the actors in the business diplomacy process and examines their role in the evolving global geo-economics characterized by a pandemic-induced world. A lot of examples have been presented from across the globe to highlight the strategic implications of business diplomacy and lobbying.

Eko et al. present the effective leadership challenges and issues during pandemic time. The dilemma of control-delegate is seen from the perspective of long periods of work-from-home arrangements, establishing and managing virtual teams, and dealing with uncertainty from various fronts. Examples from the industry are presented through case studies and the authors have highlighted the strategic management by leaders to strike a balance between taking sufficient yet proper control in the right situations and allowing autonomy to accommodate any ambiguity that may arise. The chapter has come up with strong recommendations for mangers focusing on preparation, communication, feedback and training.

Chapter 5 by Shameem Shagirbasha focuses on the effectiveness and efficiency of teams during the lockdowns and pandemic period. Virtual teams have replaced the regular workforce and a lot needs to be developed to manage these teams. It discusses the models and theories of business leadership in the "New Normal". Performance appraisal of virtual employees needs to be done in a typically different way and this becomes very important for the sectors that have never used this kind of mechanism. Also, maintaining the efficiency and effectiveness of employees and keeping them away from anxiety is another big challenge that the HR policies need to take care of. There may be many good practices being followed by industry, which needs further research and models need to be developed on them.

Mikko Mäntyneva discusses the customer relationship management strategies during the COVID-19 times. The chapter throws light on the issue by giving special reference to the business practices adopted by B2B firms. The author has conducted two separate workshops for sales managers and key account managers to seek empirical evidence of the business strategies during the pandemic. A strategic framework is presented for customer relationship management during uncertainty, which is grounded by the relevant theories and practices. The author suggests a lot of managerial implications, including risk management and compromises. Thus, the chapter provides very comprehensive strategic directions to managers for future uncertainties.

Choudhary and Chintaluri discuss the response to the pandemic by different companies in the manufacturing and services sector. The chapter presents how organizations in the manufacturing and services sector proactively responded to business difficulties in the pandemic period. The authors have used different cases from the manufacturing and the services sector to study the evolving models due to the pandemic. A lot of new strategies such as offering the same products through different infrastructure and offering different products through different infrastructure are discussed in the chapter along with the contrast between the manufacturing and service sectors. Innovative models used by the industry are nicely presented in the chapter.

Chapter 8 by Siringoringo and Kuruppuge focuses on the government policies for businesses during the pandemic and how these policies have impacted the domestic and international trade. This includes financial/non-financial support, easing and enhancing policies for different sectors and products to ensure the availability of essentials. A comparative analysis of two countries, Indonesia and Sri Lanka, is presented to illustrate the different perspectives of the policies.

The chapter by Rewari and Kalra takes up another important aspect of policy in the form of bailout packages. Governments in many countries pumped funding to support the struggling industries. These bailout packages supported a lot of small and big companies in the difficult time and helped their survival. The focus was on tax rebates, loan moratoriums, liquidity support, equity infusion, direct benefit transfers etc. The chapter presents the relief and bailout packages given by four major world economies: the United States, India, Germany and France.

The chapter on "Triple Bottom Line During Pandemic" highlights that during the recent pandemic, the focus of companies has shifted to the immediate, short-term existence of firms, making the long-term sustainability questionable. The basic essence of the three pillars of TBL gives rise to apprehension. The chapter discusses the shift of economic loss and its impact on organizations' survival solutions. The role of corporate social responsibility during the pandemic is highlighted with a special focus on CSR spending. The authors have also presented future CSR strategies to reduce the effect of the pandemic.

Chapter 11 of the book, "Online Learning Trends During the Pandemic: Case of Service Sector Professionals", by Dalal et al. explains knowledge management and the online learning environment during the pandemic, how organizations train their employees and what new models of knowledge management are being practiced. An empirical study has been conducted and the authors have proposed a framework, using which organizations can productively upskill their workforce amidst the new evolving working environment.

Due to lockdown in many parts of the world, supply chains were worst hit during the COVID-19 pandemic. In the chapter by Kumar and Gupta, the most crucial aspects of the supply chain and manufacturing industry are presented: how the supply chains were maintained among the restrictions and how the broken chains will be brought back to the track. Although the government policies were important, there have been many cases where the supply chains could not survive, even when the government supported them. A lot of human, community and health-related issues are addressed from this perspective, with both the qualitative and the quantitative perspective.

We sincerely hope that this edited volume shall provide insight into the different business strategies adopted by various stakeholders during the pandemic. This will be useful for researchers, students, practitioners, policymakers and everybody interested in strategic management. We hope that the chapters will serve as material for discussing, criticizing and thus developing our understanding of the business strategies during the pandemic. The book will serve as a wonderful academic reference for researchers and academicians and, at the same time, it will serve as a resource guide for the practitioners.

Vikas Kumar
Gaurav Gupta

Acknowledgments

A real piece of academic reference can never be created without the contribution of many intellectuals. We would like to express our heartfelt gratitude to all individuals and groups who have contributed to this book and supported us in one or the other manner.

Our sincere thanks to Prof. R. K. Mittal (Vice Chancellor, Chaudhary Bansi Lal University), Prof. Jitender Bhardwaj (Registrar, Chaudhary Bansi Lal University), Dr. Fr. Viju P. Devassy CMI (Director, CHRIST (Deemed to be University, NCR Campus)) and Dr. Joji Chandran O (Head, School of Business and Management, CHRIST (Deemed to be University, NCR Campus)) for their continued support and guidance toward the completion of this project. We are indebted to the late Prof. Anil Kumar Pundir (Guru Jambhewshwar University, Hisar), who has always been a divine force behind all our endeavors. Dr. Sachin Sinha (Christ University), Dr. Vikas Singla (Punjabi University) and Dr. Shivinder Kaur (Chitkara University) have always supported us with valuable advice and suggestions.

We should not fail to mention the name of Routledge, their administrative and editorial staff for giving us this wonderful opportunity to serve as editors for this academic project. Special thanks to Brianna Asher and Naomi Round Cahalin for providing us valuable inputs and keeping us updated. We are indebted to all the authors and contributors for reposing their confidence in us, sending their original contributions and working as per the tight deadlines. We are thankful to the reviewers from academia and industry who worked very hard to make this work a novel piece.

We would like to pen down the support from our colleagues: Dr. Mridul Dharwal, Dr. Garima Dua, Dr. Pooja Nanda and Dr. Rachna Bansal (all from Sharda University), Danijela Voljč (University of Ljubljana), Dr. Sri Aliami and Dr. Subagyo (Nusantara PGRI University), Irina Martynova (Belarusian State University), Sidney Soares Filho (University of Fortaleza), Dr. Neha Bharadwaj (IIM Rohtak), Dr. Dhiraj Sharma (Punjabi University), Dr. Mandakini Paruthi (Chaitanya Institute), Ms. Swati Oberoi (IIM Shillong), Dr. Pawan Gupta, Dr. Sunita Bharatwal and Dr. Manju Lata (all from Chaudhary Bansi Lal University), Dr. G.K.

Sethi (M L N College), Dr. Surender Kumar (Jaipuria Institute of Management), Dr. Saurabh Mittal (G L Bajaj Institute of Management & Research) and other peers from academia, who have motivated and helped us a lot in this project.

Finally, a lovely mention goes to our parents, family members and friends for the time stolen out of their share, for completing this project.

Dr. Vikas Kumar
Dr. Gaurav Gupta

1 Precursor to Lockdown Economies

Prabhat Pankaj, Varun Chotia,
Vranda Jain and Tavishi Tewary

Introduction

The whole world these days is going through a phase never thought of. The sudden outbreak of the COVID-19 pandemic has imposed an enormous health and economic shock on countries across the globe. The mitigation actions and strategies to prevent further spread and contain the adversities emanating from COVID is likely to inflict some consequences on these nations. The desire and requirement for an effective containment and prevention of further spread of this deadly virus may also warrant countries to manipulate their normal functioning, which may not yield a favorable impact on these economies. Several experts are echoing the sentiments of Mr. Kristalina Georgieva, Chief – International Monetary Fund, that the economic situation in the year 2020 is comparable with the period of the Great Depression of the 1930s and, with about 170 countries witnessing negative GDP growth rates, this could actually be a year of the worst global fallout. Global pundits have already referred it as a Black Swan event.

The term "pandemic" is not new to the world economy. Recent studies (Ferguson et al., 2020) have highlighted the outbreak of pandemics at different timelines in human history. Further, the occurrence of pandemics has been on the rise since the start of 21st century. This has led to growing interest among researchers to explore and predict pandemics of different intensities. Studies by Garrett (2007), Keogh-Brown et al. (2008), Madhav et al. (2017) and Fan et al. (2018) have predicted the outbreak of a large-scale global pandemic. However, COVID-19 is being regarded as one of the most serious pandemics in mankind's existence since the 1918 Spanish influenza pandemic (Ferguson et al., 2020).

As discussed earlier, pandemics are expected to exert a negative impact on the economy, particularly in the short run. As per Jonas (2013), this impact can be attributed to several factors:

i Decrease in the consumption levels as consumers might forego purchases of certain goods and services in the economy
ii Higher indirect costs like loss of labor and production

DOI: 10.4324/9781003125648-1

iii Offsetting and cascading effects on account of disrupted services, travel etc.

Various studies have attempted to estimate the pandemic-imposed economic loss. By examining a situation of hypothetical global pandemic for the European Union (EU), Jonung and Roeger (2006) estimated a decline in GDP by 1.6%, after considering the demand and supply factors. In another study, Barrero et al. (2020) extrapolated the death rate of 2.1% during the Spanish influenza pandemic to estimate the number of lives lost due to COVID to be 150 million deaths. They further analyzed the impact of this death rate on GDP and private consumption and concluded that these would decline by 6% and 8% respectively.

Undoubtedly, pandemics in general and COVID in particular have disrupted demand and supply conditions and result in economic slowdown. In the context of the Indian economy, this impact would be more adverse and acute, owing to the state of economy in the pre-COVID scenario. Even before the outbreak of COVID, the Indian economy exhibited a dismal performance. This is further challenged by the limited availability of policy levers at the Indian government's disposal, given the present condition of financial institutions. An examination of central government's fiscal position reveals that the fiscal deficit for 2019–20 was 4.6%, much higher than the targeted 3.5% of GDP. In the budget speech for 2020–21, the Indian Finance Minister mentioned the pegging of the fiscal deficit to 3.5% of GDP, which had already been breached in the pre-COVID period.

This scenario draws attention to the fact that the Indian government has at present little fiscal room to fight the corona crisis from an economic perspective. This may further be attenuated by events and incidents like a possible decline in tax collections, fall in public sector enterprise (PSE) revenue and a sudden rise in healthcare outlay. Even in an unlikely yet favorable scenario of the absence of additional expenditure, the decline in tax revenue and disinvestment proceeds would widen the gap, leading to unpleasantly high deficits. This may pose further challenges pertaining to financing such huge deficits.

In a nutshell, the Indian economy cannot escape the COVID-imposed brunt and will have to encounter a period of slowdown. What is uncertain is the intensity of this adverse economic impact as much would depend upon the duration of pandemic. In this chapter, we aim to assess the potential impact of the shock on various sectors of the Indian economy as discussed in the next section. Considering the recent focus of the Indian government on the MSMEs owing to their significant contribution, the subsequent section talks about the MSMEs and pandemic relationship. The chapter summarizes by presenting an outlook for the Indian economy for 2021 and beyond.

Sectoral Impact Assessment

Although COVID-19 has imposed lesser disruptions on Indian industry due to the large size of domestic market, local supply chains and lesser dependence on global value chains, yet its impact on Indian industry cannot be ignored. This is mainly due to the disruption in Chinese manufacturing capacity – the largest manufacturer and exporter in the world. This section presents a concise industry impact and the series of challenges faced by Indian industries.

Automotive

The Indian auto industry, already under the heels of plummeting sales during 2019, had a further blow owing to the outbreak of COVID-19 and consequent lockdown. With 18% of India's automobile components and close to 30% of tire imports coming from China, the Indian auto industry's dependence on China is considered to be moderate. Further, production disruptions in Wuhan – a major auto hub (IHS Markit, 2020) – and supply chain disruption led to insufficient inventories, forcing plants to produce below their normal levels. The adverse impact has been severe on the two-wheeler segment, whose import dependency on China is relatively higher. Further, the global slowdown in the auto industry will pose challenges to export-oriented ancillary component manufacturers. In the absence of sufficient liquidity, higher credit lines and a decline in market capitalization (Accenture, 2020), the industry may witness consolidation in the longer term.

Aviation, Tourism and Hospitality

The tourism and hospitality sector, contributing around one-tenth to India's GDP, is viewed as an engine of economic growth. According to a recent estimate by the World Travel and Tourism Council (WTTC, 2020), the sector generated 13% of total employment during 2018–19 and contributed INR 194 billion to India's GDP. Also, the sectoral growth in India (4.9%) has been higher than the global average (3.5%). With the outbreak of COVID-19 and international travel restrictions and visa suspensions, the industry has faced the severest downturn. The worst affected has been the aviation sector, as apart from the massive decline in passenger traffic and revenue therefrom, huge parking and housing charges of carriers had to be incurred. The hotel industry, tour operators and travel agencies were also affected due to travel bans. The overall sectoral loss is expected to be around USD 16.7 billion, with direct and indirect job losses of close to 50 million (Grant Thornton-FICCI, 2020a).

Retail Sector

The immediate aftermath of the lockdown announcement called for panic buying of consumer essential items, leading to an increase in demand and pantry loading of FMCG products like food, groceries and health, hygiene and immunity-building products like soap, sanitizer, hand wash, floor cleaners, ayurvedic products etc. Also the demand for organic food products registered an exponential growth. Non-essential items (e.g., cosmetics) saw a steep decline (BENORI, 2020). However, owing to a labor shortage and the drying up of inventory levels as a result of lockdowns, the sector experienced disruptions in supply chain, distribution and logistics and the prevailing trend could not continue. According to a recent study by Nielsen (2020), with the cumulative effects of lockdown, social distancing standards, restrictions and protocols for manufacturing plants and retailers, and store closures, the FMCG sector is most likely to register a flat growth in 2020.

Telecom

Due to the imposition of lockdown and the consequent cancellation of domestic and international travel with an evolved shift to remote working and leisure at home, the demand for data and network usage skyrocketed. According to an estimate, there has been a 10% increase in overall traffic and 20% jump in viewership on streaming platforms (Business Standard, 2020). This has placed the spotlight on the telecom sector, with Ministry of Home Affairs (MHA) granting essential services status to telecommunications, Internet services, broadcasting and cable services, IT and IT-enabled services (ITeS) (MHA, 2020). However, the enforcement of lockdown has certain fallouts for the telecom industry. As network operators currently focus on enhancing network resilience and customer retention, it may lead to a delay in the much-awaited 5G spectrum auctions and its subsequent rollout. Global supply chain disruptions are likely to have an adverse impact on handset (including 5G-enabled) and network equipment manufacturers (KPMG, 2020a). Also, due to the movement restrictions, India Ratings & Research (2020) estimates a sharp decline in average net addition of new subscribers, which would affect telecom revenue.

Healthcare and Pharma

The healthcare sector is at the epicenter of the COVID-19 crisis. Unlike other sectors, healthcare is facing dual challenges. One, the current situation warrants additional investment in equipment, manpower and consumables for patient treatment and ensuring the safety of its staff members (Economic Times, 2020). On the other hand, the sector is witnessing a decline in international patients, elective surgeries and OPD footfall (Deloitte, 2020a). As per a recent study, there has been a 80% fall in patient visits and tests, leading to around 50–70% revenue drop in the private healthcare sector (Movdawalla, 2020). Since close to 80% of hospital costs are fixed in nature, this would give a severe blow to private hospitals' cash flows and private healthcare providers. Further, due to import dependence for disposables and capital equipment (e.g., syringes, gloves, orthopedic implants etc.) on China and the restrictions imposed, the Indian medical devices industry has also been hit. Also, supply disruptions in low-cost Chinese API have impacted the operational efficiency and revenue of the Indian pharma industry.

Banking, Financial Services and Insurance Sector (BFSI)

The outbreak of COVID-19 had a significant impact on profitability and the balance sheet of the BFSI sector (EY, 2020). As businesses report losses and closure, banks may experience issues related to liquidity and capital adequacy. Banks will be required to identify, monitor and create provisions for borrowers with temporary and long-term financial ailments in both the retail and corporate segments. It would also become cumbersome to determine the sufficiency of collaterals at their end. In the short term, shareholders/investors experienced a reduction in returns due to temporary correction in valuation which may get transferred to shareholders investing their capital in organic growth opportunities and retail customers preferring asset-backed instruments as a part of a long-term financial services sector disruption (Deloitte, 2020b). Similarly, NBFCs will also experience liquidity issues which would have an adverse impact on the credit quality of loan portfolios, further affecting the expected credit loss measurement. Overcoming these challenges will require high capital infusion for maintaining regulatory and growth capital, technological investments and deepening customer relationships (Shah, 2020). It is also an acid test for the insurance sector to check their financial and operational risks and business continuity planning.

Agriculture and Allied Activities

The primary sector consisting of agriculture and allied activities occupies a place of prominence in the Indian economy as it is a source of livelihood for close to 58% of the population and provides employment opportunities to around 44% of the total population. The outbreak of the pandemic and lockdown led to a mass exodus of migrant workers, which interrupted harvesting and procurement activities, impacting liquidity and working capital requirement among farmers. It also hit the operational capacity of manufacturing plants aligned with the irrigation industry such as milk processing, cold storage and warehouses (Grant Thornton-FICCI, 2020b). Also, lockdown and other restrictions imposed led to shutting of restaurants, tea shops and other eating joints, leading to depressed milk sales. Misinformation on chicken being the carrier of the virus led to a decline in poultry sales. Imposition of global lockdown had a severe blow on Indian exports and associated jobs. The crisis disrupted the agricultural supply chain severely, with the gap between original and destination prices getting widened (ICAR, 2020).

Construction and Real Estate

The pandemic-imposed lockdown severely impaired the real estate sector's contribution in economic activity and employment-generating capacity. On the supply front, companies experienced shortage of building materials and labor and delays in construction owing to disrupted supply chains. This hit the growth of related industries like cement, steel and other building materials. It was visible in the halt of irrigation projects, flyovers and expressways. Also interior imports from other countries were affected. Mobility restrictions led to poor sales in residential and commercial segments on the demand side. Lockdowns in other countries of the world are bound to curtail potential investments in Indian commercial real estate (KPMG, 2020b). Due to the strong forward and backward linkages with other sectors and allied industries, low economic activity in other sectors would impact real estate (Deloitte, 2020c). This may also lead to postponement of REIT launches, which would put further liquidity pressure on real estate developers.

Education

The imposition of lockdown led to nationwide school closures and interruptions in conventional schooling. Continued learning was impaired due to accessibility issues pertaining to technology and Internet connectivity. Indian students from disadvantaged backgrounds found their doors to alternative ways of attending schools shut during this pandemic. The crisis brought to the fore the misalignment between resources and needs ranging from access to broadband, devices and other supporting infrastructure, inadequacies and inequalities in the Indian education system (Schleicher, 2020). However, the education community deserves applause for making concerted efforts to adapt to new teaching modes and pedagogical concepts. Travel restrictions led to a steep decline in international student mobility and affected the continuity of learning and students' exposure. Higher education institutions and other players in the education space moved to conducting online classes and thus there was a significant investment and expenditure in the EdTech sector. A recent report estimates that the EdTech sector would grow at a CAGR of 52% and would assume a size of USD 2 billion by the year 2021 (KPMG-Google, 2017).

MSMEs and Pandemic

MSMEs are the backbone of any economy (SMEfutures.com, 2020). They are responsible for propelling the 3 Es, employment, entrepreneurship and enterprise. The COVID-19 pandemic has affected over 210 countries and has disrupted the global supply chain. International trade is crucial for the growth of this sector. They earn a major portion of the revenue through exporting products by direct or indirect channels. Numerous MSMEs also rely on imported raw materials for manufacturing their products. These products can be sold in the domestic market or can be used to meet international demand. Because of the current health crises in the form of COVID-19, the MSME sector has suffered huge losses. Because of the size constraints, the sector is less resilient and flexible in dealing with the crises. It is very challenging for them to survive this phase.

The impact on the global value chain is not even for all economies. In some of the economies, this sector is highly integrated into the global value chains but in the rest of the economies this is missing (WTO, 2016). This impact not only varies from region to region, it also differs across sectors within the economy. The sectors where the MSMEs are highly integrated are the worst affected. For example, electronics and chemicals, petroleum and plastics: this sector imports the raw materials used in the production process. This can be termed as backward participation. In the area of furniture and automotive forward participation takes place and they export most of their products to foreign countries. In some of the manufacturing MSMEs export through indirect participation in the global value chain. The best examples are machinery products and equipment, publishing and printing products, paper etc. These may be affected severely because of complete closure of the economies to fight the pandemic (AMTC, 2020).

The MSME sector comprises around 64 million companies and generates employment for over 120 million people. It contributes 30% to India's GDP and 45% of Indian exports (Financial Express, 2020). Out of these, 14% are women-governed enterprises and approximately 60% are based in rural areas. The importance of this sector can be understood from the role it can play in bridging the gap between the urban and the rural areas.

It has been proven time and again that this sector is crucial for the development of the economy. It plays the role of catalyst in raising the standard of living in a developing country like India. The MSME sector in India is still underutilized and has a potential to expand further. The announcement of the nationwide lockdown dragged the small businesses to a turbulent and uncertain environment with no prior experience of handling such situations. Extended lockdown in many parts of the country had a negative impact on the procurement of raw materials and supply of the processed product. During the months of April to June 2020, they faced problems of statutory dues, payment of salaries and wages and debt repayments (Times of India, 2020). The maximum heat was faced by them because of a liquidity crunch. They did not have working capital to meet day-to-day expenses. The companies that were providing essential products during the pandemic were better off as they were allowed to function and sell their goods. Some of the MSMEs shifted from nonessential to essential commodities to take this pandemic as an opportunity. They expanded in hand sanitizers, PPE kits, face masks etc. But the MSMEs located in the interiors faced difficulties because of the interrupted supply of raw materials and intrastate restrictions in movement of goods and services (The New Indian Express, 2020).

The enterprises are facing problem at both demand and supply ends. Not only is their supply affected because of fragmented supply chains, the demand of the domestic consumers has also fallen as the pandemic has left them with lower disposable income. Many companies have resorted to salary cuts and some of them even went beyond the extent of laying off the workforce because of almost negligible or no sales and failure to pay those wages and salaries. Investments by the private sector in the economy are kept at bay because of the ambiguity of future trade scenarios.

Measures Taken by the Government

The governments have taken various incentives in terms of liquidity measures, trade support measures, resilience-focused measures (capacity-building) and measures to improve the environment in which they do their business. The governments have been quick to respond to deal with this unprecedented crisis by closing down international borders, imposing nationwide lockdowns, resorting to rigorous testing and boosting the healthcare infrastructure. Some of the governments have also announced relief packages for the economy. (Responses by the governments of different countries to support the MSMEs are shown in Figure 1.1.) The response of the Indian government is no different as India has announced a relief package to the tune of 10% of the country's GDP.

Due to the lockdown the Indian MSME sector suffered the most. The collective production has decreased by more than 90%. To overcome the negative impact of the pandemic, a series of relief packages has been announced by the Indian Prime Minister to make India "Atma-Nirbhar Bharat" or self-reliant. This will help the businesses get back on track without external support. The majority of the packages of the stimulus were targeted towards this sector in the form of providing either liquidity support loans or equity infusion support to boost capacity and expand the scale of production. There were 15 macro-economic stimulus packages declared by the government of India, out of which six centered on the MSMEs. There was a change in definition of MSMEs, credit and finance schemes, disallowing global tenders, relief in nonperforming assets, allocating funds for equity participation, and clearing odd dues (Times of India, 2020).

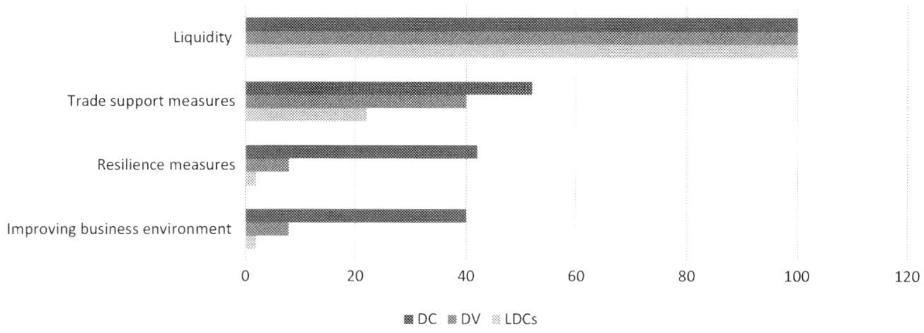

Figure 1.1 Government responses to support MSMEs.

Note: LDCs – least developing countries; DV – developing countries; DC – developed countries

Some of the relief measures taken by the Ministry of MSMEs are the setting up of kitchens to provide food to the migrant workers in cities of Delhi, Cuttack, Thane etc., providing Rs 1000/month to the registered artisans from the artisan welfare fund trust, releasing funds under market development assistance to khadi institutions through DBT.

Post-Lockdown Plan

For meeting the delivery schedule during the pandemic, in respect of government orders where, as per contract, there is provision of liquidated damages, a relaxation in the applicability of the liquidity damages clause for a period of 2 months is allowed.

To overcome the problem of delayed payments, there was immediate intervention by the government to promote release of all pending payments to this sector involved in the contract. For meeting the fixed cost, amid pressure from banks to pay the dues, the State governments can be approached for exemptions in electricity charges and other fixed charges during this crises period. The plan to deal with the COVID is presented in Figure 1.2.

To compensate for the increasing rise in prices of inputs, reductions in GST rates on raw materials have been proposed in consultation with the Ministry of Finance. To address the issue of financial compliance, a relaxing of GST filing and suitable relief measures have been undertaken. For meeting the credit requirements during such stressful times, a moratorium period of 6 months for repayment of loans has been approved along with provision of "no change" in the credit ratings. The ratings of the MSMEs will not be affected negatively. The norms for declaring an asset nonperforming has been extended to 180 days for a period of the next 2 years. This provision is made as the MSMEs require a smooth flow of funds and banking assistance to deal with the present situation.

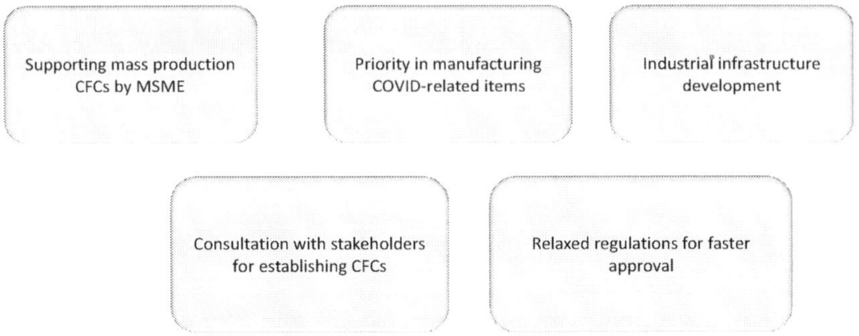

Figure 1.2 Plan to deal with COVID-19.

Long-Term Sustainability of MSMEs Post-COVID 19

The government of India has decided to focus on three initiatives. Firstly, a smart industrial village policy for achieving inclusive growth, and promoting decentralization of economic structure, and avoiding concentration of wealth in the hands of few. The government is promoting Swadeshi ideology and indigenous products. They are determined to raise the standards and quality norms and install a system to provide "non-tariff barrier" covers for promoting local products and making India a manufacturing hub.

Secondly, providing access to information technology-enabled services at an affordable rate and to integrate MSMEs to the global value chain, promoting innovations and technological upgrading of the MSMEs linking it with new technologies like block chain and artificial intelligence. They have also proposed to set up incubators in educational institutions to promote entrepreneurship.

Thirdly, they are providing financial assistance to this sector in terms of prioritized lending from banks, collateral free small loans for self-employment, and relaxing the ceiling on working capital by banks. They are devising a safe trade policy for sectors dependent on imports from China like pharmaceuticals, electronics, etc. (Ministry of MSME, 2020).

The government of India is focusing on shaping a resilient ecosystem with forward and backward integration. The sector holds a key to the critical questions like the local economy, employment generation, fiscal deficit and trade balances. Private-sector engagement is required along with the government stimulus. The government need to resolve the issues related to the procurement of raw materials, standardization, credit need and market linkages. According to Mr. Arjun Singh, global chief economist at Dun & Bradstreet, "the MSMEs will take at least 7–8 months to recover from this pandemic and the recovery rate of an enterprise will depend on factors like rate of digitization and the sector in which it is operating" (The New Indian Express, 2020). Mr. Amish Mehta, COO of CRISIL, also stressed the fact that

> Firstly, improving the sentiment around job security for formal and informal workers to boost consumption is of utmost importance. Secondly, hastening the implementation of Rs 3 lakh crore Atmanirbhar scheme to ensure flow of liquidity to MSMEs should also be done.
>
> (SMEfutures.com, 2020)

The government of India is taking various measures to help this sector during the pandemic. Recently the Ministry of MSME launched the Credit Guarantee Scheme for subordinate debt and government has also made amendments to the Essential Commodities Act that allow farmers to sell their crop to anyone. The need of the hour is to chalk out a plan to make the MSMEs sail through this difficult time with minimum impact. Only the future will tell us how successfully this sector will be able to navigate its way out of the crises with the help of government interventions.

Conclusion and Outlook for 2021 and Beyond

The talk about recovery, either V-shaped or U-shaped, and resilience to the pandemic is likely to depend upon how the economy will be doing on five key indicators.

The pace of investment in fixed assets is important for increasing aggregate demand and preparing capacity. The gross fixed capital formation as percentage of GDP has suffered and it has gone down from 30.1% to 27.4%. It looks likely that the Indian economy will do well on this count with the government putting a lot of infrastructure investment as a priority. The contribution in capital formation by the government and the public sector is about 24% and hence government spending alone is not going to help.

1 The urban economy needs to come back to running. This has been hit by a fall in consumer demand as car sales declined consequently from the last 9 months, amounting to a fall in sales by 41%. Nevertheless, the second half of 2020 started witnessing a recovery and it looks likely that urban revival is just a matter of time as the pent-up demand gets unleashed with the opening up of market.
2 However, the FMCG demand in the rural economy may take a rather longer time to come back to its old level. Here the direct transfer of income scheme, ex-gratia refund on loans etc. have worked well to

the rescue of rural consumers. The stimulus package as big, as 10% of GDP is wonderful news.

3 With the massive push to infrastructure and structural reforms in eight core sectors of the economy, it looks likely that the recovery will be speeded up. The data on the performance of the core sectors in August 2020 indicate that there is light at the end of the tunnel and the tunnel does not seem to be very long. Coal has recovered to a positive growth of 21.2% from a negative figure registered in March 2020. Among the other core sectors which have demonstrated positive growth in August 2020 are steel (0.9% from a negative 13%) and electricity (3.7% from a negative 7%). There have been marked improvements in natural gas, refinery products and cement. Good news is that fertilizer growth has registered negative 0.3% in August 2020, which was a negative 12% in March 2020.

4 As the COVID-19 vaccine is round the corner which will boost the confidence in consumers as well as producers, sectors such as food and pharma are likely to see robust growth. The India-first policy and aatmanirbhar bharat abhiyan would create the right mindset and boost domestic production capabilities. Exports have started returning and the forex reserve is high enough to support the recovery drive.

All eyes will be on the Union Budget 2021–22 as it will unfold schemes, concessions, plans and programs for boosting aggregate demand on the one hand and stepping up production on the other. The projections are positive and optimistic and it has been rightly pointed out that the Indian economy may be on a slow-run path but definitely not retired hurt.

References

Accenture. (2020). Impact on the automotive industry: Navigating the human and business impact of COVID-19 Available at: www.accenture.com/_acnmedia/PDF-121/Accenture-COVID-19-Impact-Automotive-Industry.pdf (accessed 10 October 2020).

Asia Pacific MSME Trade Coalition (AMTC). (2020). *Supporting the Small in a Pandemic*, Asia: AMTC.

Barrero, J.M., Bloom, N., & Davis, S.J. (2020). COVID-19 is also a reallocation shock (Working Paper No. 27137; Working Paper Series). National Bureau of Economic Research. https://doi.org/10.3386/w27137.

BENORI. (2020). Decoding Covid-19 disruptions: Impact of the pandemic on FMCG sector. Available at: https://benoriknowledge.com/wp-content/uploads/2020/06/Covid-19-Impact-on-Indian-FMCG-Sector-1.pdf (accessed 24 October 2020).

Business Standard. (2020). How telecom sector is coping with a 10% data demand spike amid Covid-19. Available at: www.business-standard.com/podcast/current-affairs/how-telecom-sector-is-coping-with-a-10-data-demand-spike-amid-covid-19-120032301553_1.html (accessed 12 October 2020).

Deloitte. (2020a). Changing consumer preferences towards health care services: The impact of COVID-19. Available at: www2.deloitte.com/content/dam/Deloitte/in/Documents/life-sciences-health-care/in-lshc-Deloitte_HealthcareConsumerSurvey-new-noexp.pdf (accessed 21 September 2020).

Deloitte. (2020b). COVID-19 Impact on banking in India – finding the silver lining. Available at: www2.deloitte.com/content/dam/Deloitte/in/Documents/financial-services/in-fsi-Impact-of-Covid19onBanking-in-India_BrandPart2-noexp.pdf (accessed 18 September 2020).

Deloitte. (2020c). Weathering COVID-19 impact on banking in India – Part 1. Available at: www2.deloitte.com/in/en/pages/financial-services/articles/weathering-the-covid19.html (accessed 23 September 2020).

Economic Times. (2020). Coronavirus impact on healthcare sector. Available at: https://economictimes.indiatimes.com/markets/stocks/news/coronavirus-impact-on-healthcare-sector/articleshow/75136714.cms (accessed 22 September 2020).

EY. (2020). Covid-19: Impact on the financial services sector. Available at: www.ey.com/en_gl/covid-19-financial-services (accessed 23 September 2020).

Financial Express. (2020, July 2). Covid 19: opportunity or doomsday scenario for MSMEs? Stage set for firms to decide their future. Retrieved from www.financialexpress.com/industry/msme-eodb-covid-19-big-opportunity-or-doomsday-scenario-for-msmes-stage-set-for-firms-to-decide-their-future/2011215/.

Fan, V.Y., Jamison, D.T., & Summers, L.H. (2018). Pandemic risk: how large are the expected losses? *Bulletin of the World Health Organization, 96*(2), 129–134. https://doi.org/10.2471/BLT.17.199588.

Ferguson, N., Laydon, D., Nedjati Gilani, G., Imai, N., Ainslie, K., Baguelin, M., … Ghani, A. (2020). *Impact of non-pharmaceutical interventions (NPIs) to reduce COVID19 mortality and healthcare demand.* Imperial College London. https://doi.org/10.25561/77482.

Garrett, T.A. (2007). Economic effects of the 1918 influenza pandemic. *Federal Reserve Bank of St. Louis, 26.*

Grant Thornton-FICCI. (2020a). Travel and tourism - survive, revive and thrive in times of COVID-19. Available at: www.grantthornton.in/globalassets/1.-member-firms/india/assets/pdfs/travel-and-tourism-in-times-of-covid-19.pdf (accessed 25 October 2020)

Grant Thornton-FICCI (2020b). Decoding agriculture in India amid COVID-19 crisis. Available at: http://ficci.in/spdocument/23267/FICCI-GT-Report-on-Agriculture.pdf (accessed 15 September 2020).

ICAR-National Institute of Agricultural Economics and Policy Research. (2020). Covid-19 lockdown and Indian agriculture: options to reduce the impact. Available at: www.ncap.res.in/agri_lock.pdf (accessed 15 September 2020).

IHS Markit. (2020). Coronavirus impact on automotive industry. Available at: https://ihsmarkit.com/research-analysis/coronavirus-impact-on-automotive-industry.html (accessed 15 September 2020).

India Ratings & Research. (2020). Telecom Connect: Broadband Penetration Continues to Rise; Industry Moving Towards Higher ARPU Regime. Available at: www.indiaratings.co.in/PressRelease?pressReleaseID=52553&title=Telecom-Connect%3A-Broadband-Penetration-Continues-to-Rise%3B-Industry-Moving-Towards-Higher-ARPU-Regime- (accessed 11 October 2020).

Jonung, L., & Roeger, W. (2006). *The macroeconomic effects of a pandemic in Europe: A model-based assessment*. DG ECFIN, European Commission, Brussels. https://ec.europa.eu/economy_finance/publications/pages/publication708_en.pdf.

Keogh-Brown, M., McDonald, S., Edmunds, J., Beutels, P., & Smith, R. (2008). *The macroeconomic costs of a global influenza pandemic*. Presented at the 11th Annual Conference on Global Economic Analysis, Helsinki, Finland. www.gtap.agecon.purdue.edu/resources/res_display.asp?RecordID=2755.

KPMG. (2020a). Available at: https://home.kpmg/content/dam/kpmg/in/pdf/2020/04/potential-impact-of-covid-19-on-the-Indian-economy.pdf (accessed 12 October 2020).

KPMG. (2020b). Potential impact of COVID-19 on the Indian economy. Available at: https://etinsights.et-edge.com/wp-content/uploads/2020/04/KPMG-REPORT-compressed.pdf (accessed 18 September 2020).

KPMG-Google. (2017). Online education in India: 2021. Available at: https://assets.kpmg/content/dam/kpmg/in/pdf/2017/05/Online-Education-in-India-2021.pdf (accessed 23 September 2020).

MHA. (2020). Available at: www.mha.gov.in/sites/default/files/MHA%20order%20dt%2015.04.2020%2C%20with%20Revised%20Consolidated%20Guidelines_compressed%20%283%29.pdf (accessed 12 October 2020).

Madhav, N., Oppenheim, B., Gallivan, M., Mulembakani, P., Rubin, E., & Wolfe, N. (2017). Pandemics: Risks, Impacts, and Mitigation. In D.T. Jamison, H. Gelband, S. Horton, P. Jha, R. Laxminarayan, C.N. Mock & R. Nugent (Eds.), *Disease control priorities: Improving health and reducing poverty* (3rd edn.). The International Bank for Reconstruction and Development / The World Bank. www.ncbi.nlm.nih.gov/books/NBK525302/.

Movdawalla, K. (2020). FICCI-EY report - Impact of COVID-19: private healthcare sector calls for urgent financial stimulus. Available at: www.ey.com/en_in/life-sciences/impact-of-covid-19-private-healthcare-sector-calls-for-urgent-financial-stimulus (accessed 23 September 2020).

Nielsen. (2020). FMCG to register flat growth in 2020. Available at: www.retail4growth.com/viewpoints/fmcg-to-register-flat-growth-in-2020-nielsen-808 (accessed 24 October 2020).

Schleicher, A. (2020). The impact of Covid-19 on education. Insights from *Education at a Glance 2020*. Available at: /www.oecd.org/education/the-impact-of-covid-19-on-education-insights-education-at-a-glance-2020.pdf (accessed 23 September 2020).

Shah, M. (2020). Potential implications of COVID -19 on the banking sector. Available at: https://bfsi.economictimes.indiatimes.com/blog/potential-implications-of-covid-19-on-the-banking-sector/4227 (accessed 23 September 2020).

SMEFutures.com. (2020, June 27). Can ever-resilient Indian MSMEs overcome the high tide of Covid-19 constraints? Retrieved from https://smefutures.com/can-ever-resilient-indian-msmes-overcome-the-high-tide-of-covid-19-constraints/.

The New Indian Express. (2020, August 11). MSMEs will take at least 7-8 months to recover from COVID-19 impact: Economist. Retrieved from www.newindianexpress.com/business/2020/aug/11/msmes-will-take-at-least-7-8-months-to-recover-from-covid-19-impact-economist-2182064.html.

Times of India. (2020, September, 23) Covid-19 effect on micro, small and medium enterprises (MSMEs). Retrieved from https://timesofindia.indiatimes.com/blogs/agyeya/covid-19-affect-on-micro-small-and-medium-enterprises-msmes/.

World Trade Organization (WTO). (2016). *World Trade Statistical Review 2016*. Geneva: WTO.

World Travel and Tourism Council (WTTC). (2020). Economic Impact Reports. Available at https://wttc.org/Research/Economic-Impact (accessed 24 October 2020).

2 Global Economy and Business Strategies During Pandemic

A Multi-Country Analysis

Ravinder Rena and Ifeanyi Mbukanma

Introduction

Coronavirus (COVID-19 pandemic) was initially detected in Wuhan, China, in late 2019 and sparked a global pandemic. Initially, maximum cases were originally detected in China, but the virus spread across Europe, America and the entire world. The coronavirus is a global shock "more than anything" involving a concurrent disruption of both demand and supply in the integrated world economy (Nicloa et al., 2020). The virus diminished labor availability and output on the supply side, although lockdowns, company disruptions and social distances continue to disrupt supply. On the demand side, consumer consumption and business investment are constrained by layoffs and loss of income, the burden of sickness, quarantine, unemployment and declining economic prospects. Extreme doubt about the course, duration, severity and effect of the pandemic has led to a downward cycle of declining market and consumer morale and a worsening of financial conditions that may lead to employment cuts and a continuous reduction in investment and economic development. As the tolls of infection and fatality escalate, global devastation is clear, representing the world's biggest economic shock in decades.

According to the Asian Development Bank (2020), the COVID-19 pandemic is still spreading among individuals in different nations and could cost the global economy between $5.8tn and $8.8tn. Already, different nations have started requesting financial assistance from the International Monetary Fund (IMF) to mitigate the financial shock that was caused by the pandemic. Besides, central banks around the globe have initiated aggressive policies to cut interest rates and roll out massive stimulus measures to help manage the impact of the pandemic that has rocked global economic activities and financial markets (Ozili & Arun, 2020). Possible uncertainty triggered by the pandemic and resulting behavioral changes have resulted in a temporary lack of food, price increases and disruptions to industry. These price shifts would be felt more by poor communities dependent on food markets, as well as by those still relying on humanitarian assistance to protect their living standards and food access. Consequently, different fast policy measures were implemented

DOI: 10.4324/9781003125648-2

by different nations across the globe to manage the COVID-19 impact, which includes monetary, fiscal, public health and human control measures (Ozili & Arun, 2020).

Significant conferences and events in science, architecture and sports have been canceled or delayed as the pandemic persists. Although the monetary impact on travel and trade is yet to be measured, fortunes are projected to increase. However, there have been different views from several scholars and stakeholders around the world that it's too early to properly assess the magnitude of the negative impact the pandemic has on the global economy because the situation is evolving every day. Nevertheless, going by several growth indicators and variables as provided by previous scholars, Table 2.1 provides an insight on the contributions of different authors on the indicators and variables of the global economy that are considered when assessing the impacts of a pandemic.

Accordingly, to adequately assess and quantify the impact of a pandemic such as COVID-19 on the global economy, indicators and variables are key for consideration. Perhaps, these indicators and variables are the factors that determine the economic stability of a nation (OECD, 2020a,

Table 2.1 Global economy indicators and variables affected by the pandemic

Authors	*Indicators and variables*
Bloom et al. (2018)	Unemployment, efficiency, healthcare system, business establishments, infrastructure, and public utilities.
Fan et al. (2018)	Foreign direct investment and GDP growth.
Kostova et al. (2019)	Balance of trade, GDP, production.
Ahani & Nilashi (2020)	Supply chain, traveling, export-import, manufacturing and service sector.
Haren & Simchi-Levi (2020)	Supply chain, manufacturing operations and high-tech industry.
Orlik et al. (2020) Organization for Economic Cooperation and Development (2020)	Financial markets blipping, GDP, foreign direct investment, balance of trade, financial markets, supply chain disruption, GDP, manufacturing disruption.
World Economic Forum (2020) Trading Economics (2020) Credit Union National Association (2020)	GDP, unemployment, foreign direct investment and the remittance, domestic demand, tourism and business travel.
Asian Development Bank (2020)	GDP, manufacturing, export, import, supply, interest, trade and production linkages.
Trading Economics (2020)	Balance of trade, credit rating and remittance, supply disruptions and health effects, GDP growth rate, interest rate, inflation rate, unemployment rate.

2020b). Trading Economics (2020) and Bloom et al. (2018) emphasized that the economic stability of a nation relies heavily on the positive growth in the health system, employment rate, increased productivity, a good transportation system, GDP growth and reduced interest rates and inflation rates. It is in this context that this study is conducted to evaluate the previous literature and logically reveal the impact of the COVID-19 pandemic on the global economy.

Method and Material

This study employed a qualitative literature review method. The choice of research method was informed by the purpose of this study, as the key emphasis was on the review and evaluation of previous works of literature to unfold logically and up-to-date issues as concerns coronavirus pandemic and the impact on the global economy. There are varieties of methods of literature review in this context, including narrative review, vote counting, meta-analysis and descriptive analysis of literature (King & He, 2005). A descriptive analysis of the literature was used for the benefit of this study. Thus, the descriptive analysis of literature mostly summarizes and synthesizes accessible studies on a specific subject field. However, due to the limited number of empirical research works in this field of study, a detailed descriptive analysis of previous literature was conducted, which aids in revealing current issues and challenges to the global economy as a result of the COVID-19 outbreak. Thus, various COVID-19 articles gathered from various significant and applicable websites, journals, newsletters and magazines were taken into consideration in extracting information for the descriptive analysis. It was, however, believed that the choice of research method for this study assisted in achieving and providing solutions to the study's objective.

Results and Discussion

Global Economic Contraction

An economic contraction is a plunge in national output as measured by the GDP. This involves a decline in both real personal earnings, industrial production, retail sales and other economic sectors (Palumbo, 2020). Economic indicators are used to determine when a contraction has occurred. Accordingly, the coronavirus that triggered a regional shock in Wuhan, China, in late 2019 has now triggered a big global contraction. As the coronavirus began in China and spread across the world, policymakers have acted to restrict its spread. There is no doubt that the coronavirus recession is a significant continuing world economic downturn that has triggered stagnation in most economies. It's the worst economic meltdown on a global scale since the Great Depression. The first strong sign of a recession was the downturn in the global financial meltdown of 2020, which began at the end of February and lasted until March (Elliott, 2020; Hawkins, 2020).

Both advanced economies and all developing economies have been in decline since September 2020 (IMF, 2020). The World Bank model, however, forecasts that a complete rebound in some regions will not be accomplished until 2025 or beyond (Winck, 2020). The perception of related diseases reveals that while human costs are substantial, the existence of financial costs is due to the governments' individual prevention measures and transmission control policies (Brahmbhatt & Dutta, 2008). The present experience is no different; as the epidemic spreads worldwide, many nations have now taken steps to curtail transmission, through measures of social isolation, such as closing international boundaries and educational institutions, regulating jobs and restricting people's movement. These control measures have had an immediate and significant effect on both economies and partner economies through trade and tourism. This has had significant implications for economies around the world, after a global economic recession in 2019 that has seen financial markets and consumer demand stagnate worldwide. Surviving from this contraction becomes a big challenge for most economies, as GDP growth of both advanced, emerging and developing economies is struggling in negative territory. Accordingly, in the fourth quarter of 2020, advanced economies recorded a 5.8% contraction of real GDP, while emerging and developing economies recorded a 3.3% contraction (IMF, 2020).

A significant level of contraction exists more in the advanced economies, as Spain, Italy, United Kingdom, Canada and France were the most hit. This, perhaps, relates to the infection rate in most of these countries, where the number of infections and the death rate are still on the increase. The world economy has also seen a drop in oil prices triggered by the 2020 war on oil prices between Russia and Saudi Arabia, the fall in tourism, the hospitality and mining industries, and a large reduction in economic activity compared to the previous decade (Yergin, 2020). At the end of February and March 2020, the world stock markets crashed by 20–30%, approximately. Global stock markets encountered unprecedented and volatile swings during the recession, largely due to severe uncertainty in the economy. Although stay-at-home orders affect many types of business, particularly those offering services on-site (including retail stores, restaurants and hotels, entertainment facilities and museums, medical offices, and beauty salons and spas), the financial burden and recovery roots of those businesses remains in question as the second wave of the virus hits most nations.

Similarly, unemployment around the world has risen sharply due to the global coronavirus pandemic, striking industrialized economies extremely hard and having long-term social consequences, especially on the welfare and children of those who have been laid off. The second quarter of 2020 saw a drop in full-time jobs by an estimated 400 million across the globe (Mckeever, 2020), causing a fall in income-earning by employees by 10%

in the first nine months of 2020. This 10% drop in income was estimated to be loss of over $3.5 trillion. However, unemployment continues at very high levels in many advanced economies, with little evidence of an early upturn, while economic shock has struck export-sector jobs hard in emerging and developing countries.

Impact of the COVID-19 Pandemic on the Global Economy

A detrimental effect has been felt globally from the ripple effect of COVID-19, which continues to damage the global economy in several ways. In the quest to manage and reduce the spread globally, different economies have enforced several measures, which have in turn affected economic activities around the world (Chakraborty & Maity, 2020; Nicola et al., 2020). Thus, in response to evaluating the severity of the pandemic on the global economy, this study summarized from previous literature the impact of COVID-19 on selected key sectors of the global economy as detailed below.

Agricultural Sector

Agricultural commodity prices are indications of changes in demand and supply, which reveal the abnormal conditions that attract attention on a global scale. As such, the efficiency of the agricultural commodity market has been tested by the outbreak of COVID-19. The coronavirus is a public health problem that, both directly and by the required measures to monitor the spread of the disease, has devastating consequences for the global economy. The food and farming sectors are also experiencing these impacts. Although the availability of food has been well preserved to date, the steps put in place in many countries to contain the spread of the virus have threatened the supply of agricultural food goods to markets and consumers, both within and abroad (Nicola *et al.*, 2020).

Similarly, the crash in global demand for agricultural commodities from hospitality industries and restaurants across the globe caused a drop in global prices of agricultural commodities in the second and third quarters of 2020. Thus, continuous volatility in commodity prices emerged from the uncertainty over the export of agricultural commodities, challenges of perishable commodities, and a limited number of verification and supply staff as per the regulations from lockdown rules (Atalan, 2020; He & Harris, 2020). Many agricultural commodity markets have also prompted the closure of floor trading, which has restricted the ability of traders to exchange commodities. However, this has prompted constant shifts in the prices of major agricultural commodities around the world.

Hospitality, Tourism and Aviation Industry

The spread of the coronavirus has prompted several nations to place bans on nonessential travel to countries infected by COVID-19, halting tourist travel, work visas and immigrant visas indefinitely. A full travel ban has been enforced by some countries on all modes of inward or outward travel, closing down all airports in the world. The tourism industry is obviously among the sectors that are most impacted by the coronavirus epidemic, with an impact on both travel demand and supply. The World Travel and Tourism Council warns that 50 million workers in the international travel and tourism sector could be at risk as a direct result of the coronavirus. Marriott International is poised to position tens of thousands of jobs on furlough (approximately 174,000 employees). The United Nations World Tourism Organization consequently projected that global international tourist arrivals will decline by 58% to 78% in 2020, leading to a possible reduction in international tourism receipts of US$ 0.9–1.2 trillion. Profits from the hotel industry per room available in the United States decreased by 11.6% by the weekend of 7 March 2020, although China's occupancy rate declined by 89% by the end of January 2020.

Other US hotel firms are seeking about $150 billion in direct support for employees due to a continued market slowdown, along with a forecast shortfall of $1.5 billion since mid-February. Likewise, with a current occupancy rate of 6%, Italian cities such as Rome were suddenly impacted, while London remains the most stable with an occupancy rate of around 47%. All in, the COVID-19 slowdown has resulted in global distortions in the hospitality sector and a significant slump in the European hotel industry. Africa and other parts of the globe are not excluded from this crisis because, except for the shipment of vital goods, a full ban on foreign travel has been imposed.

In Europe, the Alliance for the European Tourism Manifesto, which comprises more than 50 European public and private travel and tourism firms, has highlighted the need for immediate action. This includes temporary state funding to the tourism and travel sector from governments, and also some quick and convenient access to short- and medium-term loans to fix liquidity deficits, including EU funds accessible through the Corona Investment Response and fiscal relief initiative. The airline and transport sectors, which are complementary to the tourism industry, are grappling with an extraordinary surge of cancellations and a significant decrease in demand in the face of tight government regulations on social distance regulation and bans on unnecessary travel. Such border controls cost the tourism industry a loss of more than $200 billion worldwide on their own, excluding other tourism travel revenue losses, and a total loss of $113 billion was projected for the aviation industry, according to IATA.

Petroleum and Oil Sector

At a time when the oil industry is facing a phase of structural decline, the double blow of the coronavirus and the oil price shock has struck emerging oil countries especially hard. Although certain governments that rely on sovereign wealth funds or comparatively low levels of government debt will find some ways to resolve the current crisis, the majority of poor oil nations, many of which are resource-dependent and have already experienced high levels of debt and dynamic economic and social fragility before the current crisis, are in a situation of uncertainty (IEA, 2020). Emerging petroleum countries have been struck extremely hard by the current crisis for two reasons:

a Firstly, both of these countries' reliance on a single commodity for their exports and sales renders them extremely susceptible to fluctuations in prices.
b Secondly, before the current crisis, many of these countries were already in unstable situations, and more instability might exacerbate the underlying fragility.

The influence of the current COVID-19 pandemic has shocked many, sending oil and gas prices to a historic low. Such was the chaos that, for the first time at the end of April 2020, the US crude oil index plummeted into negative zone, along with the price of Brent Crude, the benchmark for Europe and the rest of the world, which also plunged sharply.

Although prices have changed since then, there is unlikely to be the same price buoyancy as in the aftermath of the world economic crisis of 2008. With the aid of technological advances and the steadily declining cost of green energy, the increasing contribution to decarbonization and the decreasing demand of consumers, the fossil fuel industry faces the possibility of a structural slowdown (Lahn & Bradley, 2020). The shock caused by the COVID-19 pandemic and the interruption of negotiations between the Association of Petroleum Exporting Countries (OPEC) and its allies may have led to a decrease in oil prices. OPEC planned a reduction in production of 1.5 million barrels per day (mb/d) for the second quarter of 2020 on 5 March 2020. Out of this, production cuts for OPEC nations would be 1 mb/d, and production cuts for non-OPEC but related producers, mainly like Russia, will be 0.5 mb/d. Russia dismissed the plan the next day, resulting in Saudi Arabia, the world's most powerful exporter of crude, raising demand to its highest capacity of 12.3 mb/d. Saudi Arabia has reported discounts in large economies of about 20%. This resulted in a decline in oil prices of almost 30% and the losses have continued since then. The COVID-19 dual shock and the oil price crash are interlinked, but separate.

The market share of the oil shock is related to a decline in oil use as a result of protection practices to curb the spread of coronavirus. Due to "stay-at-home" directives that have caused the global economy to slow down severely, something has happened. In the current background, oil markets cannot completely bounce back to pre-coronavirus peaks as the world moves to cleaner energy sources (BNP Paribas, 2020). In resource-rich developed nations, these predictions illustrate the risks of over-reliance on fossil fuels and provide an opportunity to place decarbonization in the front line of recovery agendas. In order to build fiscal space in emerging petroleum markets, reduce the risk of excessive debt, corruption and irregular financial flows (IFFs) and improve the change to a stable and more prosperous future, a timely and coherent solution is required, including both concessional creditors and private funders.

Manufacturing Industry

The manufacturing sector is a major part of the economy as it accounts for a reasonable percentage of global GDP. Global manufacturing activity has already seen an overall economic downturn in 2019, however; in the first quarter of 2020, production output fell significantly by 6.0%, making the manufacturing sector one of the most hit by COVID-19. This downturn is attributed to China's lockdown to curb the spread of COVID-19, as well as continuing tensions related to trade sanctions between the United States and China. Secondly, the lockdown regulations that followed the outbreak of the virus in many countries brought the manufacturing sector to a halt, derailing the whole global supply chain (Nicola et al., 2020). Consequently, a whole lot of events were triggered, including a drastic decline in global FDI inflow and a downturn in the global economy.

Owing to the volatility of supply chains and self-isolation policies, import issues and staffing shortages have been listed as key obstacles for enterprises. Indeed, for some places within a production business, "operating from home" is not a viable option. The British Plastics Federation (BPF) report analyzed the effect of COVID-19 on manufacturing sectors in the United Kingdom (UK). Over the next two quarters, approximately 80% of respondents registered a drop in sales, with 98% admitting concern about the negative effects of the pandemic on business activities. Second, a survey undertaken by the Purchasing Managers Index (PMI) among manufacturing purchasing managers around the world's major economies, using an index of 50.0 as optimism for manufacturers and 49.9 and below for pessimism, showed how major economies' manufacturing industries operated in the first six months of 2020 (Babypips Market Snapshot, 2020).

After what seemed like months of manufacturing downturn, the second quarter of 2020 seems optimistic going by the rating of PMI, after months of supply restrictions (Babypips Market Snapshot, 2020). However, it is significant that the end of the first quarter of 2020 experienced a drastic drop in the manufacturing sector of most of the economies. Perhaps, this could be aligned to the severity of the pandemic during that particular period. In view of the fact that many manufacturers began very minimal production after the lockdown, even the slightest easing of restrictions would see a rise in confidence. Therefore, rather than relying on post-lockdown optimism, stakeholders should look at patterns in export demand, development and supply shifts for clues on the road to global economic recovery.

Finance Industry

The most obvious impact of coronavirus on the financial sector was the negative effect experienced with global market prices. The global stock market lost $6 trillion between 23 and 28 February from the record of S&P Dow Jones Indices (Ozili & Arun, 2020). This drop in the stock prices continued as the spread of the virus persisted. Similarly, banks globally witnessed the same sharp drop in share prices. While the oil price battle, in which Russia and Saudi Arabia were pushing down oil prices by growing oil supply, also played a role in the decline in stock market indices, the subsequent decline in stock market indices in March was primarily attributed to investors' flight to safety following the indefinite spread of the COVID-19 pandemic.

Although at first approximation the dynamics of the financial markets during the pandemic may appear random, crazy, or even mad, they did not blindly respond to closer scrutiny. According to Albuquerque et al. (2020), Ding et al. (2020), Fahlenbrach et al. (2020), Pagano et al. (2020) and Ramelli and Wagner (2020), quite a few research studies have shown that capital markets are successful in discounting the most exposed companies, those that are more financially unstable, vulnerable to corporate social responsibility, or less resilient to social distances, subject to disruption in foreign supply chains.

However, Capelle-Blancard and Desroziers (2020) stressed four stock market facts in relation to the outbreak of COVID-19. First, after briefly avoiding the pandemic (until 21 February 2020), as disease outbreak worries grew, the stock markets reacted negatively to the spike in the number of infected individuals in each nation (23 February to 20 March 2020). Second, it appears that country-specific aspects have had next to no effect on the response of the stock market. In countries that are more prone to a disease outbreak, capital markets have not reacted more strongly, either because of structural economic fragility (e.g., indebted countries) or because of spread vector vulnerability (e.g., at-risk countries). Third, investors in neighboring (but mostly wealthy) countries were receptive to the number of COVID-19 events. Lastly, the downturn in market prices has been mitigated by credit facilities and government guarantees, lowered policy interest rates, and lockdown measures. Therefore, during the COVID-19 pandemic, the complexities of the financial markets were not entirely unintentional. However, the reaction of capital markets was affected not by the precrisis condition of the nations, but rather by the health policies introduced during the crisis to restrict the spread of the epidemic, and by the macro-economic policies aimed at helping businesses.

Healthcare and Pharmaceutical Industry

The COVID-19 outbreak has posed a major threat to global healthcare systems. In healthcare services around the world, the insecurity of healthcare personnel remains one of the major challenges. Techniques such as the early introduction of virus detection for asymptomatic and/or frontline healthcare workers have been critical because most healthcare workers are unable to function remotely (Tanne *et al.*, 2020). There are no safety precautions; even face masks, at high healthcare costs, and inadequate numbers of ICU beds and ventilators have gradually exposed gaps in the quality of medical treatment. In the United States, Brazil, Italy, Spain and many other African countries, there is concern for uninsured persons who can function in places that predispose them to viral infection, which can lead to significant impediments in the event of sickness.

In the pharmaceutical sector, deep changes in the complexities of healthcare have emerged, leading to significant investment in technology for disease prevention and accelerated technical change in healthcare delivery. The change in health policy and clinical management as new evidence arises has also been illustrated by Nicola et al. (2020). In the United States, active prescription products are mainly supplied from India (18%) and the EU (26%), while China accounts for 13%. China, accounting for 39.3%, is also the top exporter of medical devices to the United States. Shutdowns in output and shortages in supplies would eventually lead to a loss of profits. Alternatively, prospects have concurrently arisen for companies engaged in vaccine and drug production, with companies including Pfizer, Moderna and AstraZeneca having announced their COVID-19 vaccine products as approved by their national regulatory authorities, but not yet obtaining WHO EUL/PQ authorization as of early December 2020. Hence, there is an immediate need for a potential COVID-19 vaccine to manage the continuous and the second wave of the virus as well as to help restore global economic activities.

Strategic Management to Mitigate the Global Impact of the Coronavirus Pandemic

This part of the chapter provides strategic managerial initiatives that could be used to mitigate the impact of COVID-19 pandemic in most of the global economic sectors. Strategic management according to Drnevich *et al.* (2020) involves a formulation of an initiative and implementation of major goals by stakeholders to mitigate unexpected backdrops and optimize organizational goals. Thus, find below the mitigating strategies on the impact of the COVID-19 pandemic.

a *Agricultural sector* – The global agricultural sector plays a crucial role in providing food commodities for household consumption and, on the global economic scale, provides revenues that boost economic growth. The lockdown regulations and border closures have caused limited activity in this sector. As such, considering the potentials and the need for food commodity availability for global consumption, structural support and strategic limited restrictions on transportation of agricultural commodities should be implemented. This will not only sustain the progress of the agricultural sector, but also reduce the level of perishability of commodities and sustain the global food supply.

b ***Tourism and aviation sector*** – There is no doubt of the severe impact of COVID-19 pandemic on tourism and aviation industry, as travelers are restricted from moving from one part of the world to another. However, the global tourism and aviation are sectors that economies around the world cannot continue to place restriction on. As such, the focus should be on control and reduction of speed of transmission, which requires nations to improvise mandatory borders and transit point testing with instant results. Secondly, considering the potential of the tourism and aviation industry, which has proven to be an engine of economic growth, proactive measures on the scale of structural financial assistance will help in resuscitating this sector.

c ***Petroleum and oil sector*** – The petroleum sector, which has been a source of revenue for most nations, has suffered a drastic drop in oil prices that resulted from the drop in global demand. Diversification is inevitable as lockdown regulation continue to limit the consumption of oil and gas products. However, going by the rules of demand and supply, which determine the prices of oil and gas, a continuous increase in petroleum productivity with the current limited demand globally will further affect the prices of the product, thereby creating more panic in the global market.

d ***Manufacturing sector*** – Accordingly, the halt in the manufacturing sector has contributed heavily to the global economic contraction. Perhaps, the world cannot function as a globe in the absence of import and export of expertise, products and services. As such, the manufacturing sector survives mainly on human expertise and transfer of technology. Thus, this could only be sustained by first ensuring the safety of workers by maintaining and observing safety protocols as well as testing to reduce the spread of the virus. Secondly, considering the linkage between the manufacturing sector, exports and imports, a recommended logical level of limited restriction on transportation of manufactured goods would improve this sector.

e ***Financial sector*** – The threat of the COVID-19 pandemic has caused heavy panic on the global financial market, as prices continue to fluctuate as a result of the present economic uncertainty. Losses and risks are inevitable; perhaps there is an urgent need to reduce the spread of the virus, which will reflect a positive stability of the market.

f ***Health sector*** – The health sector across the globe has seen the worst level of vulnerability since the inception of the COVID-19 pandemic. The severity and fatality level of the virus across the globe have revealed the state of most health sectors in most countries. Perhaps, equal access to quality health is a basic human right. Thus, to salvage this sector in its current state, policies to improve the financing of hospital equipment, personnel training and stewardship from respective governments are greatly needed. Hence, a coherent collaboration between countries and regions across the globe is recommended.

Policy Implications and Recommendations

Policy implications and recommendations help in outlining concerns that will help policy-makers to make informed decisions. As such, stakeholders and policy-makers are advised to consider the following:

a Since the inception of the COVID-19 pandemic, there have been a reasonable number of scholarly contributions which stakeholders of different economies should employ to manage the unprecedented situation of the virus.

b To have a proper assessment of the impact of COVID-19 on the entire economic system of a nation, economic growth indicators and variables as outlined in Table 2.1 should not be ignored to have a proper evaluation of the situation.

c Although the virus is still spreading as most countries are experiencing the second wave, sourcing of vaccine and strategic policies to manage the spread as well as providing room for economic activities should be implemented by different economies.

d It is obvious that the global economy has suffered; however, the root of recovery should be encouraged by different economies through holistic reforms that encourage local economic development.

e The backdrop in the different economic sectors is obvious as economic activities were brought to a halt due to different restrictive measures. Economic sectors such as tourism, agriculture, finance and manufacturing industries which have been identified as the real engine of economic growth should be encouraged in a different capacity to salvage the economic plunge.

f Government and concerned stakeholders should lay more emphasis on extended knowledge and campaign against the COVID-19 pandemic, as a better awareness of the pandemic by individuals will help them manage the externalities that come with it.

Conclusion

Building on previous literature, this study focuses on how the COVID-19 pandemic affects the global economy as it concerns reduction in employment, closure of international borders, GDP, health systems, productivity, FDI, supply chain, a decline in demand for services that require proximity between people, imports and exports. Although different countries and regions are experiencing different forms of the severe impact of the pandemic, this study reveals on the global scale the backdrops suffered by different key economic affected areas.

Times like these call for resilient and powerful leadership in hospitals, manufacturing, government and the wider economy in the midst of a modern recession and financial crash. It is important to implement urgent relief measures and adapt them to those that can fall through the cracks. To reshape and reenergize the economy as a result of this crisis, medium to longer-lasting solutions are required. In order for those with clear and viable business models to succeed, a comprehensive social and economic growth agenda, including sector-by-sector plans and an infrastructure that encourages entrepreneurship, is also needed. Continuously reassessing and reevaluating the state of play is prudent for regimes and financial institutions.

References

Ahani, A., & Nilashi, M. (2020). Coronavirus outbreak and its impacts on global economy: The role of social network sites. *Journal of Soft Computing and Decision Support Systems*, 7(2), 19–22.

Albuquerque, R.A., Koskinen, Y., Yang, S., & Zhang, C. (2020). Love in the time of COVID-19: The resiliency of environmental and social stocks. *Covid Economics: Vetted and Real-Time Papers 11*. CEPR.

Asian Development Bank. (2020). COVID-19 outbreak to have significant economic impact on developing Asia. Retrieved from: www.adb.org/news/covid-19-outbreak-have-significant-economic-impactdeveloping-asia (accessed 6 March 2020).

Atalan, A. (2020). Is the lockdown important to prevent the COVID-19 pandemic? Effects on psychology, environment and economy-perspective. *Annals of Medicine and Surgery*, 56, 38–42.

Babypips. (2020). Market Snapshot: Global Manufacturing PMIs. Available at www.babypips.com/news/forex-global-manufacturing-pmi-h12020 (accessed 17 December 2020).

Bloom, D.E., Cadarette, D., & Sevilla, J. (2018). Epidemics & economy. *Finance & Development.*

BNP Paribas. (2020). Big oil: Staring down the barrel of an uncertain future. https://docfinder.bnpparibas-am.com/api/files/22AC4C06-8B50-4D3B-BC34-EF7A99DF9680 (accessed 14 December 2020).

Brahmbhatt, M., & Datta, A. (2008). On SARS type economic effects during infectious disease outbreaks. World Bank Policy Research Paper No. 4466. Washington DC: World Bank. http://documents.worldbank.org/curated/en/101511468028867410/On-SARS-type-economiceffects-during-infectious-disease-outbreaks.

Capelle-Blancard, G., & Desroziers, A. (2020). The stock market and the economy: Insights from the COVID-19 crisis. *VoxEU. Org, 19.*

Chakraborty, I., & Maity, P. (2020). COVID-19 outbreak: Migration, effects on society, global environment and prevention. *Science of the Total Environment*, 138882.

Credit Union National Association. (2020). Remittance changes would help mitigate coronavirus effects. https://news.cuna.org/articles/117408-remittance-changes-would-help-mitigate-coronaviruseffects.

Ding, W., Levine, R., Lin C., & Xie W. (2020). Corporate Immunity to the COVID-19 Pandemic. NBER Working Paper No. 27055.

Drnevich, P.L., Mahoney, J.T. & Schendel, D. (2020). Has strategic management research lost its way. *Strategic Management Review*, *1*(1), 1119–1127.

Elliott, L. (2020). 'Great Lockdown' to rival Great Depression with 3% hit to global economy, says IMF. *The Guardian*. Retrieved 15 April 2020.

Fahlenbrach, R., Rageth, K., & Stulz, R.M. (2020). How valuable is financial flexibility when revenue stops? Evidence from the COVID-19 crisis. NBER Working Papers 27106.

Fan, V.Y., Jamison, D.T., & Summers, L.H. (2018). Pandemic risk: How large are the expected losses? *Bulletin of the World Health Organization*, *96*(2), 129.

Haren, P., & Simchilevi, D. (2020). How coronavirus could impact the global supply chain by mid-March from the pages of Harvard Business Review. *Harvard Business Press*.

Hawkins, J. (2020). How will the coronavirus recession compare with the worst in Australia's history? *The Conversation*. Retrieved 16 April 2020.

He, H., & Harris, L. (2020). The impact of Covid-19 pandemic on corporate social responsibility and marketing philosophy. *Journal of Business Research*.

IEA. (2020). Energy market turmoil deepens challenges for many major oil and gas exporters. www.iea.org/articles/energy-market-turmoil-deepens-challenges-for-many-major-oil-and-gas-exporters (accessed 12 December 2020).

IMF. (2020). World economic outlook update. A crisis like no other, an uncertain recovery. Retrieved 11 October 2020.

King, W.R., & He, J. (2005). Understanding the role and methods of meta-analysis in IS research. *Communications of the Association for Information Systems*, *16*, Article 32, 665–686.

Kostova, D., Cassell, C.H., Redd, J.T., Williams, D.E., Singh, T., Martel, L.D., & Bunnell, R. E. (2019). Long-distance effects of epidemics: Assessing the link between the 2014 West Africa Ebola outbreak and US exports and employment. *Health Economics*, *28*(11), 1248–1261.

Lahn, G., & Bradley, S. (2020). How COVID-19 is changing the opportunities for oil and gas-led growth. https://oecd-development-matters.org/2020/07/10/how-covid-19-is-changing-the-opportunities-for-oil-and-gas-led-growth/ (accessed 2 May 2020).

McKeever, V. (2020). The coronavirus is expected to have cost 400 million jobs in the second quarter, UN labour agency estimates. *CNBC*. Retrieved 6 September 2020.

Nicola, M., Alsafi, Z., Sohrabi, C., Kerwan, A., Al-Jabir, A., Iosifidis, C., Agha, M., & Agha, R. (2020). The socio-economic implications of the coronavirus pandemic (COVID-19): A review. *International Journal of Surgery*, *78*, 185.

Nicola, M., O'Neill, N., Sohrabi, C., Khan, M., Agha, M., & Agha, R. (2020). Evidence based management guideline for the COVID-19 pandemic. *International Journal of Surgery*. DOI: 10.1016/j.ijsu.2020.04.001.

OECD. (2020a). Quarterly GDP as on 23 March 2020. Retrieved from: https://data.oecd.org/gdp/quarterly-gdp.htm#indicator-chart.

OECD. (2020b). Unemployment rate (indicator). DOI: 10.1787/52570002-en (accessed 16 December 2020).

Orlik, T., Rush, J., Cousin, M., & Hong J. (2020). Coronavirus could cost the global economy $2.7 trillion. Here's how. *Bloomberg Economics*. www.bloomberg.com/graphics/2020-coronaviruspandemic-global-economic-risk/ (accessed 21 March 2020).

Ozili, P.K., & Arun, T. (2020). Spillover of COVID-19: Impact on the global economy. Available at SSRN 3562570.

Pagano, M., Wagner, C., & Zechner, J. (2020). Disaster resilience and asset prices. CEPR Discussion Paper 14773/*Covid Economics: Vetted and Real-Time Papers 21*.

Palumbo, D. (2020). Coronavirus: A visual guide to the economic impact. BBC News. Archived from the original on 27 March 2020.

Ramelli, S., & Wagner, A.F. (2020). Feverish stock price reactions to COVID-19. Working Paper, CEPR DP14511.

Tanne, J.H., Hayasaki, E., Zastrow, M., Pulla, P., Smith, P., & Rada, A.G. (2020). Covid-19: How doctors and healthcare systems are tackling coronavirus worldwide. *Bmj, 368*.

Trading Economics (2020). GDP annual growth rate - forecast 2020-2022. https://tradingeconomics.com/forecast/gdp-annual-growth-rate (accessed 24 March 2020).

Winck, B. (2020). IMF economic outlook: 'Great Lockdown' will be worst recession in century. *Business Insider*. Retrieved 27 July 2020.

World Economic Forum. (2020). Coronavirus: US unemployment rate could hit 30% as on 25 December 2020. Retrieved from: www.weforum.org/agenda/2020/03/coronavirus-could-leave-30-of-us-workers-joblessfed-official-says/.

Yergin, D. (2020). The oil collapse. *Foreign Affairs: An American Quarterly Review*. Retrieved 15 July 2020.

3 Business Diplomacy and Lobbying During Pandemic

Faisal Ahmed and Hardik Gupta

Introduction

In a post-globalized era, the geo-economic engagements are not just based on the relationships between governments, but are also influenced by an intricate network of non-state actors like the media and policy think-tanks (Kumar & Malhotra, 2020). Hence, they are redefining the basis and instruments of diplomacy, and thus leading the world onto a more sophisticated web of geopolitical equations and power rebalance (see Saner and Yiu, 2008).

In such a complex scenario, multinational enterprises (MNEs) and even small and medium enterprises (SMEs) – which form the lead firms and participants respectively in the global value chains (GVCs) – have to regularly revisit their business models. A foreign business operating in a host country could make the local industry more competitive and increase consumer welfare. At more advanced levels of operations like greenfield and brownfield projects, the country also gains through creation of employment opportunities and an increase in investment in the country and foreign exchange reserves to finance its imports. These foreign firms also bring with them technical and administrative know-how that gets transferred to the local workforce, thus boosting the rate of innovation and domestic capacity-building in the host country. The business operations of a foreign firm thus align with the economic objectives of the host governments to create a win-win situation.

On the other hand, a firm operating globally by engaging in trade or through establishment of manufacturing and marketing operations in another country exposes itself to a new set of direct and indirect risks. It is likely that a firm sourcing raw materials through its GVCs can suffer enormously in the case of a disrupted supply for even short periods of time. Therefore, firms invest heavily while internationalizing their operations and seek measures to minimize their risks emanating from a complex political environment (Saner, 2016).

Therefore, it is imperative that firms, in order to meet their strategic intents, must secure their economic activities and business models from exposures in the external environment – especially those posed by state

DOI: 10.4324/9781003125648-3

and non-state actors in a host country. The activities of the domestic and international pressure groups, other firms operating in the region, the perception of the population, the perception of the government in power and the personal authority commanded by people in key positions of power are all important aspects to be considered for securing its interests.

In fact, today, firms can themselves act and negotiate to secure their position and preemptively attempt to solidify them through the application of business diplomacy. Business diplomacy, thus, is an instrument of deriving political power or creating favorable popular geopolitical perceptions to further its business interests and to enhance its market reputation. Business diplomacy also enables the firm to influence government policies and decisions in its favor, especially after a deeper level of understanding is reached and the communication channel is made easier. This is further aided by close collaborations with other non-state actors like non-government organizations (NGOs), media, and intergovernmental organizations too. Business diplomacy is about making the environment suitable for business and to reduce risk and uncertainty (Saner, 2016).

There have been various studies on business diplomacy and lobbying and its various aspects, e.g., Ruël and Suren (2018), Marques (2017), Riordan (2014), Ruël et al. (2013), Saner and Yiu (2003), Josselin and Wallace (2001) and Saner et al. (2000), among others. Yet, the academic discourse lacks newer and continuous research outputs in this field. Our current study therefore attempts to contribute to the discourse on business diplomacy in the following ways:

a we decipher the actors in the business diplomacy process and examine their evolving role in the context of past and current geo-economic complexities
b we outline and explain the enablers of a conducive business diplomacy process
c we identify the geo-economic instances that have been witnessed during the COVID-19 pandemic, e.g. 5G technology issues, mobile app ban, supply chain disruptions, and opportunities takeovers, and assess how business diplomacy can positively or negatively influence their global outreach.

Literature Review

For the term "business diplomacy" there is no widely accepted definition, and various scholars have conceptualized it with distinct connotations – converging at times. The use of the term with respect to international businesses and the actors therein was first proposed by Saner et al. (2000). It was also used a year earlier by London (1999) proposing business diplomacy more as a management technique that can be employed to get work done in organizations to achieve principled leadership. Henceforth, the term has been used in the context of a firm's international business operations.

In fact, Saner et al. (2000) defined it very comprehensively and stated that

> Business diplomacy management involves influencing economic and social actors to create and seize new business opportunities; working with rule-making international bodies whose decisions affect international business; forestalling potential conflicts with stakeholders and minimizing political risks; and using multiple international forums and media channels to safeguard corporate image and reputation.

A multinational enterprise (MNE) operates in a complex environment characterized by economic and geopolitical maneuverings. The MNEs in order to get their tasks accomplished in a host country may need to engage and interact with multiple stakeholders including the government, non-government organizations (NGOs), civil society organizations (CSOs), political parties, media houses and several other non-state actors. (Saner and Yiu, 2003; 2005). They thus develop an interface with such stakeholders and engage in business diplomacy to fulfill their strategic intents.

Ruël et al. (2013) also argue that through business diplomacy, corporate executives seek to establish and sustain positive relationships with government and NGOs in a host country to safeguard their corporate image and reputation. Even Saner and Yiu (2014) have also pointed out the significance of business diplomacy in managing an MNEs reputation in a foreign business environment. Also, Riordan (2014) has explained it from the perspective of risk, and argues that business diplomacy is like a strategic cooperation among firms and its stakeholders aimed to shape the firm's risk environment.

Saner et al. (2000) emphasize the importance of business diplomacy management as a core competence of modern MNEs, emanating from globalization and the rise of social media, among other factors. To succeed in the markets that the firm currently operates in, and to explore new opportunities, it is imperative to have a deeper understanding of the interests of multiple domestic and foreign pressures groups. They can, and indeed do, have a direct or indirect impact on the firm's business environment owing to changes in the already complex political and economic instruments affecting the firm's commercial interests. Ruël et al. (2013) differentiated business diplomacy with respect to other similar concepts such as corporate political activity (CPA), corporate political strategy (CPS), strategic political management (SPM), MNEs' global governance and MNEs' host government relations. They further position "corporate diplomacy" as synonymous with "business diplomacy" and argue that both these initiatives involve the same business practices, but maintain that the globally integrated firms are more involved in business diplomacy and pursue a broader approach.

There are studies in the literature which also seek to establish the linkages and interdependence between the business activities and the non-business actors in the market that the firm is operating in. For instance, Josselin and Wallace (2001) highlighted the increasing role of non-state actors, including MNEs, NGOs, CSOs etc. in international politics. Also, Saner and Yiu (2003) analyzed the changes observed in the global diplomatic framework in the modern world after the increased participation of the non-state actors in the global political and economic institutions. Later, Saner and Yiu (2005) studied the case of Switzerland and the Swiss MNEs with respect to the delicate balance that both national government and the MNEs have to maintain while interacting with international institutions – in this case, the European Union and its markets. They highlighted the influence of inter-governmental organizations on the MNEs' global market, and the dependence of these MNEs on the access to those markets. Saner and Yiu (2008) studied the interactions between the government, businesses and NGOs in the modern world. They examined the participation of non-state actors in diplomacy as a consequence of globalization, and also focused on NGOs and CSOs. Further, La Porte (2012) emphasized the newly realized impact of non-state actors on public diplomacy, exploring it as an addition to the state-pursued public diplomacy.

Interestingly, there is a significant increase in power that the MNEs have commanded at a global level in the past few decades. Muldoon (2005) has discussed the transnational corporations (TNCs) taking a pivotal position in the world economy by developing an economic clout in many countries, by managing a vast stakeholder network, and by intensely engaging with the national governments for resolution of such issues where the corporate and national interests reinforced each other. Also, they point out the fact that this added influence has led the state and non-state actors to seek more accountability in social and environmental matters from these MNEs. Earlier, Levy and Newell (2000) discussed such related convergences with reference to the environmental responsibilities of the MNEs and the industry response through the consideration of cases of climate change, ozone depletion and genetically modified food in Europe and the United States. They established a convergence among the business strategies employed in dealing with the demands of environmental activists in both regions while also maintaining that there exists a process of negotiation in such policy formulations by the national governments.

There is no doubt that the thematic discourse has also tried to justify the growing need for business diplomacy in modern times and attributed it to growing complexities in the global socio-political sphere and the fast-evolving geo-economic environment. Ruël (2013) discussed the global economic balance shifting to create a more interdependent system where the government, businesses and non-state actors all have a role to play. Kesteleyn et al. (2014) discussed the relevance of global markets now for a multitude of factors ranging from market and labor to attractive investment opportunities. The need for business diplomacy begins here. They also argue that the businesses cannot remain dependent upon the economic or commercial diplomacy of the state when a huge sum of money is at stake.

Riordan (2014) also attempted to study business diplomacy management in terms of the capabilities that the firms acquire. The study argued that larger firms make their own capabilities, whereas the smaller firms buy them in. The need to develop these capabilities include the fall of the US hegemony, the rise in international governance, the rise of ICT and social media, and other threats such as terrorism and organized crime (Riordan, 2014). In addition to this, a general helplessness of the home country's government on international issues may raise the need for a firm to develop its own capabilities. Haynal (2014) and Ruël and Wolters (2016) have discussed the complexities that the businesses have to deal with in the evolving global business environment. Ruël and Wolters (2016) also highlight the subsequent changes in the relationship between state and non-state actors primarily caused by globalization. They also laid emphasis on the development of geopolitical analysis skills, stakeholder management skills, intercultural communication skills and negotiation skills, to navigate through the complexities of the external environment. The corporate role in peace-building and peace-making activities for the mutual benefit of business and state has also been affirmed by Westermann-Behaylo et al. (2015).

There have been studies on the actual impact of business diplomacy on specific companies. These studies have either taken specific examples or used samples in some cases. Saner and Yiu (2014) identified the challenges where business diplomacy is required by taking the example of OECD guidelines for MNEs. Taking the examples of various industries like extractive industries including the energy sector and their OECD guidelines, they determined that for fulfillment of several commercial requirements, core competence in the form of business diplomacy is required. Thus, the appointment of business diplomats by MNEs is becoming increasingly important. In a relatively recent study, Pantoja (2018) explained the need for business diplomacy as a tool to establish inter-linkages between businesses, governments and various non-state actors. In doing so, the paper analyzes the motivation of the businesses and the governments to take part in conversations attempting to build a long-term sustainable relationship. The paper recognizes business diplomacy as a subset of public diplomacy. Taking the case of biotechnology companies that bargain for commercialization, deregulation or intellectual property enforcement, the paper lists different instruments of business diplomacy such as reactive strategic communication, proactive strategic communication, relationship-building strategic communication, lobbying networks, etc. The paper studies them as a situation-specific measure that ultimately aims to contribute to long-term relationship-building. These instruments have been listed by taking into account the experience of the biotechnology companies promoting GMOs in Mexico.

Marques (2017) studied business diplomacy in Brazil and concluded through empirical research that the Brazilian firms that have entered the world market need to develop their competency in the domain to maintain legitimacy and leverage their presence. Later, Ruël and Suren (2018) attempted to identify the relationship between the international business diplomatic activities of MNEs and a firm's performance. The study, which involved interviews with five large MNEs operating in different industries, found a positive effect of international business diplomacy on the firm's performance. Non-financial indicators like marketing possibilities, knowledge sharing, company image and reputation were the ones that experienced an increment. They further stated that these non-financial gains can lead to financial gains in the long run.

Actors in the Business Diplomacy Process

The essence of business diplomacy should also be understood with reference to the exposure that the businesses face from non-business actors. Business diplomacy's primary aim is to address this exposure and ease the process of conducting operations in another country (Saner et al., 2000). Therefore, to formulate policies aimed at building a sustainable positive relationship with various non-business stakeholders in the international business environment, it is crucial to identify the actors that impact the firm's immediate environment. These actors vary greatly with respect to the degree of interaction with the firm and the decision-making power they carry over the elements of the business environment. These actors can be divided into two groups, viz. primary participants and secondary participants. The primary participants have direct decision-making authority over various elements that affects a firm's operations and can individually affect the business. On the other hand, the secondary participants affect the firms' operations indirectly, but have the ability to influence the primary participants too.

Primary Participants

The following actors can be classified as primary participants:

(a) Host Country Government: The government grants the MNE permission to operate in the country and lays down the code of conduct through laws and regulations. Therefore, the first sign of legitimacy and the "license to operate" is provided by the government of the host country. On one hand, the government carries the authority to change laws or provide exceptions in the present laws to invite the foreign firms to operate in the country.[1] It is the government's responsibility

to introduce policies and regulation that helps the country's economy prosper and grow (Beales et al., 2017). On the other hand, it alone can decide to take extreme measures such as nationalization or expropriation rendering the foreign firms exposed to the greatest of political risks (Hajzler, 2012). Further, through the formulation of competition, labor laws, environmental protection laws, taxation policies etc., the government can directly impact the profitability and, in some cases, survivability of foreign firms in the country.[2] High degrees of cooperation are therefore required at all levels of the government: local, state and national. Even though other factors may play a role in influencing the decision-making process, the final authority to consider or ignore the pleas of other parties remain with the government.[3]

Another important aspect of involvement that has been observed by *The Economist* (2012) and emphasized by Ruël (2013) are the state-owned enterprises (SOEs) that operate in a number of countries. These enterprises are partially or fully owned by the government and are especially popular in developing countries such as China and India – the two emerging major economies in Asia. This makes their governments a direct participant in the market system, further increasing the interaction between the state and the MNEs. Here, the interests of the government are more complex and difficult to analyze as the SOEs function both for public welfare and as a government source of revenue. SOEs are fully backed by the government's financial resources and also garner support from allied government machinery.

In the case of a business facing hostile government policies and strict regulatory actions, the only recourse that is generally available to business is the judiciary – domestic or international – which in itself is a very long process in many countries. With ceased operations and further legal expenditures, the firm can be expected to face serious financial implications on top of what can now be considered as the sunk costs, without the assurance of any returns. Also, the reason that the judiciary cannot be stated separately as a participant in the business diplomacy process is because the businesses have much less room for relationship-building with a country's judicial structure. The conversation with the judicial system starts and ends with the assessment of actions on the basis of the law of the land.

An aggrieved firm may also approach international fora and seek justice on the basis of the international laws and conventions that the country's government has already ratified. However, the government may still choose to stand its ground and take the heat of international pressure. The country's credibility may get affected but the company still may not receive appropriate financial compensation for the losses it may have suffered. For instance, under President Hugo Chavez, Venezuela embarked on the mission to nationalize several of its industries, ranging from steel and cement to food processing and packaging.[4] A notable example in the series of nationalizations carried out by the government is that of the "Siderúrgica del Orinoco", also known as Sidor, the largest steel manufacturer in the country. After demands from the workers for increased salaries, the government decided to jump in and re-make the company as a socialist company, entering into negotiations in April 2008. Ternium, controlled by the Argentine-Italian conglomerate Techint Group, demanded $4 billion for its 60% ownership of Sidor. The government valued the company at $800 million.[5] Refusing to pay the demanded amount, President Chavez threatened by saying "if they don't want to reach an agreement with us, I'll sign an expropriation decree. I'll take immediate control".[6] Eventually, Ternium settled for an amount of $1.97 billion.[7]

(b) Host Country's Population and Local Communities: Depending upon the amount and type of involvement, an international business requires varying degrees of cooperation from the local communities in order to exist and operate in the country. This cooperation is what provides the firm with market access, the employee base and ability to operate safely. At even the most minimum level of operations in a foreign country, it is of extreme importance that the local community is not hostile to the firm's interests. For instance, Compañía Minera Malku Khota (CMMK) was incorporated in Bolivia to explore and develop the Malku Khota mining project on 7 November 2003. South American Silver Limited (Bermuda) (SAS), a fully owned subsidiary of Gold Springs Resource Corp., a Canadian mining firm, owned all the shares of CMMK. In 2010, the local community accused CMMK of polluting sacred spaces, abusing its authority, deceiving and threatening community members, and condoning the rape of women from the community.[8] This led to violent clashes shortly after forcing the Bolivian government to step in to aid the local community. Soon, on 1 August 2012, a Supreme Decree was issued that reversed the ownership of the mining concessions to the State of Bolivia.[9]

In addition, the local population carries immense weight in decision-making, especially in democratic countries. This can be thrown around to influence government in changing its directives. The situation can get further complicated with social media narratives and disinformation mechanisms in the current times. The local issue can well turn into an international fiasco hurting the company in other markets and financial losses and its spillover effects globally. Even with a good standing with the country's government and other actors in the region, the firm's operations will be significantly compromised just due to a hostile relationship with the people. This was well highlighted by Saner et al. (2000) through an example of Shell Oil's experience in Eastern Nigeria with minority tribes. Shell Oil started operations in Nigeria through the formation of a joint venture with the Nigerian National Petroleum Corporation (NNPC). The operations in the Ogoni territory led to deterioration of their living conditions, compelling them to ultimately sabotage some of Shell's oil wells. The story was picked up by the NGOs, which additionally caused a severe reputation loss for the company.

Secondary Participants

The secondary participants include the following:

(a) Media: Media refers to the means of communication that are used to disseminate information and data, which can be news, entertainment, promotional messages etc.[10,11] Here we are talking about media with special reference to free press and news dissimilation (Kumar & Svensson, 2015). As evident from its widespread use during World War II and then the Cold War, media has always been used as a key instrument to shape public opinion for or against a cause.[12] This position has only solidified in the recent past with the rise of the Internet making it much easier and cost-effective to reach truly huge numbers of people across geographic boundaries and political barriers, leaving the business activities prone to much deeper levels of investigative journalism (Saner, 2016).

With the increased availability of a firm's information and government policies on the Internet, the media now has the ability to detect any wrongdoings or ignored regulation that can lead to legal actions, government scrutiny and reputation loss (Saner, 2016). The media reports about a business can also have huge financial implications especially in the capital markets created through panic or euphoria.[13] Even wrongly stated facts or out-of-context statements can lead to a devastating effect on the firm.[14]

The situation has been further complicated with rise of social media, which allows smaller news agencies and independent news investigators to disseminate news and information at a much grander scale and far too quickly, not giving the company time to take corrective actions or issue clarification before the damage has been done. Influencers on YouTube, Twitter and other such sites have especially emerged as a pressure group in recent times.[15] For instance, a report surfaced in April 2017 accusing Evan Spiegel, Snap Inc. CEO, of making the remark "This app (Snapchat) is only for rich people. I don't want to expand into poor countries like India and Spain".[16] Indian users reacted immediately, bringing down the rating of Snapchat on Apple App store from 5 to 1 and trending #boycottsnapchat on Twitter calling for mass uninstallation by the app users. The alleged remark – claimed to have been made in 2015 – came forward as a result of a lawsuit by a former company employee and was backed by no concrete facts. Snapchat denied such statements ever being made but the damage had been done. This shows that a company in current times need to be extremely pro-active in shutting down fake news and explaining its position at the earliest.[17]

(b) Inter-Governmental Organisations: The international and inter-governmental organizations, and regional congregations, such as the United Nations, World Trade Organization or the European Union, carry significant weight in their ability to influence decision-making by national governments. This was also pointed out by Saner and Yiu (2005) in their study of Swiss companies operating in Europe. This has arisen after the

establishment of various international institutions to promote peace and prosperity in the post-World War 2 era that witnessed calls for independence by many countries worldwide, and also the growing political friction between the two power blocs – led by the USA and USSR. Over the years, several regional congregations were established to promote economic integration and socio-cultural cooperation. Both multilateralism and economic integration were accepted as the way forward for development.

Countries have also gradually moved toward accepting a more standardized international rules and regulations, and to create a level playing-field in international trade – though it is not without exceptions! The purpose, however, has also been broadened to include the agenda of environmental protection and human rights, among many others (Riordan, 2014). Due to this, as stated by Ruël et al. (2013), international business operations are now exposed to the rules and regulations prescribed by the multilateral agreements negotiated and ratified by the national governments of countries that they want to operate in. Therefore, any new proposal or framework is expected to have an impact on firms' having simultaneous operations in multiple countries, thus making it difficult to cope with and introduce compliance measures.

This also provides an advantage to the business group seeking to secure its interests in multiple countries at the same time. A firm may establish a positive relationship with the institutions to seek favorable policies in all member countries at the same time. Thus, they can save crucial time and effort that would have been utilized in interacting with each member country separately. The same has been observed in the case of the European Union, where the five biggest oil and gas companies, and their industry groups, namely BP, Shell, Chevron, ExxonMobil and Total, spent €251 million from 2010 to 2018 in their lobbying efforts for more favorable climate policies.[18] A Greenpeace Report also stated that the efforts have yielded results for the firms, much to the dismay of the environmental activists.[19]

It is also important to note that there exist a few inter-governmental organizations that supersede the rights of the national governments in policy formulation and law-making, leaving only the execution of policies to the government agencies. In such cases, businesses need to consider such organizations as the primary participants in the business diplomacy process that are capable of proactively and individually changing the elements of the business environment. The European Union is one such example. The "precedence principle", one of the fundamental principles in European law, gives supremacy to the European law in the case of a conflict with national laws. Therefore, a member country is obligated to adhere to the laws of the European Union.[20]

(c) Non-Governmental Organisations (NGOs) and Activists: NGOs are entities that function to achieve political or social goals for the betterment of society. They can operate locally, nationally or internationally. In current times, with the increased access to the Internet, more accurate and

detailed information is now accessible to these organizations. Moreover, they have better public outreach than perhaps most governments or the international community. Additionally, the number of international NGOs has increased consistently in the recent past and so has the number of people associated with them (Turner, 2010).

For the MNEs, these organizations are extremely important mainly due to the increased assertiveness of such entities in the global arena after the rise of Internet connectivity (Saner et al., 2000). Even with the absence of any legal grounds, NGOs and CSOs can raise awareness about an issue on an international scale, taking the social, environmental or humanitarian ground to explain their point of view, leading to huge implications for the firm's reputation and threatening its local and global agenda (Saner and Yiu, 2005; Ruël, 2013). However, when the firm is working in the favor of the general public and local communities, the NGOs can act as pressure groups against local government pressure and unwarranted scrutiny (Riordan, 2014). NGOs operating locally can also aid the business to converse better with people and increase the focus of a firm's corporate social responsibility (CSR) activities, thus creating a positive relationship with local communities.[21] An example of the interaction between the NGOs and businesses would be Greenpeace's allegations about the US fast-food industry for destroying the Amazon rainforest by participating in soya purchase in the continent.[22] The environmental organization first started looking into the firm's practices in 2003 and finally released its research in 2006 in the form of a report titled "Eating Up the Amazon". The report linked the soya crisis in the South American continent with the US-based multinational company. The issue was widely published and disseminated through various media platforms in addition to the protest by Greenpeace at various locations in the United Kingdom. The fast-food chain faced much heat and finally decided to abstain from using the Amazon soya from the deforested parts of the forest. The incident resulted in a worldwide reputation loss for the company.[23]

Enablers of an Effective Business Diplomacy Plan

Given this backdrop, we outline some of the essential enablers that must be considered by MNEs to develop an effective business diplomacy plan. These include the following:

(a) Home Country's Policies and Global Diplomatic Dynamics: The host government is also influenced by global geopolitics and the economic diplomacy pursuits of the firm's home country. For instance, any protectionist measure by one country on another is expected to bring retaliation causing much harm for the businesses of both countries. In the US-China trade war, both countries proceeded to apply country-specific tariffs on bilateral imports. This posed significant risks to companies from both sides. For example, the US technology giants suffered a decline in market

capitalization summing up to hundreds of billions of dollars.[24] Similarly, any hostile strategic or military move can also have its consequences on bilateral trade. The same can be observed from the experiences of European aircraft-maker Airbus and US aircraft-maker Boeing in their dealings with Iran, after the United States decided to pull out of the Iran nuclear deal or the Joint Comprehensive Plan of Action. The two firms had signed contracts for sale of aircrafts to the tune of $39 billion.[25] The subsequent US sanctions will render the aircraft makers unable to fulfill their commitments.[26] Therefore, it is necessary to draft a business diplomacy policy after careful consideration of the home country's economic policy and geopolitical dynamics relevant at the time. Subsequently, the policy needs to be revised to solidify or hedge the position in turbulent times.

(b) Setting up Communication Channels: A necessary step after due consideration of the home country's policies and economic diplomacy pursuits is to set up a conducive and reliable communication channel with all participants of the business diplomacy process. These channels need to be used in order to deepen the understanding and relationship in relatively stable business periods, thus helping the business to explore new opportunities. In turbulent times, these channels can be used to gather information and take proactive measures against any and all threats to the stability and performance of the firm. Pantoja (2018) also discussed it in the context of strategies and activities in the case of biotechnology companies in Mexico. The paper discussed different types of communication strategies in a business diplomacy set-up.

(c) Multi-Stakeholder Development: The firm needs to build a network of stakeholders that have their business interests aligned to that of the firm. Through this, the foreign company with seemingly less influence or standing with the national government and authorities can instead influence them through the domestic stakeholders. With aligned objectives, it is to the benefit of the authorities to act positively towards the firm to, in turn, benefit the local stakeholders. These can be in the form of suppliers, customers, employees or investors. It is generally advisable that the firm aims to build a network that has a large number of people who engage with the firm either directly or indirectly. For instance, in the Indian market, Uber displayed this through the way it engaged with customers and drivers. As a result of this, in 2014, when the app was banned, a large community of cab drivers protested against the government in support of Uber.[27] The firm may also seek a few stakeholders with significant bargaining power with the primary participants of the business diplomacy process. To this effect, many firms seek large domestic investors that can throw their weight around on the negotiating table. The availability of financial resources can help the firm take social initiatives in the country or promise developmental interventions, directly leading to the creation of a long-term relationship with the parties involved. On

the other hand, the firm may also use the financial leverage as political funding, but that may have ethical and legal issues in the future.

(d) Development of Counter-Pressure Groups: A counter-pressure group may act as a diplomatic support to the business in times of distress. They may negotiate on behalf of the business or take up the case of unfair treatment or legal bias with the relevant parties. Domestically, these groups can be in the form of an industry association, NGO, research agency, etc. that has relevant communication channels available to it to stage formal protest against any other party. For instance, a company manufacturing eco-friendly paper bags will use environmental activists as a pressure group to advocate a plastic ban. Similar dynamics can play out on a global level but with much larger consequences. An issue that can be discussed with a single international agency will have the potential to be picked up by other global institutions outside the reach of the government. Such counter-pressure groups can bring governments to the negotiating table where the businesses can discuss the issue at par with the opposite party.

Key Business Diplomacy Instances During the Pandemic

In this section, we outline and examine some of the key examples of business diplomacy and lobbying that were evident during and immediately prior to the pandemic. These include the following:

5G Technology: 5G, the term used for fifth generation mobile networks, is the latest breakthrough in global wireless standards.[28] Designed to create a network between machines, objects and devices, it can benefit every field ranging from entertainment to security through a more uniform and enriched user experience.[29] The technology is also expected to aid the development of the Internet of Things (IoT) ecosystem.[30] Since 2019, 5G has emerged as a major international issue with several countries being worried about the security implications of a network connected to innumerable devices in its vicinity with the core hardware provided by a foreign firm.

The issue was first raised when the Chinese technology giant Huawei was accused of spying on people by the US authorities in early 2019.[31] In the later months, more allegations poured in on account of Huawei being mandated by Chinese law to comply with government requests on security and intelligence.[32] The controversy with Huawei is, however, older than these acquisitions. The first legal charge against the company came in late 2018. It accused Huawei of "conspiracy to defraud multiple international institutions" saying that the company has violated the Iran sanctions.[33] The list of charges increased in January 2019 with the addition of bank fraud and stealing trade secrets.[34] In addition to the aggressive US lobbying for a ban on Chinese technology firms, these charges decreased the global trustworthiness of Huawei and paved the way for further charges, including the spying allegations.[35] As a result, by the end of 2019, the company was banned in Australia, New Zealand, Japan, Taiwan and the United States, while many more countries were still on the fence about the decision.[36]

The COVID-19 pandemic has already resulted in a general rise in anti-China sentiments all across the globe.[37,38,39] This is expected to have a severe impact on the countries that were on the fence about allowing Huawei into their technological ecosystem. In early May 2020, the United States launched another strike on the firm, restricting it to use American technology in design and manufacture of semiconductors produced for it abroad.[40] The United Kingdom, which had earlier allowed the Chinese company to operate in limited capacity, put out an all-inclusive ban in June 2020.[41] The European Commission, the executive branch of the European Union, also directed the European Union member countries to take urgent steps in favor of diversification of their 5G supply needs.[42] Similarly, India also decided not to include Huawei and ZTE (another Chinese technology firm) in its 5G rollout.[43] In other markets like Portugal, dominant companies in the mobile phone market expressed their disinclination to use Chinese 5G infrastructure despite there being no ban by the government.[44]

Though the company has continuously denied the allegations, the case of Huawei is a good example of how a firm loses its major negotiating power globally due to legal charges against it. Huawei was all but powerless in international markets due to a lack of an understanding with local governments. The matter for Huawei became worse with the absence of any substantial international opposition to the US lobbying – except that by China.

However, the chain of events has also played out to the benefit of other telecommunication giants like Nokia (Finland), Ericson (Sweden) and Samsung (South Korea). As counter-measures to Huawei's presence across the globe, the United States decided to support such companies to strengthen their presence in the telecommunication industry.[45] Also, other governments entered into talks with these giants for their national rollouts of 5G technologies, as seen in the example of the United Kingdom,[46] Singapore,[47] Portugal and Spain[48] etc. This has led to the formation of deeper ties of these firms with governments and provided them with a sense of relative security. Further, these giants now have to employ business diplomacy and use their ties to further their interests by filling the gap left by the Huawei ban or its intentional unacceptance in various countries.[49] For instance, Nokia joining the Open RAN Policy Coalition allows it to use the organization as a pressure group to lobby for favorable telecommunication policies with the US government.[50]

Mobile Apps Ban: A press release by the Ministry of Information Technology, Government of India, was issued on 29 June 2020 banning 59 Chinese apps (mobile applications) from the Indian market with the stated motive to "ensure safety and sovereignty of Indian cyberspace".[51]

Then at the end of July 2020, the Indian government further banned 47 more apps, classifying them as clones or variants of the apps banned earlier. Further, a list of 275 more apps was drawn up to be examined for violations of national security and user privacy.[52] With another order passed on 2 September 2020 to ban 118 new Chinese apps, the total tally has increased to 224.[53] The list of apps that have been banned includes the likes of TikTok, ShareIt, CamScanner, etc. that have a huge user base in India and would severely affect the overall profitability of the respective firms. The ban came after a series of events that began with increased border tensions between the two neighbors in the face-off that began in early May.[54] The heat from this incident was not limited to the political platforms, but it was reflected in social media discourse too. Whereas a part of the Indian population demanded a boycott of Chinese products and services, the Indian government too started questioning the heavy involvement of China in key sectors of the Indian economy.[55]

Coupled with the COVID-19-affected global supply chain, this was also seen as one of the reasons leading up to a direct call to the citizens of the country to use goods and services that have originated in India, launching the motto of "Aatma Nirbhar Bharat" or "Self-Reliant India" by Prime Minister Narendra Modi on 12 May 2020.[56] This further gained momentum after the India-China border tensions escalated to the point of a violent clash that took place on 16 June 2020.[57] This led to a rise in anti-China sentiments in India with the people calling for boycotting Chinese products on social media and a series of measures taken by the Indian government to reduce the participation of Chinese companies in the Indian market.

With this background information, the ban was seen in a more political light all across the world.[58] However, it can also be seen as an example of the failed business diplomacy of Chinese businesses in the Indian market. The apps were unable to address the concerns of the Indian government and failed to take proactive measures to handle the situation. To study it in detail, we take the example of TikTok, a small video-sharing app owned by the Chinese firm named ByteDance.[59] With 611 million downloads, India made up 30% of the total download figures of the app.[60] According to a Chinese news article, the firm may lose $6 billion due to the app ban.[61] However, this ban was not the first for the company. The troubles first started in February 2019 when the Tamil Nadu government called for a ban on the app due to the presence of obscenity.[62] The app then faced approximately a 3-week ban in April 2019 after a high court termed it as being dangerous to children. Subsequently, TikTok ensured that it cracked down on inappropriate content and the ban was lifted.[63] The firm had stated that it was facing a $500,000 daily loss due to the ban, putting over 250 jobs at risk.[64]

Additionally, Sensor Tower, an independent market intelligence firm, estimated that the ban also cost the app over 15 million first-time users in India.[65] The app had also been accused of "interfering in the Indian election process through its social media applications" on 29 March 2019 in a complaint to the Election Commission of India (ECI) which resulted in the company being told to take down the content that violated the ECI guidelines. Three months after the incident, the issue of TikTok sharing confidential information with China was discussed in the lower house of the Parliament of India (Lok Sabha) by a prominent politician. Though no action was taken, it did invite a clarification from the firm stating that the claims are untrue and giving assurance of no sharing of data with the Chinese government.[66] When studied in this light, the current app ban can be seen to have its roots in the events that transpired earlier. From a business diplomacy perspective, the company failed on multiple fronts, and it can be summarized as follows:

- The concerns regarding the security of the app had already started in 2019. Even so, the firm failed to act proactively to establish deeper understanding with the Indian government to showcase the claimed security of the user data.
- The local stakeholders of the firm were limited to its users, influencers and 2,000 strong workforce.[67] With a general absence of local investors or association with local industries, the firm lacked any substantial stakeholder support. When the anti-China sentiment in India rose and the call for a boycott of Chinese products and services intensified, the limited user base could not act as a relevant pressure group against the government agencies and anti-China lobby.
- The company failed to react proactively to the changing relationship between India and China. The effects of regional diplomacy on the business were ignored and the company did not make any moves to solidify its position in the wake of changing geopolitical landscapes.

Supply Chain Disruptions: In the wake of the COVID-19 pandemic, China was criticized for its inability to share information that could have been crucial in controlling the pandemic in the early phases of global transmission of the virus. This invited a huge criticism on the world stage, especially beginning from the United States for its alleged mishandling of the pandemic.[68] China, however, rejected the allegations that it concealed the spread of the pandemic.[69] It was further claimed that the Chinese government is using its position as the biggest trade partner to countries around the world as a tool to silence criticism.[70] Evidence was cited from Australia, where a 80.5% tariff was laid on Australian barley exports.[71]

This unpredictability gradually led various countries to seek to reduce their dependence on Chinese imports.[72] For instance, Japan was one of the first countries to take a concrete step in order to build a more resilient supply chain amid disruptions caused due to the pandemic. In early April, Japan created a 243.5 billion yen (i.e. $2.2 billion) fund to incentivize Japanese firms to move their production facilities out of China. Of this, 220 billion yen was for firms moving back to Japan, while 23.5 billion yen was allocated for firms moving to other countries.[73] On 17 July 2020, the list of the first group of 87 firms was released by the Japanese government, availing themselves of up to 70 billion yen from the fund.[74] A total of 57 of these firms were moving production to Japan and the remaining 30 intended to expand production capacities to Southeast Asia.[75] Another example of such sentiment was reflected in the statement by the US Secretary of State Mike Pompeo on 29 April 2020, who announced that the United States was working with Vietnam, South Korea, Japan, New Zealand, India and Australia to restructure supply chains to avoid the possibility of disruptions in future.[76] Further, the United States pushed for an "Economic Prosperity Network", and the Under Secretary, Keith Krach, in a Press Brief on 25 June 2020, called for the creation of "a global framework for trusted geo-economic partnerships". This is generally seen as an initiative by the Trump administration to reduce the reliance of global value chains on China.[77]

Similarly, coupled with the effects of US-China trade war that began in 2017, these events have also motivated businesses to diversify, if not completely move their production units to places outside of China.[78] On the other hand, countries around the world are keen to be the destination for such firms. In this regard, the Indian government began development of a land pool in early May 2020 spread all across the country totaling up to 461,589 hectares to make it easy for foreign firms trying to shift production from China to India. With the special focus on Japanese firms leaving China[79], the Bangladesh government has also set up a high-level task force aimed at laying the groundworks to attract such investment to the country's ecosystem.[80] There are other similar examples across the globe.[81] In such a situation, the importance of business diplomacy rises due to the flexibility of national governments in policies aimed at attracting huge chunks of foreign direct investment (FDI) inflows.

FDI, FII and Opportunistic Takeovers: The global financial markets too have been affected by the economic disruptions caused by the COVID-19 pandemic. Market capitalizations of various companies have eroded in the wake of the pandemic. This has left the firms vulnerable to takeovers by foreign cash-rich parties that can now attempt to take over the firm at heavily discounted prices. The shifting of domestic businesses to foreign hands has got governments concerned all over the world. As a result, major governments are now keen on protecting their domestic companies, compelling them to formulate stricter legislations for FDI and foreign institutional investment (FII). In Europe, there has been a general onset of such legislations first at the European Union level and then at the country level by Italy, Spain, Germany,[82] the United Kingdom[83] and France. Other than that, countries like Australia, Canada[84] and India[85] too have already followed suit. Many of these measures are attributed to the supposed risk posed by China, though such dispositions may not be real, given the fact that China has already started building its supply and value chain and has increased its domestic output. In April–June 2020, China was the only major economy in the world to attain a positive gross domestic product (GDP).[86]

However, in such an unpredictable environment, it is of utmost importance that the relations that foreign businesses have with the host governments be used to showcase transparency and good intentions in future investments. Any misinterpreted or exploitative investment prospects may lead to even stricter legislation as a retaliatory measure, causing the MNEs even more harm. It is also important to notice that the foreign businesses are in the middle of a cash crunch due to disrupted economic activities and still have to incur the fixed cost associated with operations. It is therefore essential that the businesses and government representatives cooperate for mutual benefit. One such example would be Tata Steel's efforts to raise 900 million pounds through the UK government.[87] It is one of the steps that the steelmaker had to take due to disruptions emerging from the COVID-19 pandemic. The cooperation with the government shows how businesses can use the local governments to bail themselves out in crisis situations like this.

Moreover, the pandemic has already directly affected the rate of economic development all over the world. As a result, contractions are expected in some major economies of the world while others are expected to show a sharp decline in predicted growth rates. Unemployment rates are expected to rise and purchasing power is expected to decline, thus further pushing down business activities. This will affect the tax income of the governments at various levels and may affect the efficiency of the government to handle the crisis. Moreover, as the unemployment rate rises in several countries, including the United States and India, and as the healthcare situation deteriorates, the dependence of the population on government welfare programs increases.

In the current pandemic, it has been repeatedly observed that national governments are acting upon the findings, research and suggestions of the international community. Here, the role of international institutions like the IMF, World Bank Group and the World Health Organization has to be recognized. Firms should maintain their communications and relationship with these institutions to help them decipher their demand and supply-side constraints.

Also, the non-state actors including NGOs and CSOs operating in the host countries have stepped up their efforts to ensure that the healthcare guidelines prescribed by the government are being met by the businesses. Media is another key non-state actor that needs to be considered while designing a business diplomacy policy in today's scenario. Its importance has grown with respect to its ability to influence public opinion on a mass scale after the pandemic has already instilled fear and uncertainty among the population across the world. However, the media in many developing countries has often been criticized for being politically motivated or spreading disinformation too. A firm's business diplomacy outreach plan with the media must factor-in this aspect too.

Conclusion

Due to the extraordinary situation created globally as a result of COVID-19, business diplomacy is now more important than ever for firms operating internationally. There is no doubt that the dynamics of the relationship between a firm and a foreign state and non-state actors have been affected as a result of this pandemic. Also, the geopolitical landscapes have witnessed a dramatic transformation during this pandemic.

Business operations all over the world have been disrupted as a direct result of the pandemic. This has mainly stemmed from the government policies and actions aimed at controlling the spread of the virus and enhancing the healthcare infrastructure for any future pandemic. Imposition of national or localized lockdowns in countries forming a part of the global value chains had led to temporary halts in the production process. With tightly planned financial and operating cycles, this halt resulted in huge losses for big and small firms conducting business internationally. This created a spillover effect resulting in reduced availability of resources for these businesses, rendering them even more dependent on government support and stimulus packages. Also, with adverse economic conditions and reduced consumer demand, the firms continue to face an increased level of uncertainty in current times. The governments will definitely have a significant influence on the firms in these matters. International organizations (e.g. IMF and WHO) are also actively giving directives and recommendations to the national governments and the businesses alike.

The interdependence between the business and government is now deeper. Businesses need governments to adopt policies that are conducive to economic growth and development with respect to the new situation at hand. This is where business diplomacy steps in to act as a bridge between the governments and the businesses. Both the parties need to be aware of each other's needs and also of the function they are supposed to perform according to the other's mandate and strategic interests. This will help the governments in policy formulation and the businesses in getting prepared for the upcoming changes in the business environment. Also, with the introduction of the economic relief packages by the governments, the need for the businesses to capitalize on their long-standing relationships is now greater than ever. At this juncture, it is crucial that the governments make sure that the foreign businesses do not withdraw from the country. The businesses need to assure the government of their commitment to stay and act for the public good in supporting the measures to fight the pandemic. Business diplomacy is thus a positive tool for strengthening the supply and value chains, boosting investor confidence and making the business environment more liberal and structurally robust.

Acknowledgment

The infrastructural support provided by FORE School of Management in completing this study is gratefully acknowledged

Notes

1 India to ease foreign investment rules in push for $5tn economy, NIKKEI Asian Review, 5 July 2019. Available at: https://asia.nikkei.com/Economy/India-to-ease-foreign-investment-rules-in-push-for-5tn-economy. Accessed 22 July 2020.
2 The Effects of Government Policies on Businesses, Chron, 8 March 2019. Available at: https://smallbusiness.chron.com/effects-government-policies-businesses-65214.html. Accessed 22 July 2020.
3 Government ignores advice of expert group on business and human rights, Human Rights Law Centre, 18 October 2017. Available at: www.hrlc.org.au/news/2017/10/17/government-ignores-advice-of-expert-group-on-business-and-human-rights. Accessed 24 July 2020.
4 5 Ways Hugo Chavez Has Destroyed the Venezuelan Economy, ABC News, 17 January 2013. Available at: https://abcnews.go.com/ABC_Univision/News/ways-chavez-destroyed-venezuelan-economy/story?id=18239956. Accessed 24 July 2020.
5 Chávez orders nationalization of Venezuela's largest steel maker, The New York Times, 1 May 2008. Available at: www.nytimes.com/2008/05/01/business/worldbusiness/01iht-1venez.12477847.html. Accessed 25 July 2020.
6 Hugo Chavez threatens takeover of steel maker, The Daily Reporter, 29 April 2008. Available at: https://dailyreporter.com/2008/04/29/hugo-chavez-threatens-takeover-of-steel-maker/. Accessed 26 July 2020.
7 Venezuelan Industries Hugo Chavez Nationalized (Besides Oil), Foundation of Economic Education, 10 January 2020. Available at: https://fee.org/articles/8-industries-hugo-chavez-nationalized-besides-oil-on-venezuelas-road-to-serfdom/. Accessed 26 July 2020.
8 Tribunal finds expropriation of investment by Bolivia due to non-payment of compensation but awards only sunk costs to British investor, International Institute of Sustainable Development, 23 April 2019. Available at: https://cf.iisd.net/itn/2019/04/23/tribunal-finds-expropriation-of-investment-by-bolivia-due-to-non-payment-of-compensation-but-awards-only-sunk-costs-to-british-investor-trishna-menon/. Accessed 28 July 2020.
9 Ibid.
10 Communication Media, Technopedia, 19 June 2017. Available at: www.techopedia.com/definition/14462/communication-media. Accessed 28 July 2020.
11 Media, Business Dictionary. Available at: http://www.businessdictionary.com/definition/media.html. Accessed 29 July 2020.
12 Cold War Propaganda, Alpha History, 24 September 2018. Available at: https://alphahistory.com/coldwar/cold-war-propaganda/. Accessed 1 August 2020.

13 Fake news can cause 'irreversible damage' to companies — and sink their stock price, NBC News, 25 April 2019. Available at: www.nbcnews.com/business/business-news/fake-news-can-cause-irreversible-damage-companies-sink-their-stock-n995436. Accessed 3 August 2020,
14 Ibid.
15 How social media could ruin your business, BBC News, 9 July 2019. Available at: www.bbc.com/news/business-48871456. Accessed 4 August 2020,
16 Snapchat CEO row: Here's the full context around that 'Poor India' remark, The Indian Express, 18 April 2017. Available at: https://indianexpress.com/article/technology/tech-news-technology/snapchat-ceo-evan-spiegels-alleged-anti-india-remark-anthony-pompliano-here-are-details-from-the-lawsuit-4616133/. Accessed 4 August 2020,
17 Snapchat controversy: Did Evan Spiegel really say India is poor? IndiaToday, 17 April 2017. Available at: www.indiatoday.in/technology/features/story/snapchat-controversy-did-evan-spiegel-really-say-india-is-poor-971864-2017-04-17. Accessed 4 August 2020,
18 Fossil fuel big five 'spent €251m lobbying EU' since 2010, The Guardian, 24 October 2019. Available at: www.theguardian.com/business/2019/oct/24/fossil-fuel-big-five-spent-251m-lobbying-european-union-2010-climate-crisis. Accessed 7 August 2020,
19 Big oil and gas buying influence in Brussels, Fossil Free Politics. Available at: https://storage.googleapis.com/planet4-eu-unit-stateless/2019/10/0a8d2624-20191024-report-big-oil-and-gas-buying-influence-in-brussels.pdf. Accessed 7 August 2020.
20 Precedence of European law, EUR-Lex, 1 October 2010. Available at: https://eur-lex.europa.eu/legal-content/EN/TXT/?uri=LEGISSUM%3Al14548. Accessed 8 August 2020.
21 Can Businesses and NGOs Create Purposeful Partnerships? Medium, 12 January 2017. Available at: https://bthechange.com/can-businesses-and-ngos-create-purposeful-partnerships-d1dd4f1cbbe. Accessed 8 August 2020.
22 Greenpeace accuses McDonald's of destroying the Amazon rainforest, Mongabay, 7 April 2006. Available at: https://news.mongabay.com/2006/04/greenpeace-accuses-mcdonalds-of-destroying-the-amazon-rainforest/#:~:text=Greenpeace%20accuses%20McDonald's%20of%20destroying%20the%20Amazon%20rainforest,-by%20Rhett%20A&text=After%20a%20year%2Dlong%20investigation,to%20deforestation%20in%20the%20Amazon.. Accessed 8 August 2020.
23 Greenpeace defends Amazon rainforest against McDonald's, others, Global Nonviolent Action Database, 6 April 2006- 26 July 2006. Available at: https://nvdatabase.swarthmore.edu/content/greenpeace-defends-amazon-rainforest-against-mcdonalds-others-2006. Accessed 8 August 2020.
24 Why Apple, Tesla, and Intel Are Helpless in the U.S.-China Trade War, Fortune, 14 May 2019. Available at: https://fortune.com/2019/05/13/tech-companies-china-trade-war/. Accessed 11 August 2020.
25 Boeing and Airbus will miss out on a combined $39 billion payday because of Trump's Iran deal decision, Business Insider India, 9 May 2017. Available at: www.businessinsider.in/politics/boeing-and-airbus-will-miss-out-on-a-combined-39-billion-payday-because-of-trumps-iran-deal-decision/articleshow/64099452.cms. Accessed 11 August 2020.

26 Ibid.
27 Uber Drivers Protest Ban on Cab Service in Delhi, NDTV, 12 December 2014. Available at: www.ndtv.com/delhi-news/uber-drivers-protest-ban-on-cab-service-in-delhi-712130. Accessed 11 August 2020.
28 Everything you need to know about 5G, Qualcomm. Available at: www.qualcomm.com/invention/5g/what-is-5g. Accessed 14 August 2020.
29 What is 5G? T-mobile. Available at: www.t-mobile.com/5g. Accessed 11 August 2020.
30 Introducing 5G technology and networks (speed, use cases and rollout), Thales Group. Available at: www.thalesgroup.com/en/markets/digital-identity-and-security/mobile/inspired/5G. Accessed 12 August 2020.
31 The US says Huawei has been spying through 'backdoors' designed for law enforcement - which is what the US has been pressuring tech companies to do for years, Business Insider India, 12 February 2020. Available at: www.businessinsider.in/tech/news/the-us-says-huawei-has-been-spying-through-backdoors-designed-for-law-enforcement-which-is-what-the-us-has-been-pressuring-tech-companies-to-do-for-years/articleshow/74101258.cms. Accessed 14 August 2020.
32 U.S. officials: Using Huawei tech opens door to Chinese spying, censorship, NBC News, 15 February 2020. Available at: www.nbcnews.com/politics/national-security/u-s-officials-using-huawei-tech-opens-door-chinese-spying-n1136956. Accessed 14 August 2020.
33 Huawei and Top Executive Face Criminal Charges in the U.S., The New York Times, 28 January 2019. Available at: www.nytimes.com/2019/01/28/us/politics/meng-wanzhou-huawei-iran.html. Accessed 12 August 2020.
34 Huawei: Banned and Permitted in which countries? List and FAQ, CHANNELe2e. Available at: www.channele2e.com/business/enterprise/huawei-banned-in-which-countries/. Accessed 12 August 2020.
35 Europe Edges Toward 5G Restrictions After Blast of U.S. Lobbying, Bloomberg, 9 December 2019. Available at: www.bloomberg.com/news/articles/2019-12-09/europe-edges-toward-5g-restrictions-after-blast-of-u-s-lobbying. Accessed 12 August 2020.
36 Which Countries Have Banned Huawei? Statista, 30 January 2020. Available at: www.statista.com/chart/17528/countries-which-have-banned-huawei-products/. Accessed 14 August 2020.
37 Amid rising anti-China sentiments, European powers send stern messages to Beijing, 24 April 2020. Available at: https://economictimes.indiatimes.com/news/international/world-news/china-strikes-a-diplomatic-low-note-in-europe/articleshow/75262927.cms?from=mdr. Accessed 14 August 2020.
38 Rising Anti-Chinese Sentiment in Indonesia, The ASEAN Post, 4 July 2020. Available at: https://theaseanpost.com/article/rising-anti-chinese-sentiment-indonesia. Accessed 16 August 2020.
39 Chinese in India say they are being harassed amid rising anti-China sentiment following border clash, Global Times, 24 June 2020. Available at: www.globaltimes.cn/content/1192596.shtml. Accessed 15 August 2020.
40 US adds new sanction on Chinese tech giant Huawei, The Economic Times, 16 May 2020. Available at: https://economictimes.indiatimes.com/news/international/business/us-adds-new-sanction-on-chinese-tech-giant-huawei/articleshow/75770660.cms. Accessed 15 August 2020.

41 UK bans Huawei from its 5G network in rapid about-face, CNN Business, 14 July 2020. Available at: https://edition.cnn.com/2020/07/14/tech/huawei-uk-ban/index.html. Accessed 13 August 2020.
42 European Commission Asks EU Nations to Diversify 5G Suppliers, NDTV, 24 July 2020. Available at: https://gadgets.ndtv.com/telecom/news/european-commission-eu-countries-diversify-5g-suppliers-huwaei-uk-ban-2268408. Accessed 16 August 2020.
43 China's Huawei, ZTE set to be shut out of India's 5G roll out plans, Business Standard, 13 August 2020. Available at: www.business-standard.com/article/companies/china-s-huawei-zte-set-to-be-shut-out-of-india-s-5g-roll-out-plans-120081301645_1.html. Accessed 15 August 2020.
44 Exclusive: Portugal telcos won't use Huawei for core 5G networks though no government ban, Reuters, 31 July 2020. Available at: https://in.reuters.com/article/huawei-5g-portugal/exclusive-portugal-telcos-wont-use-huawei-for-core-5g-networks-though-no-government-ban-idINKCN24W08T. Accessed 14 August 2020.
45 US wants to help Ericsson, Nokia and others develop 5G alternatives, TechradarPro, 17 February 2020. Available at: www.techradar.com/in/news/us-wants-to-help-ericsson-nokia-and-others-develop-5g-alternatives. Accessed 19 August 2020.
46 UK government is in talks with Samsung to replace Huawei network gear, Sammobile, 8 June 2020. Available at: www.sammobile.com/news/uk-government-talking-samsung-replace-huawei-network-components/. Accessed 14 August 2020.
47 Singapore chooses Nokia, Ericsson over Huawei to build core 5G networks, CNET, 25 June 2020. Available at: www.cnet.com/news/singapore-chose-nokia-ericsson-over-huawei-to-build-core-5g-network/. Accessed 14 August 2020.
48 Exclusive: Portugal telcos won't use Huawei for core 5G networks though no government ban, Reuters, 31 July 2020. Available at: https://in.reuters.com/article/huawei-5g-portugal/exclusive-portugal-telcos-wont-use-huawei-for-core-5g-networks-though-no-government-ban-idINKCN24W08T. Accessed 15 August 2020.
49 Ericsson, Nokia say ready to step in after UK 5G Huawei ban, TechXplore, 14 July 2020. Available at: https://techxplore.com/news/2020-07-ericsson-nokia-ready-uk-5g.html. Accessed 14 August 2020.
50 Nokia throws its weight behind Open RAN lobby group, TelecomTV, 22 May 2020. Available at: www.telecomtv.com/content/5g/nokia-throws-its-weight-behind-open-ran-lobby-group-38740/. Accessed 19 August 2020.
51 Government Bans 59 mobile apps which are prejudicial to sovereignty and integrity of India, defence of India, security of state and public order, Press Information Bureau Government of India, 29 June 2020. Available at: https://pib.gov.in/PressReleseDetailm.aspx?PRID=1635206. Accessed 14 August 2020.
52 Govt bans 47 more Chinese apps citing risks to national sovereignty, integrity and defence, The Economic Times, 27 July 2020. Available at: https://economictimes.indiatimes.com/tech/software/government-bans-47-more-chinese-apps-citing-risks-to-national-sovereignty-integrity-and-defence-source/articleshow/77195821.cms. Accessed 16 August 2020.

53 India bans 118 more Chinese mobile apps including PUBG Mobile over privacy concerns, The Financial Express, 2 September 2020. Available at: www.financialexpress.com/industry/technology/india-bans-118-more-chinese-mobile-apps-including-pubg-mobile-over-privacy-concerns/2072830/#:~:text=The%20list%20included%20apps%20like,of%20the%20previously%20banned%20apps.. Accessed 19 August 2020.
54 India-China faceoff 2020: Why this border clash is different, The Economic Times, 16 June 2020. Available at: https://economictimes.indiatimes.com/news/defence/india-china-faceoff-2020-why-this-border-clash-is-different/articleshow/76357645.cms. Accessed 16 August 2020.
55 China reacts cautiously to mounting boycott calls of its products in India, says it values ties, India Today, 19 June 2020. Available at: www.indiatoday.in/india/story/china-reacts-cautiously-to-mounting-boycott-calls-products-india-says-values-ties-1690801-2020-06-19. Accessed 16 August 2020.
56 From March 19 to May 12, Here is How Long Each of PM Modi's Addresses to Nation on COVID-19 Lasted, India.com, 12 May 2020. Available at: www.india.com/news/india/from-march-19-to-may-12-here-is-how-long-each-of-pm-modis-addresses-to-nation-on-covid-19-lasted-4027406/. Accessed 16 August 2020.
57 India says 20 soldiers killed on disputed Himalayan border with China, The Guardian, 17 June 2020. Available at: www.theguardian.com/world/2020/jun/16/india-says-soldiers-killed-on-disputed-himalayan-border-with-china. Accessed 28 August 2020.
58 India Bans Nearly 60 Chinese Apps, Including Tiktok and WeChat, The New York Times, 29 June 2020. Available at: www.nytimes.com/2020/06/29/world/asia/tik-tok-banned-india-china.html. Accessed 24 August 2020.
59 TikTok report shows India sends highest number of user information and content takedown requests, The Economic Times, 9 July 2020. Available at: https://economictimes.indiatimes.com/tech/internet/tiktok-report-shows-india-sends-highest-number-of-user-information-and-content-takedown-requests/articleshow/76875109.cms#:~:text=TikTok%2C%20owned%20by%20Chinese%20startup,were%20mentioned%20in%20these%20reports. Accessed 28 August 2020.
60 10 TikTok Statistics That You Need to Know in 2020 [Infographic], Oberlo, 3 September 2020. Available at: www.oberlo.com/blog/tiktok-statistics. Accessed 24 August 2020.
61 ByteDance loss may hit $6b after India bans Chinese apps, Global Times, 1 July 2020. Available at: www.globaltimes.cn/content/1193243.shtml. Accessed 28 August 2020.
62 Indian politicians accuse China-made app Helo of election interference and call for TikTok to be banned, Business Insider India, 17 April 2019. Available at: www.businessinsider.in/indian-politicians-accuse-china-made-app-helo-of-election-interference-and-call-for-tiktok-to-be-banned/articleshow/68916044.cms. Accessed 24 August 2020.
63 India's two-week ban cost TikTok 15 million users, CNN Business, 2 May 2019. Available at: https://edition.cnn.com/2019/05/02/tech/tiktok-ban-india-users/index.html. Accessed 25 August 2020.
64 Indian court lifts ban on TikTok in India, TechCrunch, 24 April 2019. Available at: https://techcrunch.com/2019/04/24/indian-court-lifts-ban-on-tiktok-in-india/. Accessed 25 August 2020.

65 India's TikTok Ban Cost the App at Least 15 Million New Users There—and Its Biggest Month Yet, SensorTower, 1 May 2019. Available at: https://sensortower.com/blog/tiktok-ban-downloads. Accessed 24 August 2020.
66 TikTok shares user data with Chinese government, Tharoor tells Lok Sabha; company denies his claims, Medianama, 3 July 2019. Available at: www.medianama.com/2019/07/223-tiktok-shares-user-data-with-chinese-government-tharoor-tells-lok-sabha-company-denies-his-claims/#:~:text=On%20July%201%2C%20during%20the,a%20%E2%80%9Cnational%20security%20issue%E2%80%9D.. Accessed 28 August 2020.
67 TikTok CEO's Message to India Employees After Government Blocks App, NDTV, 1 July 2020. Available at: www.ndtv.com/india-news/tiktok-ceos-message-to-india-employees-after-government-blocks-app-2255067#:~:text=We%20have%20also%20assured%20more,of%20its%20employees%20in%20India.
68 Shift of supply chains from China accelerates, Tribune India, 8 May 2020. Available at: www.tribuneindia.com/news/comment/shift-of-supply-chains-from-china-accelerates-81847#:~:text=The%20spurt%20in%20the%20relocation,and%20even%20its%20internal%20stability. Accessed 3 September 2020.
69 China Hits Back at Report That It Hid Coronavirus Numbers, Time, 2 April 2020. Available at: https://time.com/5814313/china-denies-hiding-coronavirus/.
70 In addition to propaganda, China uses trade to coerce compliance with its dictates: US NSA, The Times of India, 27 June 2020. Available at: https://timesofindia.indiatimes.com/world/us/in-addition-to-propaganda-china-uses-trade-to-coerce-compliance-with-its-dictates-us-nsa/articleshow/76659720.cms.
71 China confirms over 80 per cent tariff on Australian barley exports, South China Morning Post, 18 May 2020. Available at: www.scmp.com/economy/china-economy/article/3084930/china-confirms-over-80-cent-tariff-australian-barley-exports. Accessed 5 September 2020.
72 President Trump ordered US firms to ditch China, but many already have and more are on the way, CNBC, 1 September 2020. Available at: www.cnbc.com/2019/09/01/trump-ordered-us-firms-to-ditch-china-but-many-already-have.html. Accessed 5 September 2020.
73 Japan to Fund Firms to Shift Production Out of China, Bloomberg Quint, 10 April 2020. Available at: www.bloombergquint.com/global-economics/japan-to-fund-firms-to-shift-production-out-of-china. Accessed 5 September 2020.
74 Japan reveals 87 projects eligible for 'China exit' subsidies, Nikkei Asia, 17 July 2020. Available at: https://asia.nikkei.com/Economy/Japan-reveals-87-projects-eligible-for-China-exit-subsidies. Accessed 5 September 2020.
75 Japan helps 87 companies to break from China after pandemic exposed overreliance, The Washington Post, 21 July 2020. Available at: www.washingtonpost.com/world/asia_pacific/japan-helps-87-companies-to-exit-china-after-pandemic-exposed-overreliance/2020/07/21/4889abd2-cb2f-11ea-99b0-8426e26d203b_story.html. Accessed 3 September 2020.
76 Trump administration pushing to rip global supply chains from China: officials, Reuters, 4 May 2020. Available at: www.reuters.com/article/us-health-coronavirus-usa-china/trump-administration-pushing-to-rip-global-supply-chains-from-china-officials-idUSKBN22G0BZ. Accessed 5 September 2020.

77 Under Secretary Keith Krach Briefs the Press on Huawei and Clean Telcos, U.S. Department of State, 25 July 2020. Available at: www.state.gov/telephonic-briefing-with-keith-krach-under-secretary-for-economic-growth-energy-and-the-environment/. Accessed 7 September 2020.
78 New Data Shows U.S. Companies Are Definitely Leaving China, Forbes, 7 April 2020. Available at: www.forbes.com/sites/kenrapoza/2020/04/07/new-data-shows-us-companies-are-definitely-leaving-china/#322c266740fe. Accessed 7 September 2020.
79 China exit: Japanese firms keen on moving to BD, The Financial Express, 27 May 2020. Available at: https://thefinancialexpress.com.bd/economy/bangladesh/china-exit-japanese-firms-keen-on-moving-to-bd-1590214572#:~:text=At%20least%2034%20Japanese%20companies,of%20foreign%20affairs%20on%20Wednesday.. Accessed 3 September 2020.
80 Bangladesh eyes foreign firms leaving China, The Business Standard, 16 October 2020. Available at: https://tbsnews.net/economy/trade/bangladesh-eyes-foreign-firms-leaving-china-94240#:~:text=Bangladesh%20has%20initiated%20groundwork%20to,dependence%20after%20Covid%2D19%20pandemic. Accessed 7 September 2020.
81 Southeast Asia vies for foreign manufacturers leaving China, Nikkei Asia, 4 July 2020. Available at: https://asia.nikkei.com/Economy/Southeast-Asia-vies-for-foreign-manufacturers-leaving-China. Accessed 7 September 2020.
82 Merkel's Government Approves Tighter Rules on Takeovers, Bloomberg Quint, 8 April 2020. Available at: www.bloombergquint.com/business/merkel-s-government-approves-tighter-rules-on-foreign-takeovers. Accessed 11 September 2020.
83 Coronavirus: New rules to protect British firms amid virus, BBC News, 21 June 2020. Available at: www.bbc.com/news/business-53127737. Accessed 3 September 2020.
84 Covid-19: Canada moves to protect companies from takeover by 'predatory foreign investors', Hindustan Times, 20 April 2020. Available at: www.hindustantimes.com/world-news/covid-19-canada-moves-to-protect-companies-from-takeover-by-predatory-foreign-investors/story-8hGFKFbpkpTdHbhCjyWAaI.html. Accessed 11 September 2020.
85 India has become the latest country to bolster its foreign takeover regulations in response to the public health crisis caused by COVID-19., Reed Smith, 19 April 2020. Available at: reedsmith.com/en/perspectives/2020/04/manda-protectionism-following-covid19-pandemic-expands-to-india. Accessed 3 September 2020.
86 China GDP: first major economy to show a recovery from coronavirus damage with 3.2 per cent growth in second quarter, South China Morning Post, 16 July 2020. Available at: www.scmp.com/economy/china-economy/article/3093371/china-gdp-economy-avoids-recession-second-quarter-growth-32. Accessed 3 September 2020.
87 Tata Steel in talks with UK Government for 900-million-pound investment, Money control, 26 July 2020. Available at: www.moneycontrol.com/news/business/tata-steel-in-talks-with-uk-government-for-900-million-pound-investment-5598941.html. Accessed 11 September 2020.

References

Beales, H., Brito, Brito, J., Davis, J.K. Jr., DeMuth, C., Devine, D., Dudley, S., Mannix, B., & McGinnis, J.O. (2017). Government regulation: the good, the bad, & the ugly, released by the Regulatory Transparency Project of the Federalist Society. 12 June 2017. https://regproject.org/wp-content/uploads/RTP-Regulatory-Process-Working-Group-Paper.pdf.

Hajzler, C. (2012). Expropriation of foreign direct investments: Sectoral patterns from 1993 to 2006. *Review of World Economics, 148*, 119–149.

Haynal, G. (2014). Corporate statecraft and its diplomacy. *The Hague Journal of Diplomacy, 9*(4), 393–419.

Josselin, D., & Wallace, W. (2001). Non-state actors in world politics: A framework. In Josselin, D., & Wallace, W. (Eds.), *Non-state Actors in World Politics* (pp. 1–20). London: Palgrave Macmillan.

Kesteleyn, J., Riordan, S., & Ruël, H. (2014). Introduction: Business diplomacy. *The Hague Journal of Diplomacy, 9*(4), 303–309.

Kumar, V., & Malhotra, G. (Eds.). (2020). *Examining the role of IT and social media in democratic development and social change*. IGI Global.

Kumar, V., & Svensson, J. (Eds.). (2015). *Promoting social change and democracy through information technology*. IGI Global.

La Porte, T. (2012). The impact of 'intermestic' non-state actors on the conceptual framework of public diplomacy. *The Hague Journal of Diplomacy, 7*(4), 441–458.

Levy, D.L. & Newell, P. (2000). Oceans apart? Business responses to global environmental issues in Europe and the United States. *Environment: Science and Policy for Sustainable Development, 42*(9), 8–21.

London, M. (1999). Principled leadership and business diplomacy: A practical, values-based direction for management development. *Journal of Management Development, 18*(2):170–192.

Marques, J.C. (2017). Business diplomacy in Brazil: Early lessons from an emerging economy. *International Business Diplomacy*. Published online: 28 November 2017, 219–239.

Muldoon, J.P., Jr. (2005). The diplomacy of business. *Diplomacy & Statecraft, 16*(2), 341–359.

Pantoja, M.Y. (2018). Business diplomacy strategies and instruments: Biotechnology companies promoting GMOs in Mexico. *The Hague Journal of Diplomacy, 13*(4), 457–482.

Riordan, S. (2014). Business diplomacy: Shaping the firm's geopolitical risk environment. Clingendael. www.clingendael.org/publication/business-diplomacy-shaping-firms-geopolitical-risk-environment.

Ruël, H. (2013). *Diplomacy means business. Windersheimreeks Kennis en Onderzoek 46* (p. 41). Zwolle: Windesheim. www.academia.edu/6054918/Diplomacy_means_business_Commercial_and_business_diplomacy_as_key_factor_in_IB.

Ruël, H., & Suren, L. (2018). Introduction to the volume. *International business diplomacy* (pp. 3–31) (Advanced Series in Management, Vol. 18). Emerald Publishing.

Ruël, H., & Wolters, T. (2016). Business diplomacy. In C. Constantinou P. Kerr & P. Sharp (Eds.), *The SAGE handbook of diplomacy* (pp. 564–576). London: Sage.

Ruël, H.J.M., Betlem, F., Wolters, T., & Kaap, H. van der (2013). Business diplomacy in MNCs: A study into its determinants. Paper presented at the European International Business Academy (EIBA) 39th Annual Conference, 2013. Universität Bremen, Germany. www.academia.edu/6054810/Business_diplomacy_in_MNCs_an_empirical_study_on_its_determinants_Paper_presented_at_the_EIBA_2013.

Saner, R. (2016). Effective business diplomacy. *Diplomatist*, pp. 16–18. www.academia.edu/30585501/Effective_Business_Diplomacy.

Saner, R., & Yiu, L. (2003). International economic diplomacy: Mutations in post-modern times. Discussion Paper No. 84, Clingendael.

Saner, R., & Yiu, L. (2005). Swiss executives as business diplomats in the new Europe: Evidence from Swiss pharmaceutical and agro-industrial global companies. *Organizational Dynamics, 34*(3), 298–312.

Saner, R., & Yiu, L. (2008). Business-government-NGO relations: Their impact on global economic governance. In Cooper A.F., Hocking B., & Maley W. (Eds.), *Global governance and diplomacy. Studies in diplomacy and international relations*. London: Palgrave Macmillan.

Saner, R., & Yiu, L. (2014). Business diplomacy competence: A requirement for implementing the OECD's guidelines for multinational enterprises. *The Hague Journal of Diplomacy, 9*(4), 311–333.

Saner, R., Yiu, L., & Søndergaard, M. (2000). Business diplomacy management: A core competency for global companies. *The Academy of Management Executive, 14*(1), 80–92.

Turner, E.A. (2010). Why has the number of international non-governmental organizations exploded since 1960? *Cliodynamics, 1*(1).

Westermann-Behaylo, M.K., Rehbein, K., and Fort, T. (2015). Enhancing the Concept of corporate diplomacy: Encompassing political corporate social responsibility, international relations, and peace through commerce. *Academy of Management Perspectives, 29*(4), 387–404.

4 To Control or to Delegate?

Effective Leadership in Challenging Times

Eko Liao, Amy Yamei Wang and Cheryl Qianru Zhang

Introduction

According to the World Health Organization, the COVID-19 pandemic has (up to now) resulted in 46,840,783 confirmed coronavirus cases in 219 countries, areas and territories (World Health Organization [WHO], 2020a). In addition to its adverse health effects, this unprecedented global pandemic is also severely impacting business management practices. The survival and development of enterprises have become a major concern for firms all over the world as the pandemic has caused the largest global recession in history due to more than a third of the world's population being placed on lockdown to limit the spread of the disease (WHO, 2020b). Additionally, due to practiced and enforced measures of social distancing, quarantine and isolation, many employees are mandated to work from home, reduce their working hours, or postpone non-essential work tasks or events in accordance with local regulations and guidance. As a result, many business leaders are pressed to rethink new solutions to adapt to the public health crisis and to dedicate themselves to exploring "unknown unknowns" related to human resource management (Carnevale & Hatak, 2020). The transition to a virtual team reality has been swift: due to the rapid development of new communication technologies such as Zoom, Microsoft Teams and Skype, organizations are able to coordinate their work electronically despite members being geographically dispersed. However, much remains to be known about the effective management of virtual teams, particularly against the novel backdrop of the coronavirus. Therefore, leaders of business organizations are faced with the critical challenges of not only adjusting their business communication strategies to reflect a virtual workplace but also doing so in a way that addresses their employees' needs during this uncertain time.

Balancing Control and Autonomy

In management, supervisors and organizational leaders must balance the needs of themselves and the organization with those of their employees.

DOI: 10.4324/9781003125648-4

In deciding how to lead employees, organizational leaders may encounter a paradox in the need of managing control and autonomy; that is, how much control should they exert over their employees versus how much autonomy they should allow their employees? In the management of organizational affairs, team leaders need to determine the degree to which they delegate, referred to as the assignment of responsibilities to team members and the conferral of authority to execute work tasks. From a manager's perspective, effectively delegating work is important because it frees up managers' time and resources, improves the speed and quality of decisions, and also helps employees develop their skills while viewing leaders as participative (Ayodeji & Kumar 2019; De Pater et al., 2010). From an employee's perspective, proper delegation can increase their intrinsic motivation as it enables empowerment, facilitates efficacy, and enhances supervisor-subordinate relationship-building (Chen & Aryee, 2007). From an organization's perspective, appropriate delegation augments task coordination, productivity and performance as employees with different skills specialize in different tasks; indeed, research has found that proper delegation improves team members' working efficacy (Akinola et al., 2018). In the context of virtual teams, delegation coincides with higher flexibility and time control with higher responsibilities, work motivation and empowerment of the team; in other words, virtual teams may be managed more effectively by delegating managerial functions to the members (Hertel et al., 2005).

Delegation can be an attractive strategy to use as it is a relatively low-cost approach for managers. Effectively communicating desired outcomes to employees is also conducive to the development of business productivity, flexibility, as well as job satisfaction (Gur & Bjørnskov, 2017). However, although managers aim to achieve positive results through delegation, there are three major challenges that can explain the unwillingness of managers to delegate. First, some employees may be inefficient in their jobs. No matter how well the manager delegates, it will be a waste of time and resources as the subordinate is simply unable to carry out their assigned tasks. Secondly, there may be a shortage of employees, which reduces the necessity to delegate. For example, if there are only a few employees in a firm, the division of labor is relatively straightforward. Thirdly, a principal-agent problem may arise between the manager and the subordinate. As managers and employees may have conflicting interests, the employee (the agent) may engage in self-serving behaviors that benefit himself/herself, rather than the manager (the principal). For example, although a manager delegates a work assignment to an employee, the employee may spend their working hours organizing their personal vacation plans or family affairs. To address the principal-agent problem, scholars have discussed the importance of management control systems on corporate governance by monitoring and evaluation (Faeni et al., 2020). As such, in the pursuit of performance goals, some leaders tend to adopt controlling management styles (e.g., authoritarian leadership) to ensure that employees are doing their jobs. Thus, managerial control, by focusing on the processes involved in a subordinate's performance, is also an important part of the management process.

On the other hand, although control processes aim to contribute to business operation quality by ensuring that employees work in the interests of the firm, from a subordinate's point of view, he/she may perceive being observed or watched, which leads to negative feelings of distrust, nervousness, or insecurity on the job. This is because employees value job autonomy – the extent to which a job allows the discretion, freedom and independence to make work decisions and choose the methods used to complete tasks (Hackman & Oldham, 1975). Job autonomy motivates employees to master new tasks and develop their skills as they have increased control over their work environment. Increased job autonomy also allows employees to find non-routine solutions, develop new and useful ideas and demonstrate originality at work. Likewise, reduced job autonomy reduces personal accomplishment and increases burnout and turnover intentions (Spector, 1986). In the context of virtual teams, leadership is a focal challenge because managerial control is difficult when team managers are not in the same location as their subordinates (Hertel et al., 2005). One way in which managers can monitor their employees digitally is through electronic performance monitoring (EPM) which includes controls such as performance recordings by the computer hardware software (e.g. log-in data, number of keystrokes). Using network technology, this allows managers to control employees' log-in and log-out times and employees' working pace, and gain an understanding of their employees' direct performance (Aiello & Kolb, 1995). However, it is difficult to utilize this managerial control without experiencing some negative effects on employees' stress and work satisfaction (Hertel et al., 2005). Managers, therefore, face an essential but paradoxical dilemma – how can they effectively balance a manager's need for control versus an employee's need for autonomy?

COVID-19 and Businesses

The COVID-19 pandemic has created severe challenges to managers all over the world, which have forced them to make quick decisions to adapt to the changing business environment. Disease prevention measures such as travel bans and restrictions, closures of non-essential businesses, social distancing measures and regulations have significantly impacted businesses across multiple industries. For example, undoubtedly the tourism industry is one of the most impacted economic sectors hit hard by the COVID-19 pandemic. Due to quarantine restrictions, fears of illness abroad, reduction of flights abroad, and travel bans, the United Nations World Tourism Organization estimated that global travel may decrease by 58% in 2020, which is equivalent to a potential loss of US$0.9–1.2 trillion in international tourism receipts (United Nations

World Tourism Organization, 2020). Although some have argued that the tourism industry can be resilient (e.g., Prayag, 2020), the future remains ambiguous as the pandemic has shown no signs of slowing down. Globally, in April of 2020, the International Labour Organization predicted a 6.7% loss of job hours in the second quarter of 2020, equaling 195 million full-time jobs (International Labor Organization, 2020). In March of 2020, more than 10 million Americans were unemployed and applied for government aid (Long, 2020). All in all, COVID-19 has caused the largest global recession in history. For small businesses especially, it is still unknown whether shutdowns are temporary or permanent (Carnevale & Hatak, 2020). Statistical data reported by the Kenan Institute of Private Enterprise (2020) show that 18 million jobs from small businesses are at risk in the United States and face further layoffs this economic year. Although governments have tried to alleviate the financial burden on small businesses by providing financial and political support, employees who have lost jobs have found it difficult, if not impossible, to find employment in the economic recession. For those small businesses still holding on, managers need further guidance on how their business can adapt and survive as the pandemic continues.

The COVID-19 crisis has impelled leaders to think and operate small businesses differently. Some of the challenges that small businesses currently face are limited financial capabilities due to weakened economic activity, the instability of inventory supply and logistics, the changing market demand and competition with larger companies that have more resources. Additionally, a shift from traditional face-to-face working environments to virtual home offices triggers small business leaders to find feasible resources and tools to delegate or control.

These circumstances lead to critical research questions such as:

1. What are the effects of COVID-19 on different industries?
2. How should leaders, particularly those of small businesses, respond to the ongoing challenges? How much should managers delegate to their employees? How much autonomy should managers allow their employees?
3. How much should managers delegate/control within virtual teams?

Methodology

To gain further understanding as to how companies with different sizes, business natures and industrial backgrounds deal with the difficulties and challenges from COVID-19, the author team has chosen three firms, which are a small-sized family business in the food industry, a large-sized international firm in the hotel and tourism industry and a large-sized local logistics company. For each firm, a series of interviews were conducted with either the firm owner (case 1), the team leaders (case 2) and/or employees (cases 1, 2, & 3) to acquire information as to the details of management functionality and effectiveness in managing teams during COVID-19.

Case 1: Management Dilemma of a Small Business

Mr. Choi has owned a food and ingredient supply business for decades in Hong Kong. The company mainly supplies small local restaurants with wholesale food ingredients and engages in business-to-business transactions (B2B). Although this family business is small with only ten employees, it is a busy and beloved company on which many local restaurants in the community depend for high -quality ingredients.

Prior to the COVID-19 pandemic, Mr. Choi had hired six full-time back-office employees, who were mainly responsible for support functions such as accounting, marketing and administrative duties. There were also three part-time staff members assisting with the daily operations such as product deliveries, packing and handling goods, and taking care of urgent or expedient orders. These part-time employees are paid by the hour.

Like many other places around the world, Hong Kong was hit hard by the pandemic, from the first to the third wave, during which a large number of cases were recorded daily (Cheung et al., 2020). The local restaurants were among the worst-hit victims. Not only did people avoid leaving their homes (specially to places which required them to take off their masks), but also many people were furloughed from their jobs, which limited their spending ability. Additionally, the Hong Kong government quickly imposed strict lockdown and social distancing requirements; for example, restaurant tables must be spaced at least 1.5 meters apart and restaurants were only allowed to seat 50% of their restaurant's capacity. At one point, no more than two diners were allowed to dine together, and restaurants were no longer to provide dine-in service after 6:00 p.m. As a result, people have changed their dining habits from frequently eating in restaurants to mostly staying at home. As restaurants saw their number of customers decreasing, Mr. Choi's food supply company was also experiencing a decline in orders from local restaurants. Clearly, the B2B model is not sustainable amidst this change and crisis. However, with a positive reputation built over the years within the community, Mr. Choi was pleasantly surprised to find that there were more individual customers coming over to his business to shop for ingredients needed for home cooking. As Mr. Choi started to cater more to individual buyers, Mr. Choi considered switching the focus of his company to a business-to-customer (B2C) model. After brainstorming with his employees about how to further sustain the business with a shift in customers, Mr. Choi decided to provide door-to-door delivery services for individual purchases if the order quantity reached a certain amount.

As the COVID-19 situation is showing no signs of slowing down and is threatening a new wave of the virus, and despite some government subsidies, many businesses continued to layoff many of their workers

(Anonymous, 2020). Observing all of these social and economic tensions, employees at Mr. Choi's company have also started to worry. Joe Tam, one of the most senior staff, had a long conversation with Mr. Choi to express the staff's concerns and worries. The staff were deeply troubled and influenced by job insecurity. Regardless of whether their position was full-time or part-time, the employees were fearful that they could lose their jobs at any given time. To address these fears, Mr. Choi and Joe sat down and structured a detailed plan as a response to the changing business environment and employees' needs.

As he firmly believes that a small local business (such as his own) is built mostly on a positive reputation, Mr. Choi understood that these employees are his most important assets. As such, he was determined to compromise his own short-term profit for their satisfaction and loyalty. Mr. Choi planned to carry out his self-deemed three-step approach to achieve this. First, after a weekly clearing, Mr. Choi ordered milk tea for his staff and gathered them for a heart-to-heart, honest chat. He verbally assured them that he will strive to keep everything the same as usual, to not lay off any employees and not cut down any work hours. Moreover, after finding out that some of his part-time employees had encountered financial difficulties due to their family members losing their jobs, Mr. Choi decided that he could initiate some new projects (e.g., reorganizing the warehouse, conducting a thorough cleaning of company premises, restructuring his customer files) as a way to create more working hours for his employees. Therefore, he decided to increase his part-time employees' work hours to increase their pay. Of course, this extra work scheme is arranged based on their willingness to enroll. This contingency plan – which requires additional costs for employees' compensation – means a compromise to his profit, yet it creates more opportunities for future development as his business reputation will continue to rise. For full-time employees, Mr. Choi switched them from working in the back office to working from home most of the time, as technology has reduced the necessity for them to be physically around to complete their jobs. This signifies a decreasing control, yet it receives much appreciation from people as they can avoid the risk of contracting COVID-19.

To balance the manpower management with elements of autonomy, Mr. Choi chose not to monitor his employees' work progress. The employees were required to only report their progress twice a week and to seek help from the manager if needed. This change seems to loosen managerial control, yet employees feel empowered with important delegation and feelings of trust. As a result, they did not show any procrastination at work and their performance increased during this time.

Mr. Choi's plan was also extremely appreciated by those who were suffering from financial difficulties. They were gratefully surprised that Mr. Choi not only refused to reduce their work hours to keep the business profitable, but also applied the extra work scheme to allow them to earn a higher pay during this difficult time. They felt extremely grateful and appreciative of Mr. Choi's actions to increase their pay. Because they also felt less job insecurity after Mr. Choi's promise, they were better able to focus on and perform better at their jobs.

Case 2: Engagement and Expectation Management from Big-Size Firms

Across different countries under the COVID-19 pandemic, the hotel and tourism industry is one of the hardest hit industries in Hong Kong. Due to imposed travel bans and restrictions on incoming travelers, the United Nations World Tourism Organization estimated that foreign arrivals in Hong Kong fell by a staggering 99.7% year-on-year in September of 2020 (Yau, 2020). As it is one of the top three sources of income for Hong Kong, resolving its challenges and crises remains a priority in restoring the city's economic health.

With approximately 5000 employees, the customer experience enhancement department that Shelly Wong works in is from one of the largest organizations in the hotel and tourism industry. The organization oversees an iconic tourist spot in the city, and the company earns its revenue mainly from tourists visiting this attraction spot.

Before COVID-19, the company was running smoothly on a very well-functioning system and business model and its yearly profit had been relatively stable in recent years. Shelly is in charge of one team in the customer experience enhancement department.

Since January of 2020, the hotel and tourism industry had started to experience the influence of COVID-19. As Hong Kong is closely located near China (where the first cases were reported), and as travelers frequently and freely travel between the two places, the number of tourists visiting Hong Kong quickly declined. From late June to July, the tourist spot was completely shut down due to the Government's imposed lockdown and social distancing regulations. Shelly's team, together with almost all of the teams in the company, began a drastic restructure of staff scheduling due to a slowdown in tourist activities. Before COVID-19, the employees had to work according to a set schedule assigned by the scheduling team. However, after COVID-19, Shelly decided to provide more flexibility for employees to schedule their working days, especially those who had children at home. She decided to fine-tune the schedule to fit employees' needs and to balance work and family issues.

Shelley evaluated the situation before making this decision. She found that most team members were extremely worried about the pandemic and that the company might lay off the employees due a lack of activity. However, as Shelley did not own the company, she did not have any say or influence over manpower decisions and was similarly worried about her own job as an employee. Regardless, as a responsible team leader, Shelly strived to do whatever she was able to do to keep the psychological contract (mutually understood work agreements) with her team members. First, she focused on keeping everyone informed with the most updated information on hand. In times of uncertainty, Shelly knew that it was important to provide as much information as possible to reduce the employees' stress and worries. Therefore, whenever there was a policy change from upper management, Shelly would immediately inform her team and communicate about what may happen in the future so that employees were mentally prepared for any organizational change. Moreover, Shelly actively engaged herself in more frequent chats with the employees to understand more about their worries, opinions about company policies, and special needs about their working schedule. Due to her practice of active listening and frequent interactions, Shelly is better able to manage the employees' expectations within the scope of her decision-making power.

Dyadic Communication: Although a work-from-home policy was adopted, Shelly did not closely monitor the working schedule of the employees; instead, they had a meeting every week for updates. She continually updated the employees about the latest policies from the company and likewise, the employees updated her of their work progress. As there are basically no ongoing projects for the team (due to the absence of tourists), members mainly focused on the preparation for future tourism events and they did not work at a rushed pace so they had time to work carefully on the details of their tasks.

In evaluating what Shelly had done for her team, most of her team members appreciated and understood that she had tried her best to sustain their employment opportunities. Also, with the new flexible scheduling, team members were better able to concentrate on their work tasks as they are better able to balance their work and family issues.

Case 3: Precaution or Hindsight?

Turbo Express is a large-scale integrated express logistics service leader in Hong Kong. Their business activities include providing transportation for various types of goods, cargo and documents with efficiency and punctuality. With a decades-long history of their business in Hong Kong, Turbo Express had gained a great reputation in the city from customers for their fair prices and for their online tracking function, which allows senders and recipients to track the shipping process from receiving to delivery.

The automatic logistics arrangement system in Turbo Express was designed for accuracy, effectiveness and efficiency. When receiving clients' shipping orders by phone calls or from the online platform, the system will quickly evaluate the occupancy of vehicles, and sort an optimal solution by assigning a driver and a delivery team to process the goods receiving, integrating and transiting. For the nature of its business, drivers, warehouse employees and clients often have close physical contact during their work progress such as transferring, checking and signing for delivered goods.

Before COVID-19, in the management of facilities and transportation, the company only had clean-up routines for their cars and other equipment during weekends through an outsourced cleaning company. Limited additional cleaning services were provided for special situations (e.g., accidental liquid leakage) by the end of the working day.

When COVID-19 cases started to increase suddenly in February, many companies decided to allow their workforce to work from home because of safety concerns. Unfortunately, the nature of Turbo Express's business is one that cannot afford such accommodations. Considering the nature of work, it was not feasible to allow work-from-home arrangements for the majority of their employees. Yet, in facing the emergent COVID-19 situation, management teams need to step up the precaution mechanisms. In order to maintain their business, the management teams decided to enhance the hygienic level at work with the purpose of reducing the risk of front-line employees getting infected. They thus embarked on a four-step control system:

Step 1. Turbo Express explored their vendor network and placed a bulk purchase of epidemic prevention products such as face masks and hand sanitizer. This was remarkable given that in a time of increased demand and not enough supply, everyone – including the Hong Kong government – faced difficulties in obtaining basic hygienic products such as face masks. All front-line employees who had opportunities to interact with clients were equipped with a full set of such supplies including glass shields, protection apparels and disinfectants.

Step 2. Originally, Turbo Express had a laundry allowance budget for employees' staff uniform cleaning. After the pandemic situation in Hong Kong got worse, the company doubled the amount of the laundry allowance, which allowed the employees to get their uniform cleaned more frequently to reduce risks of infection.

Step 3. Before the pandemic, the driver and delivery team would usually stay in a small and cramped lounge between shifts during the daytime for their breaks. With COVID-19, the company aimed to free up more vacant rooms for the teams to comply with social distancing rules.

Step 4. As many front-line employees such as drivers could not avoid interacting with various customers on a daily basis, it was highly possible that they may serve or be involved with a close contact with suspected cases of infection. As a result, the managers required their employees to have at least 14 days of quarantine if they showed any symptom of COVID-19 or it had been confirmed that they had served a customer who was diagnosed as a positive COVID-19 case.

While the four-step solution seemed to be considerate in certain ways, more problems were presented. Due to the quarantine policy, the company started experiencing a serious staff shortage, especially as many employees were required to have a quarantine for the positive cases caused by the second wave in Hong Kong. There was inadequate manpower to plan the roster to maintain regular business functioning. Therefore, the company offered an overtime work scheme during this special time. It is a voluntary-based policy that employees who are available for extra time work would get a higher hourly pay as compensation and incentives. This special arrangement was expected to deal with the problem of insufficient human resources, and also helped in striking a balance between a shortage of manpower and workload increase.

In terms of facilities and transportation management, the company increased the frequency of the cleaning service for all vehicles and any other equipment. Drivers and delivery teams became responsible for conducting basic cleaning after every route finished. Then, an outsourced cleaning company was hired to carry out further comprehensive cleaning at the end of a working day.

With these changes in policy and work arrangements, Turbo Express received mixed feedback. For the voluntary extra work plan, employees felt empowered and showed more motivation to explore different schedules to accommodate their needs at work and from home. The increased contingent payment plan also attracted sufficient employees to engage in the plan, which helped relieve the manpower shortage to a great extent.

However, between making effective problem-solving decisions and taking precautionary actions, some employees felt that the company did not do enough. They believed that the company reacted too slowly and too late, which did not match up to their reputation as a market leader in logistics. When the first wave of pandemic started, the company had not done much to increase protection or allow any flexibility. They were considered to be too reactive and not sufficiently proactive in their response to the changing work environment. For instance, the organization only provided face masks for their staff when they were at work but no other additional services. After a while, some customers expressed their concerns about the health condition of the employees who continually interacted with different people every day. Finally, but perhaps too late, the company started being aware of the hygiene concerns and gradually made some arrangements.

Results and Discussion

Lesson Learned: The Control-Autonomy Balance

Dealing with paradox – the coexistence of conflicting yet interconnected elements – is naturally embedded in a leader's role. One of the most pertinent paradoxes for any leader stems from the need to manage control and autonomy. The *control-autonomy paradox* signifies a leader's need to address the conflicting yet complementary control and autonomy simultaneously, which is traditionally viewed as an "either-or" relationship. Extant leadership literature primarily focuses on either one of these two elements. For example, transactional leadership focuses on how to effectively control for maximum output, while empowering leadership emphasizes the importance of giving employees power (Pieterse et al., 2010). Increasingly, however, both organizational power and employee autonomy are being recognized as essential for effective leadership in modern leadership literature. Proper control and appropriate autonomy are both needed, yet the mismanagement paradox (i.e., excessive control and excessive autonomy) causes problems. Without proper mechanisms for leveraging, instead of getting the best of both worlds (i.e., benefits of proper control and autonomy), both leaders and employees may suffer, whereby the former lose control and the latter are left to shoulder the blame.

The COVID-19 situation only intensifies such a control-delegate dilemma. Long periods of working from home, establishing and managing virtual teams, and dealing with uncertainty from various fronts challenge leaders to strike a balance between taking sufficient yet proper control and allowing autonomy to accommodate situational ambiguity. For example, to actively engage work-from-home employees, leaders need to assign challenging but not too over-the-top tasks so that employees are likely to spend sufficient time and effort to produce achievements. However, it remains unclear to managers who are used to face-to-face communication when deciding how much they should intervene to check employees' progress, or advise appropriate approaches, or show support by empowering employees with critical decision-making power. In this chapter, the authors use three examples from virtual workplace management during the pandemic in exploring effective ways for leaders to adopt in engaging and motivating employees using various approaches.

COVID-19: Challenges to Leaders on Delegation and Control

The cases presented demonstrate that companies and organizational leaders are facing difficulties from various fronts. However, the three cases show only part of the picture as many more constraints and challenges remain. Below, we identify critical issues that companies are continuing to face:

1. *Remote work.* Leaders have to adapt to the new workplace reality, particularly to those organizations that seldom rely on remote workforces.
2. *Communication.* How to communicate directly and effectively is a central consideration to leaders.
3. *Decision-making.* Due to the uncertainty of the pandemic, emergency decision-making depends on the "superpower" of leaders' judgments.
4. *Psychological safety.* Most of the organizations face struggles to maintain productivity in an environment of change and ambiguity, which would affect the psychological safety of leaders and employees.

5 *Mental health.* Social distance and quarantine policies bring stress, anxiety and other mental issues to employees.
6 *Employee commitment.* Without proper supervision and motivation, employees' morale and commitment to tasks and to organizations are likely to decrease.
7 *Financial stability.* Most companies are likely to be affected by the pandemic, which causes a high risk to organizations' financial stability.
8 *Manpower shortage.* One of the biggest challenges is manpower shortage because of the quarantine policy, traveling constraints, etc.
9 *Customer loyalty.* During the COVID-19 pandemic, without sufficient resources and manpower to conduct regular marketing campaigns, companies find it difficult to maintain the customer loyalty level.
10 *Work flexibility.* Not all jobs are suitable for flexible working arrangements, such as public service sectors, thus leaders often need to develop contingency plans with limited resources.

Moving Forward: Strategies for Effective Control

There are pragmatic approaches to enforcing control. Liao and Hui (2016) argued that supervisors can adopt at least two types of monitoring to keep informed of how employees perform at work: *observational monitoring* and *interactional monitoring*. On one hand, in order to keep an eye on employee's work behaviors and progress, some managers choose to conduct close and strict surveillance via gathering employees' work progress and outcomes without consulting or interacting with employees. This kind of monitoring is of a controlling nature and is often practiced with a top-down mechanism. Supervisors decide when to monitor, what information is to be gathered, and how to use and evaluate the employee's work based on the monitoring results. For instance, team leaders of frontline manufacturing workers would walk around in the workplace, peering over employees' shoulders or following closely how employees carried out their work. With these practices, supervisors can directly observe how employees deal with new tasks or work problems. This type of monitoring allows for quick observation when efficiency is a top priority for firms. However, without face-to-face communication, the information collected may be biased and employees often perceive less job autonomy.

There exists an alternative way to balance the need to check in on employees' work progress and the need to involve employees in the progress. Liao and Hui (2016) identified this work information-gathering mechanism – which involves employee's side of the story – as interactional monitoring. One of the most common and straightforward ways to achieve this is via holding formal or informal discussions with employees. Such meetings focus on knowing more of employees' expectations and concerns of work tasks, their feedback of certain work requirements or policy changes, as well as their views regarding issues such as work scheduling or team projects. This dyadic interaction not only allows supervisors to collect valuable information, but also creates a sense of empowerment for employees. They are enabled to better understand their supervisor's expectations and requirements and given the opportunity to provide explanations regarding unachieved tasks, mistakes, or unsatisfactory performance.

Delegation for Outstanding Performance

The difficult situation arising from COVID-19 forces every leader to think of ways to allocate resources smartly and to keep employees engaged and well-motivated. In addition to implementing control measures, organizational leaders have a balance to keep in empowering employees. On the one hand, they need to delegate to cultivate empowerment and engage employees because delegation is a sign of trust, respect and involvement. On the other hand, there are multiple factors that influence a leader's delegation decisions such as the importance of the decision that needs to be made, the employee's capabilities, and the efficiency. Zhang et al. (2015) argued that leaders now have at least five different paradoxes to manage including "enforcing work requirements, while allowing flexibility" (p. 538) as one critical element. Without a balance, leaders who demonstrate a controlling style in dealing with decision-making and interpersonal interaction (e.g., authoritarian leadership) are more likely to be perceived as closed-minded and less considerate, which may negatively influence employees' engagement and sense of belonging. Conversely, leaders who always delegate may be regarded as irresponsible (e.g., laissez-faire leadership). Given that the negative influence of excessive control-autonomy is well established, it is essential to find ways to tackle this paradox. The notion that higher- and lower-level actions can coexist provides an alternative perspective for investigating the control-autonomy paradox. Sagie's (1997) loose-tight principle also promotes a similar argument that leaders' direction and employees' participation in decision-making can coincide and have complementary effects. Thus, while the authors of many studies in this field have focused on only one side of leader behaviors, there is a possibility that leaders can practice both control and autonomy simultaneously (and preferably at different levels of identification). In fact, a leader can execute control at a higher level (e.g., having a shared vision for the firm, and aligning management goals of all units with the vision) as the nature of controlling action is more regulatory-oriented, while allowing autonomy at a lower level (i.e., the operational level; such as allowing employees to make decisions as to work procedures, priority of tasks, etc.) because autonomy is often associated with operational conduct (Shalley & Gilson, 2004).

During difficult times, organizational leaders need to leverage various resources and their own capabilities to maximize the sustainability of the business and increase the morale of manpower. The common paradoxes that they face from regular management practices will be more prominent during times of change and crisis. Finding solutions for effective management of the leader paradox, consistent with the Chinese yin-yang philosophy, Zhang and colleagues developed insightful research on leadership practices that facilitate functional solutions to five paradoxes: (1) combining self-centeredness with other-centeredness; (2) maintaining both distance and closeness; (3) treating subordinates uniformly, while allowing individualization; (4) enforcing work requirements, while allowing flexibility; and (5) maintaining decision control, while allowing autonomy (Zhang et al., 2015). They argue that "leaders will confront ongoing, competing demands to meet organizations' structural needs and followers' individual needs" (p. 541).

To develop effective solutions, their study proposed that leaders should adopt three practices. First, leaders should adopt holistic thinking, which requires leaders to include various factors that influence the decision-making process and build a "whole picture" instead of focusing on one aspect. As such, leaders are better able to understand in-depth work problems and use an open mind to explore different possible solutions. Second, leaders should exhibit integrative complexity, which refers to one's cognitive abilities and willingness to recognize the coexisting nature of the two opposite poles of a paradox. For example, leaders who believe that they can both execute control on certain work elements while practicing delegation on others achieve high levels of integrative complexity. As such, these types of leaders welcome different – even conflicting – perspectives. They also have the cognitive capacity to process various perspectives before delivering an optimal solution. Lastly, Zhang et al. (2015) suggested that an organic structure (e.g., a high level of decentralization) instead of a mechanical structure (e.g., a strict hierarchy and tall organizational structure) is more likely to allow leaders to better deal with paradox. For example, with an organic structure, leaders have more autonomy to practice their creative problem-solving ideas. They also face fewer barriers and challenges in promoting promising yet drastic change initiatives.

Building Employee's Initiatives: Job Crafting

During a time of change and crisis such as COVID-19, for leaders to lead effectively and efficiently, they not only need to pay attention to how they manage their leadership styles and behaviors, it also becomes more important for them to understand how to cultivate employees' initiatives of self- and work-improvements. Researchers argued that employees' proactive behaviors such as crafting their jobs across different work elements not only prove to be beneficial for their growth at work, but also generate value for organizations. The topic of job crafting has been receiving increasing attention from management researchers and practitioners. Job crafting refers to employees' voluntary behaviors in changing the *task*, *relational* or *cognitive* elements of their jobs (Wrzesniewski & Dutton, 2001). To enhance favorable job experiences and fulfill personal needs, employees craft their jobs by making decisions about how much to engage in tasks, how frequently to communicate with colleagues, or what professional image they wish to build. Effective crafting behaviors have positive implications not only for employees themselves, but also for organizations and other stakeholders.

During difficult times, organizations and leaders often face the challenge of not having enough resources to allocate to achieve organizational goals. As such, companies have to rely on employees' motivation and the capability to proactively engage in job crafting themselves. For employees to craft their jobs, they can work from two main aspects. First, employees as job crafters may choose to design their jobs in terms of their task-related aspects. For example, they can actively take up more challenging tasks, engage themselves in skill and knowledge learning for better work performance, and optimize their work procedures for better effectiveness and efficiency. With a task focus, employees concentrate on delivering outstanding job performance and thus psychologically and physically engage more with their jobs. For instance, they spend more time on fulfilling requirements, involve themselves with more skill learning and performance refining activities, or dedicate themselves to tackling difficulties and challenges. As a result, their job-related behaviors would be enhanced and deliver better results.

When employees craft aspects of their jobs with a task focus, they are drawn toward fulfilling duties and improving their performance at work. Crafting job-focused elements – for instance, by exploring more effective ways of completing tasks – strengthens employees' sense of fit in their roles (Tims et al., 2016) and their engagement with work activities (Petrou et al., 2015). In such cases, they are more dedicated to their roles and strive to achieve outstanding performance on all fronts and avoid destructive actions that put their effective work functioning at risk. When they spend more psychological and physical effort on fulfilling work-related goals, employees are more likely to enjoy higher job performance and engage in work initiatives such as finding better ways to complete tasks. Counterproductive behaviors such as taking too many breaks or intentionally working slowly are also reduced, as such behavior is inconsistent with a focus on a favorable job experience.

Secondly, employees can also engage in the crafting about relationship-related aspects. For example, they can actively engage in more coworker bonding activities, initiate communications with other team members or clients, or spend extra time and effort in building more effective relationships at work (Wrzesniewski & Dutton, 2001). With a relational focus, employees emphasize strengthening their relationships and the quality of their interactions with coworkers. Thus, they engage in more instrumental behavior toward coworkers (e.g., helping), and in turn enjoy enhanced relationships and more effective teamwork.

When job crafting has a people focus, employees' crafting behavior aims to develop high-quality relationships with coworkers. Employee's perceived importance of coworkers (Barrick et al., 2002) is adopted to measure the focus on people. For example, employees actively search for opportunities to work with team members they consider worth having quality relationships with, and invest in such relationships accordingly (Niessen et al., 2016). Employees who regard relationship-building as an important goal engage more in effective teamwork and cooperative behavior (Barrick et al., 2002).

One example is that crafting job elements with a people focus should motivate employees to spend more time and effort building a harmonious teamwork environment. They should also respect coworkers' opinions and offer support and assistance when needed. Thus, coworkers are more likely to perceive and appreciate such efforts, leading to a higher quality of exchange relationships (Seers, 1989; Seers et al., 1995). Coworkers would also be less likely to engage in exclusionary behavior toward employees who contribute and are perceived as having a positive value for the group's functioning (Scott & Duffy, 2015). Consequently, employees should experience high-quality relationships.

Managing Virtual Teams during COVID-19: Recommendations for Managers

1. *Preparation.* In order to help employees necessarily transition from a traditional workplace to a work-from-home arrangement, it is important that leaders provide employees with an execution plan as to how to navigate virtual teams. In addition to articulating a vision that is motivating and inspiring, managers must also set clearly defined goals. Establishing well-defined goals provides directions to employees as to how to function in a non-traditional workplace and reduces stress that employees may experience in adapting to virtual team arrangements (Konradt et al., 2003). Setting quality goals also increases team performance in virtual teams; in a study by Hertel et al. (2004), there was a significant correlation between the quality of set goals (as perceived by the employees) and the effectiveness of the virtual team (as rated by the manager).
2. *Communication.* Virtual teams reduce employees' ability to make sense of events through physical observation; therefore, to facilitate communication, managers must make good use of the available technology to ensure that information is shared among members in a consistent and explicit manner. As there may be a lack of cohesion and difficulty in integrating the work from different team members, managers need to establish norms as to how information is to be shared and communication technology will be used (Malhotra et al., 2007). For example, managers can set and enforce norms regarding

how to post information, where to post it, when to post it, and etiquette for electronic communication.

3 *Providing Feedback:* To allow virtual team members to continue to improve and to keep them in the loop, managers should provide timely, frequent and concrete feedback. Feedback helps to better inform virtual team members about team processes and increases their motivation, satisfaction and performance (Hertel et al., 2004). For example, managers can hold regular meetings to provide consultations with their employees and keep everyone on the same page.
4 *Training for Managers and Virtual Teams:* As many managers are also adapting to virtual team leadership, organizations should consider providing training opportunities for their managers and employees. In a study of virtual team training, Jokisch et al. (2004) identified three main areas of improvement: (1) clarification of team goals, (2) effective use of communication media and (3) establishing commonly shared norms for intra-team processes (e.g., electronic communication etiquette). The authors found that after a 3-month training program focusing on these topics, questionnaire results revealed that participants perceived significant improvements as well as observing an increase in the team's overall effectiveness and working climate.

Conclusion

In situations of unprecedented uncertainty and organizational change caused by COVID-19, the importance of managers cannot be overstated. Managers and organizations are facing tremendous external challenges ranging from government-imposed lockdowns and public health measures to a widespread fear of contracting the disease that have severely impacted their businesses. In addition, these challenges have necessarily transformed the traditional work environment into a virtual, ever-changing landscape. While direct leadership strategies are possible in conventional times, managers of virtual teams must adapt their leadership to overcome the disadvantages of a geographically dispersed work group. As working from home has become the "new normal" for many companies and managers are no longer physically situated with their employees in a shared workspace, interesting questions have arisen for managers. That is, how much should managers delegate to their employees and allow them the autonomy to work from home? How much should managers monitor and exert control over their employees from afar? On the one hand, providing autonomy allows employees to perceive a higher degree of trust which can motivate them to perform better. On the other hand, exerting control over employees can reassure managers of the activities of employees at home. Thus, managers are faced with a compelling paradox of managing control and autonomy and are relied upon more than ever to not only achieve organizational goals and meet bottom lines to keep their companies afloat, but also to meet the needs of their employees and lead them effectively through uncertain times and circumstances.

Realistically, managers need to assess the specifics of their external environment and their organizational goals to properly determine the level of control versus autonomy. Overall, we suggest firms and their management teams should provide autonomy to employees as a motivational mechanism to maintain their loyalty and commitment so that the firm can develop in the long term. In addition, more control over the employees is needed to pacify the safety concerns of the employees and customers as well as to minimize the risk of exposure to the virus. Lastly, allowing for flexible scheduling and showing trust in employees working from home are effective ways to reduce uncertainty within the firm so that employees can concentrate on their tasks. In terms of effectively managing virtual teams, managers are advised to explore ways to enhance employees' self-initiatives such as ways to craft their jobs cognitively and behaviorally. Motivating employees via virtual teams can be more challenging than face-to-face teams, yet finding the right motivation for employees can be exceptionally rewarding. Ultimately, managers will be depended upon to make careful considerations about how much to control – versus delegate – their employees through uncertain times.

Acknowledgment

The work described in this paper was supported by a grant from the Research Grants Council of the Hong Kong Special Administrative Region, China (Project No. UGC/FDS14/B05/19).

References

Aiello, J.R., & Kolb, K.J. (1995). Electronic performance monitoring and social context: Impact on productivity and stress. *Journal of Applied Psychology, 80*(3), 339.

Akinola, M., Martin, A., & Phillips, K. (2018). To delegate or not to delegate: Gender differences in affective associations and behavioral responses to delegation. (Report) *Academy of Management Journal, 61*(4), 1467–1491.

Anonymous. (2020). Hong Kong 2020 Latest News on retrenchment, layoff and job cut. (November 11). Employee at Work. https://employeeatwork.com/layoff-hongkong/.

Ayodeji, O.G., & Kumar, V. (2019). Social media analytics: A tool for the success of online retail industry. *International Journal of Services Operations and Informatics, 10*(1), 79–95.

Barrick, M.R., Stewart, G.L., & Piotrowski, M. (2002). Personality and job performance: Test of the mediating effects of motivation among sales representatives. *Journal of Applied Psychology, 87*(1), 43.

Carnevale, J., & Hatak, I. (2020). Employee adjustment and well-being in the era of COVID-19: Implications for human resource management. *Journal of Business Research, 116*, 183–187.

Chen, Z.X., & Aryee, S. (2007). Delegation and employee work outcomes: An examination of the cultural context of mediating processes in China. *Academy of Management Journal, 50*(1), 226–238.

Cheung, E., Lau, C., & Cheng, L.L. (2020, July 28). Hong Kong third wave: 'No place for complacency' on Covid-19, health officials warn, as city records small drop in new cases. South China Morning Post. www.scmp.com/news/hong-kong/health-environment/article/3094974/hong-kong-third-wave-city-register-more-100-new.

De Pater, I.E., Van Vianen, A.E., & Bechtoldt, M.N. (2010). Gender differences in job challenge: A matter of task allocation. *Gender, Work & Organization, 17*(4), 433–453.

Faeni, D.P., Faeni, R.P., Septiyanti, R., & Yuliansyah, Y. (2020). The role of management control system on firm performance. *Talent Development & Excellence, 12*, 1629–1639.

Gur, N., & Bjørnskov, C. (2017). Trust and delegation: Theory and evidence. *Journal of Comparative Economics, 45*(3), 644–657.

Hackman, J. R., & Oldham, G. R. (1975). Development of the job diagnostic survey. *Journal of Applied Psychology, 60*(2), 159.

Hertel, G., Geister, S., & Konradt, U. (2005). Managing virtual teams: A review of current empirical research. *Human Resource Management Review, 15*(1), 69–95.

Hertel, G., Konradt, U., & Orlikowski, B. (2004). Managing distance by interdependence: Goal setting, task interdependence, and team-based rewards in virtual teams. *European Journal of Work and Organizational Psychology, 13*(1), 1–28.

International Labour Organization. (2020, November 9). Rebuild tourism safely to save 300 million jobs worldwide. www.ilo.org/global/about-the-ilo/multimedia/video/institutional-videos/WCMS_756336/lang--en/index.htm.

Jokisch, W., Haardt, C., & Schöckel, D. (2004). Entwicklung, Durchführung und Evaluation eines Basistrainings für virtuelle Teams bei der Siemens AG. *Human Resource Management **im** Inter-und Intranet, 313*.

Kenan Institute of Private Enterprise. (2020. April). The COVID-19 Pandemic and Small Business Employment. https://kenaninstitute.unc.edu/kenan-insight/the-covid-19-pandemic-and-small-business-employment/.

Konradt, U., Hertel, G., & Schmook, R. (2003). Quality of management by objectives, task-related stressors, and non-task-related stressors as predictors of stress and job satisfaction among teleworkers. *European Journal of Work and Organizational Psychology, 12*(1), 61–79.

Liao, E.Y., & Hui, C. (2016). Supervisor monitoring and subordinate innovation. *Journal of Organizational Behavior, 37*(2), 168–192.

Long, H. (2020, April 2). Over 10 Million Americans applied for unemployment benefits in March as economy collapsed. www.washingtonpost.com/business/2020/04/02/jobless-march-coronavirus/.

Malhotra, A., Majchrzak, A., & Rosen, B. (2007). Leading virtual teams. *Academy of Management Perspectives, 21*(1), 60–70.

Niessen, C., Weseler, D., & Kostova, P. (2016). When and why do individuals craft their jobs? The role of individual motivation and work characteristics for job crafting. *Human Relations, 69*(6), 1287–1313.

Petrou, P., Demerouti, E., & Schaufeli, W.B. (2015). Job crafting in changing organizations: Antecedents and implications for exhaustion and performance. *Journal of Occupational Health Psychology, 20*(4), 470.

Pieterse, A.N., VanKnippenberg, D., Schippers, M., & Stam, D. (2010). Transformational and transactional leadership and innovative behavior: The moderating role of psychological empowerment. *Journal of Organizational Behavior, 31*, 609–623.

Prayag, G. (2020). Time for reset? Covid-19 and tourism resilience. *Tourism Review International, 24*(2-3), 179–184.

Sagie, A. (1997). Leader direction and employee participation in decision making: Contradictory or compatible practices? *Applied Psychology, 46*(4), 387–415.

Scott, K.L., & Duffy, M.K. (2015). Antecedents of workplace ostracism: New directions in research and intervention. *Mistreatment in Organizations, 13*, 137–165.

Seers, A. (1989). Team-member exchange quality: A new construct for role-making research. *Organizational Behavior and Human Decision Processes, 43*(1), 118–135.

Seers, A., Petty, M.M., & Cashman, J. F. (1995). Team-member exchange under team and traditional management: A naturally occurring quasi-experiment. *Group & Organization Management, 20*(1), 18–38.

Shalley, C.E., & Gilson, L.L. (2004). What leaders need to know: A review of social and contextual factors that can foster or hinder creativity. *The Leadership Quarterly, 15*, 33–53.

Spector, P.E. (1986). Perceived control by employees: A meta-analysis of studies concerning autonomy and participation at work. *Human Relations, 39*(11), 1005–1016.

Tims, M., Derks, D., & Bakker, A.B. (2016). Job crafting and its relationships with person–job fit and meaningfulness: A three-wave study. *Journal of Vocational Behavior, 92*, 44–53.

United Nations World Tourism Organization. (2020, May 7). International tourism numbers could fall 60-80% in 2020, UNWTO reports. www.unwto.org/news/covid-19-international-tourist-numbers-could-fall-60-80-in-2020.

World Health Organization. (2020a, November 9). WHO Coronavirus Disease (COVID-19) Dashboard. https://covid19.who.int/.

World Health Organization. (2020b, November 9). Coronavirus. www.who.int/health-topics/coronavirus#tab=tab_1.

Wrzesniewski, A., & Dutton, J. E. (2001). Crafting a job: Revisioning employees as active crafters of their work. *Academy of Management Review, 26*(2), 179–201.

Yau, C. (2020). Coronavirus: Hong Kong tourism almost non-existent, with visitor numbers for September down 99.7 per cent from last year. www.scmp.com/news/hong-kong/hong-kong-economy/article/3106109/coronavirus-hong-kong-tourism-almost-non-existent.

Zhang, Y., Waldman, D.A., Han, Y.L., & Li, X.B. (2015). Paradoxical leader behaviors in people management: Antecedents and consequences. *Academy of Management Journal, 58*(2), 538–566.

5 Managing Efficiency and Effectiveness in the "New Normal" Work Environment

Shameem Shagirbasha

Introduction

COVID-19 entered the public consciousness and made many businesses to decide to let most of their employees work from home. Now, it has become the biggest challenge to manage the employees virtually. Though we have many models used to manage the performance of the employees, some of them have failed to meet their desired objectives during the lockdown period. The two common measures to assess organizational performance are effectiveness and efficiency (Bounds et al., 1995; Robbins, 2000). For managers, suppliers and investors, these two terms might look synonymous, yet, according to Mouzas (2006), each of these terms have their own distinct meaning. While some organizations focus on effectiveness to assess organizational performance, a few others assess performance using efficiency (Chavan, 2009). To measure effectiveness, companies focus mainly on their vision, mission and goals. For those who rely on efficiency, they emphasize the optimum utilization of resources to get the desired output. Now, the interesting question is, what must organizations do to manage their performance, in other words, to manage their employees in this new normal work environment?

Most organizations are working under pressure. This makes it necessary for the employees to carry out the correct tasks (effectively) in the right way (efficiently). More efficiency means more production with the same level of resources. This lowers costs and increases return, which in turn exerts less pressure on the organization. Efficiency, in other words, doing things in the right way, is of two types – static and dynamic. Static refers to improvements within the existing conditions whereas dynamic refers to continuous improvements of the conditions.

Needless to say, efficiency can be termed as the ability of employees to act/behave and produce effectively with less expenditure of resources, minimizing waste and effort. The effectiveness of employees is determined by their goals, objectives, mission and vision and their ability to achieve the same in the right way. Although efficiency and effectiveness are central measures in assessing employees' performance, many organizations find it challenging to balance effectiveness with efficiency in the workplace.

DOI: 10.4324/9781003125648-5

Now, in a virtual work environment, it has become even more challenging than ever before. This chapter describes managing the efficiency and effectiveness of employees and highlights the importance of assessing the performance of employees in the new normal work environment.

Efficiency and Effectiveness

The term "performance" is extensively used in all fields of management. Often, performance is associated or equated with effectiveness and efficiency. We can say that efficiency and effectiveness are the two sides of the coin to understand performance management system. Most traditional performance tools concentrate on financial or productivity aspects. Later, the subsequent generation performance management systems focused mainly on the strategic perspective. Strategic performance management highlights different performance measures or KPIs (key performance indicators) to quantify quality and productivity in terms of efficiency and effectiveness of employee actions so as to monitor, manage, control and perform the work activities (Akhtar & Sushil, 2018). Other traditional strategic performance management tools such as TQM, Six Sigma, BSC (Kaplan & Norton, 1992) and performance prism (Neely et al., 2007) have been developed over the years to manage the efficiency, effectiveness and quality of the work. These performance models are not free from implementation failures like other management frameworks and tools, particularly during the new normal environment. Performance management has some issues which managers face while using it to evaluate or improve the performance of employees (Halachmi, 2005).

Many managers in today's world find it challenging to acquire business opportunities that increase their organization's market value. Often most organizations emphasize efficiency rather effectiveness. Organizations can run efficiently without being effective in managing the employees' performance. An organization is a platform for pursuing and realizing the vision of employees. It is the excellence of an organization derived from the collective power of its structure, systems, and multidimensional proficiencies that shapes its performance and makes effective execution of strategies through their employees. Getting people to consciously move in a preferred direction and path, guiding them to embrace a thought or action with enthusiasm, and facilitating their performance and success form the crux of an organization's vision. At the strategic level, it is about creating, sustaining and enhancing organizational energy for institutional excellence. Top management need to formulate and communicate the vision, consistently articulate cultural imperatives and values, and build desired core competencies, apart from ensuring structural adequacy. At the operating level, managers are required to set direction to the performance of their teams and make sure that the team members get the sense of it, gain their commitment to performance expectations, help

Table 5.1 Comparison between efficiency and effectiveness

Comparison criteria	*Efficiency*	*Effectiveness*
Meaning of the term	The virtue of being efficient is known as efficiency.	The degree of closeness of the actual with the intended result is known as effectiveness.
Way of doing	Doing work in a correct manner.	Performing accurate work.
Importance on	Inputs and outputs	Means and ends
Time orientation	Short run	Long run
Approach	Introverted	Extroverted
Process	Strategy implementation	Strategy formulation
Focus	Operations	Strategies

them to succeed through feedback and coaching, and support them in developing required competencies. In all, it is evident that the role of managers is designed to be committed to ensuring performance readiness in the organization, to manage efficiency and effectiveness in the work and to facilitate employees to perform and succeed individually and collectively. Efficiency can be defined as a component of the career growth and progress of employees and organizations. It requires the willingness of an employee and ability to function to master his work (Alwehabie, 2017). Similarly effectiveness indicates the degree to which the objectives are achieved. Both the terms are linked with each other. While efficiency means achieving targets with least cost, time and effort, effectiveness indicates reaching the desired goal. Table 5.1 presents a comparison between the terms efficiency and effectiveness.

Traditional Frameworks to Manage Performance

The Performance Pyramid

As in any performance management system, the performance pyramid is also an attempt to incorporate the financial and non-financial performance indicators. The pyramid, as the name suggests, provides us the hierarchy of the measures including financial and non-financial performance aspects. The performance pyramid is also known as the SMART pyramid, which stands for strategic measurement and reporting technique. This pyramid was developed by Lynch and Cross (1991). The performance pyramid supports the need to focus on internal efficiency as well as the external effectiveness measures of performance. The performance pyramid emphasizes the actions to achieve the organization's vision. This can be done by cascading down through a number of different levels; for example, the pyramid presents how strategy and day-to-day operations

Figure 5.1 The performance pyramid.

can be linked to achieve performance. There are four levels (Figure 5.1) and each one is described below.

Level 1: At this level, the company's mission including goals, objectives, strategies and vision including the company's future position in the market are described. The organization's vision and mission form the top of the pyramid. The organization's vision or mission also gives us an idea of how companies will achieve long-term success and gain competitive advantage.

Level 2: This level focuses on market and financial measures. To achieve the corporate vision and mission, it is ideal to start with market-related issues and financial aspects.

Level 3: Now, the market- and compensation-related measures set at the previous level (level 2) are linked with customer satisfaction, increased productivity and greater flexibility at level 3. These linkages become the guiding forces that help organizations to drive their strategic objectives and to maintain the efficiency and effectiveness of the business.

Level 4: The base level in the pyramid captures various departmental measures such as cycle time, quality, waste, delivery which helps to monitor the level 3-related issues.

The pyramid highlights non-financial aspects (external focus) and financial measures (internal efficiency) of the organizations. One of the shortcomings of the performance pyramid is that it focuses on only two groups of stakeholders – customers and shareholders. Hence, it lacks the holistic capture of the business and it is essential to make certain that other stakeholders' measures are included in the model. Due to the lack of inclusion of all stakeholders, this model is not suitable to measure the efficiency and effectiveness of the workplace in the COVID era.

The Balanced Scorecard

The application of developing operational measures including all functional areas and relating them to individual objectives gives rise to four perspectives of the balanced scorecard (BSC) (Figure 5.2). Building this scorecard helps the organizations to link today's action to tomorrow's goal (Kaplan & Norton, 1992). BSC supplements the traditional financial measures with additional indicators that reveal customer satisfaction, internal business development and the ability to learn and grow. It enables organizations to track their financials simultaneously observing the feasibility of identifying and executing their respective intangible assets that they would need to survive in the market and further grow. Hence, this framework of four perspectives (customer perspective, internal business perspective, learning and career growth perspective and financial perspective) not only replaces the conventional financial measurement system but also complements it. This framework provides the balanced illustration of present operating performance and the drivers for future performance as well. These four perspectives allow equilibrium between the long-term objectives and short-term operations and also between the desired outcomes and their respective driving force.

The customer perspective is a value-adding view with the mission of delivering value to their customers. The internal business perspective depicts the process view functioning with the mission to promote efficiency and effectiveness in the business process. The learning and career growth perspective is from the point of shareholders with the mission to succeed financially, by delivering value to the shareholders. The learning and career growth perspective is the futuristic view portraying the organization's mission to achieve innovation and transformation

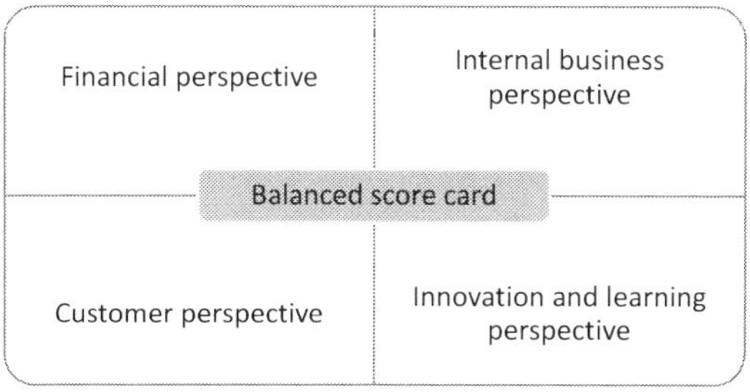

Figure 5.2 The balanced scorecard.

capabilities, through uninterrupted improvement and preparation for future challenges. Thus, BSC attempts to contribute in the transformation of intangible assets to long-term financial success, making the process unambiguous and controllable as well.

The Performance Prism

The performance prism is an innovative performance management framework of the second generation. It is unique in managing efficiency and effectiveness as it focuses on stakeholders in addition to the strategies of the organizations. It is an overall framework encompassing investors, customers, employees, suppliers, communities and regulators. It takes into account two important aspects.

1 The prism considers the needs and wants of the stakeholders.
2 The prism considers the needs and wants of the organization from their stakeholders.

In this way the reciprocal relationships with each stakeholder is included in the performance prism.

There are five facets of the performance prism – stakeholder satisfaction, strategies, processes, capabilities, stakeholder contribution. These facets are distinct and all of the facets are interlinked logically. The performance prism works on the belief that considering today's business environment, most organizations are aspiring to be successful in the long run. The organizations who adopt the performance prism will have a clear picture of where they stand, what they want from stakeholders and what stakeholders require from them. This will in turn help the efficiency and effectiveness of the business. The performance prism (Figure 5.3) answers the following questions.

1 **Stakeholder satisfaction**: Who are the key stakeholders? What are their wants and needs?
2 **Strategies**. What can be the different strategies organizations can adopt to satisfy the wants and needs of these key stakeholders?
3 **Processes**. What are the critical processes that need to be followed to execute these strategies?
4 **Capabilities**. What are the different capabilities required to operate and to improve these processes?
5 **Stakeholder contribution**. What will be the contributions from the stakeholders? If we need to retain, maintain and develop the capabilities, what do we require from the various stakeholders?

The performance prism has demarcated what strategies they will follow to make sure that value is delivered to these stakeholders. This framework understands what processes the organizations need if these strategies are

Figure 5.3 The performance prism.
Source: author

to be delivered. The capabilities to execute the processes are well-defined. Most organizations have also thought cautiously about what it is that they want from their stakeholders. It can be customer centricity, customer service, employee satisfaction, employee loyalty, employee experience, investments, returns, profits etc. In essence, the performance prism provides us a clear business model and an unambiguous understanding of what constitutes and drives good performance.

As prism refracts light and illustrates the concealed complexity of something which appears outwardly as simple as white light and decomposes it to its elements. The performance prism works on the same principle. It illustrates the unseen complexity of the organization. While the traditional frameworks, mostly one-dimensional, even pick out the element of the complexity in business, we cannot rely on them as performance is not a unidimensional concept. Therefore the performance prism meets this shortcoming, by including multiple stakeholders and interlinked perspectives to understand the concept holistically and to ensure efficiency while being effective.

In spite of the advantages of traditional performance systems, there are disadvantages as well with respect to continuous feedback mechanisms. To overcome these shortcomings, the agile performance management system was introduced by organizations. A comparison of the traditional and agile performance management systems is given in Table 5.2.

Automated Performance Management Process

With the increasing shift toward flat organizations, many businesses are under tremendous pressure to perform more with less. To manage

Table 5.2 Comparison between traditional and agile performance management systems

Traditional PMS	*Agile PMS*
Performance reviews happen only once a year.	Performance reviews happen on a regular basis.
As it is not done on a continuous basis, remembering the good performers will become difficult and subjected to biases.	Continuous review and feedback given to employees.
Minimum scope for employee career growth as there is absence of proper supervision or developmental plans.	As continuous feedback is given, there is scope for employees to work on their weaknesses and develop themselves.
Only focuses on giving performance feedback, no plans for developments.	Constructive feedback to improve performance and to develop employee career growth.
Retrospective in nature.	Prospective in nature.
Makes employees anxious as it does not report their challenges effectively.	Employees' challenges are discussed properly with intervention, support and guidance.
Poor employee engagement as they are often not recognized for their good performance. They feel underrated.	Better employee engagement as they are rewarded and recognized on a regular basis for their performance.
Expectations and goals are often not communicated clearly. They are not aligned with the business objectives.	Goals are defined clearly. They are prioritized as per the objectives of the organization.
One-way communication, manager gives feedback and convinces employees on results.	Supported with technology, multi-channel communication happens and 360-degree feedback is solicited from multiple sources, including internal and external stakeholders.
There is no team work and minimal autonomy is given to employees while performing their tasks.	Improved team collaboration and regular flow of ideas. Enhanced innovation and team development and increased sense of belonging to the organization.

efficiency and effectiveness, it is required for the performance evaluation system to evolve into more comprehensive processes which include different activities driving performance such as goals, expectations, reviews, feedback (London & Mone, 2014). In order to improve efficiency, most of the performance management systems were automated (Aguinis, 2013). These automated systems evaluate "how" employees perform (behaviors) and "what" they deliver (results), in other words, the efficiency and effectiveness of activities performed (Pulakos, 2009).

Most performance management measures start by defining objectives and targets for every employee to help and direct them toward expected behaviors. Goals are often used to link the organization's strategic goals to each employee. These linkages will help organizations to achieve efficiency and effectiveness in their business performance. Principles of MBO (management by objectives) and SMART (Specific, measurable, attainable, realistic and time-based) are used in these automated performance management systems. Despite the fact that connecting individual and organizational goals bodes well, O'Leary and Pulakos (2017) listed the following practical issues:

1 Cascading goals demand time and effort and make it difficult for managers who are not familiarized to link goals between levels.
2 These goals often become detached from organizational goals and get concealed.
3 Though goals for each job are predictable at the beginning of the year, even automated systems cannot account for unexpected events during the year, for example, the COVID pandemic and subsequent lockdown.
4 It becomes difficult for the managers to assess the relative contributions of the different employees when their objectives/goals are not comparable (Pulakos, 2009).

New Approaches to Manage Efficiency and Effectiveness

Much thought has gone over the past few years into gaining more value from performance management systems that can be differentiated from traditional models. Most companies are moving from formal to informal processes to assess the behavior of employees and to ensure the efficiency and effectiveness of the performance. There are predominantly two approaches. The first is to change the formal system to reduce the low-value-added steps, unnecessary steps that result in high cost and low ROI. The second approach is to improve day-to-day practices by giving more real-time feedback to drive employee performance and to overcome challenges by implementing agile plans that are ad hoc and easy to adjust as per the changes in the environment. While some organizations have concentrated on the first strategy (make a more efficient process), other organizations have focused more on the second strategy (drive more effective performance management behavior), and some organizations have made modifications and interlinked and leveraged both the approaches.

Over almost a few decades, we can see the evolution of performance management systems. Right from rating scales such as graphic rating, to more complex and sophisticated automation processes, performance management systems have seen tremendous modifications. All these changes are an attempt to improve managing the efficiency and effectiveness of employees and the business as a whole. Most of the countless efforts to improve performance management systems have concentrated on executing formal steps, tools and practices to bring them into line with the goals, identify and improve the performance gaps, improve accuracy of the rating scales and ultimately make better decisions. On the other hand, many researchers argued and debated the importance of informal systems in place. They emphasized giving real-time feedback to employees to improve their performance. Pulakos et al. (2019) have highlighted the transformation of the performance management approach. Organizations follow periodical performance reviews now; it is high time to focus on continuous feedback to improve efficiency of employees. Ledford et al. (2016) have suggested that one or two well thought-out and considered changes to make a more efficient formal system or adding new aspects such as rating-less reviews and crowdsourced feedback can result in positive outcomes. Therefore, in future the emphasis can be on the ways to add various interventions to the formal systems and make them more effective to manage and improve the efficiency and effectiveness of the performance. Though the significance of teams in accomplishing tasks has been argued about comprehensively, very few organizations have made an attempt to implement team-based performance management systems. One another area that needs attention and seems promising for future work is further rigorous definition of the context in which performance management occurs. The contextual factors need to be identified for the effective management of the performance management process and practice. To understand the new approaches to manage efficiency and effectiveness, focused group discussion was carried out among contemporary managers.

Methodology

Given the context of the new normal work environment, this chapter attempts to present a detailed content analysis of a focused group discussion with some of the industry practitioners. The focused group discussion aimed to answer the following questions:

1 How did they manage the efficiency and effectiveness of virtual teams' performance?
2 What are the organizational-level, team-level and individual-level challenges they faced?
3 What did they do as employers to manage the new normal work environment?

Purposive sampling was employed to recruit the managers. Managers having work experience of more than five years participated in the focused group discussion. All the managers belong to the IT/ITES sector as they have to manage their teams during work from home. The details of the sample are given in Table 5.3. Three rounds of discussion were conducted to get practical insights on how they managed their team members during

Table 5.3 Respondent's Profile

Respondent	*Age*	*Gender*	*Experience*	*Location*	*Qualification*
1	34	Female	7	Chennai	Postgraduate
2	32	Female	6	Bangalore	Postgraduate
3	43	Male	10	Chennai	Undergraduate
4	35	Male	7	Hyderabad	Undergraduate
5	32	Male	6	Chennai	Postgraduate
6	42	Male	11	Bangalore	Postgraduate
7	36	Male	9	Chennai	Postgraduate
8	30	Female	6	Chennai	Postgraduate
9	31	Male	6	Bangalore	Postgraduate
10	30	Male	7	Hyderabad	Undergraduate

working from home. The results are consolidated and presented in the next section as "Insights from industry practitioners".

Insights from Industry Practitioners

The objective of the focus group discussion is to understand the contemporary challenges managers face in the "work from home" (new normal) environment in handling their teams.

Organizational Level

Infrastructure Support

Every organization has invested a huge amount of money in their infrastructure to give the best experience to their employees. This was also considered by the employees to define the work environment of the company and to spread positive word of mouth to the outside world. Most employees choose their jobs or change their jobs for the below listed three reasons.

1 Compensation
2 Career growth
3 Work environment and work culture

Few people get all the above-mentioned in their companies, few people settle for either of the two and the fewest people settle for at least one of the above if it is satisfying. If employees are compensated well, the most important criterion for millennials and almost most generations, they stay at the job. If compensation is satisfied in an exemplary way, they don't further look out for the career growth or work environment much until it becomes an issue. A few years into the role will make the employees look out for career growth. The work culture will not come into picture until there is discomfort created for the employees in the work environment. There are quite a few employees who change their job for the work culture/environment. The work environment is not created by one single employee. It is the combination of clusters of employees and the infrastructure of the company. If the work environment is not user-friendly it will degrade the effectiveness and efficiency of the employee.

Compensation and career growth mainly concern a few employees who look to the future and focus on their long-term goals. If the employee has received a salary hike or promotion, he/she will know that they will not have any changes in their compensation or career growth aspects for the next few months or years. But as far as the work environment is concerned, the scenario is different. It is the day-to-day aspects for the employee where he/she needs to survive. That is why if the work environment is impacted for the employee, firstly it will create an impact on efficiency for the individual, then at the team level and it finally impacts the organization. After a while, this inefficiency will have an impact on the business performance. Examining this will help us understand that the reason for the inefficiency of the individual can be attributed to the work environment rather than compensation or career growth aspects. Therefore the fundamental concern for any manager is to look into the work environment/culture as it plays a major role in the efficiency and effectiveness of the employee.

Now, let's come to the present scenario. So far in the normal way the work environment provided by the company was common to every employee. Now in the "new normal" the work environment for every individual is their own home. All the infrastructure created by the organization is not accessible to its employees as they are working from different locations. Internet connectivity is the basic necessity for all the employees working from home and that is not up to standard for certain employees due to their locations.

Employees have already started missing the work environment in terms of the cafeterias (of course, the breaks), recreation rooms, gyms, high-speed Internet connection, air conditioners, chairs and tables which made them comfortable to work at. Imagine if the Internet connection is too slow and when the employee clicks the mouse, the click happens with a 2-second delay on the monitor, how long will the employee survive to work with that Internet connection? It will frustrate the employees and put them in a difficult position to compete with their peers. This will pull down his motivation, efficiency and effectiveness of the work being performed.

Organizations should try to fix the few things which are possible from their end to enhance the efficiency of employees. For example, providing chairs and tables to the employees. Employees can buy the chairs and be reimbursed the amount by the company. A few other things are not possible, like high-speed Internet connection or cafeterias, but still companies can think of something as an alternative to keep the employees satisfied with the work environment and their health which would show a significant improvement in their efficiency.

Information Technology (IT) Support

Information technology support is another major aspect of change that happened at the organization level. When all the employees were asked to work from home, the IT support teams did not have enough time to set up all the systems with the requirements and most of all they did not have the time to test that the systems were working. Their goal was to ensure every employee had a laptop in their hands before the COVID situation got worse. This had a cascading impact on the efficiency and effectiveness of the employees as they lost days in fixing their laptops or desktops. It was even more difficult to manage as almost in every organizations 60% of the workforce employees were without prior experience.

In the normal work situation, the IT support team staff would walk up to the employee who is having an issue and they will fix the issue. Now in the new normal they have to guide the employees to perform a few steps and make the employees fix the issue by remote control of the desktops or laptops. This is tough when it is done through a zoom call. First and foremost, the aspect which causes discomfort is the availability of the IT support team and the employee at a common time. The ticket would have been raised and the IT support team would reach them through the chat and if the employee is not available in the system the ticket will be updated and moved to pending status. Now if the employee comes back and responds to that chat message, the IT support team will be looking into another ticket. This causes a delay and discomfort for both the employee and the support team staff. Previously any information technology issues are a problem of the IT support team and the employee will be working on an alternative system due to which the issue does not affect him but now if the employee's system is not working it is the employee's responsibility to get it fixed, which was not done by them before. There are some improvements and new tools provided to the support team to ensure the dependency is reduced but still this reduces the efficiency of the employees. Also we can't run with the tools or software which we were used during pre-COVID as now the situation requires something more advanced.

Team Level

Employees who are working in the same role from the pre-COVID period are easily able to connect themselves with their team members but employees who joined the company during March or later after the COVID lockdown initiated are finding it difficult to collaborate with their team members as they don't know each other. When we know each other in person and get oriented for few weeks after joining the company it will always make us feel better than interacting or working with team members only through virtual means. Employees compete, collaborate and work together in physical teams as compared to virtual teams. There is no constant supervision in virtual teams, and most of the time they have to be self-managed teams. Healthy competition improves the efficiency of the individual and the team, which is missing in virtual teams as compared to the physical teams. Now in the new normal employees do not know where their peers stand or what they are doing on a daily basis.

As a solution to the above, "huddles" should be conducted every day within the team. During a huddle, the manager or team leader should initiate the discussion of the team members and allow them to interact. Each and every team member should speak about what they did yesterday, what they are going to do today and any other important information they want to share with the team. This will ensure at least they are communicating with the team once a day. Also video calls should be conducted once a week. When people see each other and converse it creates more impact rather than just exchanging voice notes. There can also be some informal meetings where employees do some chit-chat on the video calls as a part of their fun Fridays. These chit-chats give them the lively environment, a break from the usual work, and happiness and a sense of belonging to the company. Now they may be in their homes which is their comfort zone but still adding a little bit of fun and a smile will boost their performance. Lastly, the managers should provide periodic communication on what the company is doing to their team members. They can inform them about the strategic decisions of the companies, information about the leadership meeting or any other information. Managers can choose the information that can be communicated without breach of confidentiality and share it with their teams. This will give a positive note to them that they know what is happening in the company. The most important question in mind for most employees is about the layoffs and shutting down of companies happening in the corporate world. As much as possible, make sure to give the team members the correct information. Any panic or chaos created will directly impact the efficiency and effectiveness of the employee performance.

Employee Level

The COVID pandemic has increased digital connections and decreased physical connections. In other words, we are living in the physical environment. This environment has actually created a disconnection and an imbalanced state among the employees, contributing to the dip in their efficiency. In this COVID lockdown, employees face many problems in their day-to-day work-life context. Employees should make a note of their problems, be it IT issues or network issues, and update the same to their upline managers on a weekly manner. Only if the data are collected for some period can a pattern be found in them and a permanent solution can be provided or else these temporary issues will be prolonging themselves on the employee side.

Employees should come up with flexible shift timing where they do not get distracted by their family members provided their company allows them. The interruptions from the family members will reduce their efficiency. Also employees should be working from a place where they do not have any television or entertainment which will also distract them and impact their performance. Team members can constantly communicate with each other or their managers using an internal chatbot which makes them feel in an "office-like environment". This will in turn improve their efficiency.

Because employees are working from home, it should not be necessary for them to log in and log out several times in a day. They must ensure they are working in their 8 hours of shift timings, not to split time and work, for example, for 2 hours, 3 hours, and 3 hours. These split hours will impact their efficiency to a greater extent. Employees should check with the managers on their previous month's performance score to ensure that they are going on the right path. By doing this, any dip in their performance can be immediately rectified.

A common space should be created by the employees and all their activities should be updated there. They can design those pages in a more aesthetic way as they wish. This actually replaces their desire to decorate their workplace desk with dolls, paintings and other stuff. We can recreate the same in a digital way. More liveliness in these aspects will bring more liveliness to their working space, enhancing the efficiency and effectiveness of their work.

Discussion

Reasons for the Failure of Existing Performance Management Models

Performance management is a strategic tool as the entire process is orchestrated toward the success of the organization in respect of its strategic pursuits. It facilitates organizational integration by seeking to get all its constituents tuned to a common set of purposes. Also, clarifying and establishing inter-role and inter-functional linkages contributes to unleashing the power of teamwork. Put together, it enables the organization to inculcate and institutionalize a culture of focused and purposeful performance.

The performance management system in most organizations seems to have caused more problems and dissatisfaction rather than leading to positive organizational and business outcomes. The reasons for this are manifold; however, central to them is the failure to recognize it as a way of achieving the organization's well-being. This has resulted in several flaws in the manner in which the system is designed, positioned, and administered.

Positioned as a tool to evaluate the performance of people. Goals are sought to be set not primarily to get people goal-oriented and to work toward organizational outcomes, but more because goals and targets make evaluation of performance possible. Not surprisingly, often goals and targets assigned to individuals do not reflect organizational priorities.

Positioned as a task /project of the human resource management department. The entire process is seen as owned and administered by the HRM department as part of their "people management routine". The rest of the organization hence does not assume ownership of it. Consequently, attention gets focused on filling in forms and going through the motions instead of genuinely and purposefully managing the process

Inadequate top management commitment and visible involvement for implementing a holistic performance management system. This is due to a lack of understanding of the purpose and potential benefits of the system and/or to the inability to see the top management's role and responsibility in getting the organization aligned and integrated through performance. It is ironic that while the top leadership group is the body primarily accountable for enterprise results, they do not assume responsibility for providing stewardship to organization-wide performance management which alone has the potential to deliver those results.

Failure to position performance management as leadership accountability in the organization. Many among those who have the responsibility to lead confine themselves to "managing" or are insensitive to the idea of leadership itself. They tend to hold a preference for "control" over "facilitation". This results in peripheral interest and involvement of most of them in the performance management process .They tend to see the processes as mere routines and as administrative requirements. The senior leadership group also seem unmindful of this, which probably explains the lack of focus on developing skills of performance planning, reviewing performance, carrying out performance conversations, providing feedback etc.

Linking performance assessment with remuneration/compensation decisions. Most organizations tend to see in the performance management system a "convenient" way of establishing a basis for arriving at organization-wide compensation/remuneration-related decisions. Hence, they choose to impose on the system the requirement of rating. People see evaluation and rating as the main purposes of the system and turn defensive in their approaches.

This is further complicated by the practice of "rationalization" of ratings to arrive at a "normal distribution" of rating. Organizations and managers have at no time been able to explain the post-assessment "rating corrections", leading to widespread resentment among employees and erosion of trust in whatever process that preceded it (the good news is that many organizations, including those that had pioneered the practice of engineering a "normal distribution" of rating, have of late begun to consider abandoning this).

Recognize the centrality of performance management systems for organizational performance and business results, and position it accordingly. Hold the senior leadership group in the organization, including the chief executive, accountable for organization-wide performance management. Let the people-management specialists be responsible for designing the sub-systems, helping people to understand them, creating platforms for leaders to develop skills for managing the processes, and for facilitating the processes. The responsibility for execution of the processes and steering the teams to success must rest with leaders in each function. The performance management system sets the platform for aligning individual and team efforts with the organization's objectives. Deployment of corporate priorities and goals through the organization ensures that everyone is able to see how one is contributing to a larger purpose and focus on a set of common outcomes. Establishing clearly expectations of results, actions and behaviors provides everyone the much-needed "direction" to their efforts. Ongoing reviews provide the opportunity to recognize opportunities, problems, constraints and contingencies at an early stage and prepare to respond to them. They also highlight "learning needs" in individuals, leading to competency development initiatives. It is thus a set of proactive processes and practices for achieving organizational results by facilitating people's performance in an integrated manner.

The performance management system addresses these imperatives through a set of sub-systems, the combined efficacy of which facilitates performance across the organization. Some of the key point to note are as follows.

1 Establishing, communicating, and clarifying the organization's vision, mission, priorities, strategies and performance indicators.
2 Role clarification – designing meaningful roles, developing clear role descriptions and specifying competency requirements for effective performance of the role.
3 Performance planning – deploying corporate priorities through the entire organization structure – business divisions, units, functions, departments to individuals in accordance with their roles.
4 Establishing Individual performance plans and specifying performance indicators (lead & lag) for measuring progress and outcomes against set targets/benchmarks; ensuring that goals at each level are aligned vertically and are integrated laterally.
5 Ongoing review of performance – taking stock of performance and progress towards goals as well as emerging performance requirements; carrying out performance conversations with team members, providing feedback and determining further courses of action.
6 End of cycle review of performance – assessing quality of performance (what has contributed to a given outcome) and identifying areas for

improving performance in the ensuing cycle, assessing competencies, and working out plans for improving performance and developing competencies.
7 Rewarding – designing and administering reward mechanisms for recognizing those who excel in their jobs by meeting/exceeding performance expectations.

Adopt a "segmented" approach to performance management. Design different sets of processes as relevant to those who are required to pursue individual goals and group goals. "One fit for all" does not work. Likewise, schedule and carry out performance reviews and performance conversations as appropriate or relevant to performance plans of individuals and teams instead of fitting into a "standard schedule for all". Let not these processes be seen as "time-specific rituals". Also, provide for ongoing assessment of performance instead of making it an "end of the year task". Dispense with the requirement to "rate" performance, and delink remuneration/compensation administration from performance management. Position "rewards" *only* for "high performers". Organizations may also "rethink" the need to continue the practice of annual remuneration enhancement across the board. Even if the policy and practice are sought to be continued, organizations will do well to seek approaches for determining the basis for effecting such enhancement outside the framework of the performance management system. Establish "measures of efficiency and effectiveness" of the system and related processes at organizational, functional and team levels, and at individual levels, and carry out structured assessments.

Conclusion

Performance management in its intended form is a systemic and orchestrated endeavor for crafting organizational performance and outcomes. Recognizing that everything an organization does and achieves is due primarily to the performance of its people, performance management systems seek to align and facilitate the efforts of individuals and teams to organizational priorities. Thus, while the purpose of performance management is achievement of organizational results, the focus is on shaping individual and team performance toward these results. Efforts made in the right direction, with commitment and enthusiasm, and backed by relevant competencies alone have the potential to generate the required performance and through it the desired outcomes. People will be the prime movers in future organizations too even as the nature of their work, roles, tasks, performance parameters and required competencies are likely to undergo substantial change, just as it has happened at every stage of the introduction and advance of automation and adoption of technology and the current new normal work environment. Aligning and integrating their performance toward the achievement of organizational objectives will continue to be the most comprehensive and potentially impactful system in organizations.

References

Aguinis, H. (2013). *Performance management* (3rd edn). Upper Saddle River, NJ: Pearson/Prentice Hall.

Akhtar, M., & Sushil, S. (2018). Strategic performance management system in uncertain business environment. *Business Process Management Journal, 24*(4), 923–942. https://doi.org/10.1108/BPMJ-05-2017-0102.

Alwehabie, A.M. (2017). Criteria for measuring the efficiency and effectiveness of human resources management strategy and its relation to institutional performance at Al Rajhi Bank at Al Qassim in Saudi Arabia from the employees' point of view. *International Journal of Business and Management, 12*(10), 111.

Bounds, G.M., Dobbins, G.H., & Fowler, O.S. (1995). *Management: A total quality perspective*. South-Western Publishing Company.

Chavan, M. (2009). The balanced scorecard: A new challenge. *Journal of Management Development, 28*(5), 393–406. https://doi.org/10.1108/02621710910955930.

Halachmi, A. (2005). Performance measurement is only one way of managing performance. *International Journal of Productivity and Performance Management, 54* 7), 502–516. https://doi.org/10.1108/17410400510622197.

Kaplan, R.S., & Norton, D.P. (1992). The balanced scorecard: measures that drive performance. *Harvard Business Review, 83*(7), 172.

Ledford, G.E., Benson, G., & Lawler, E.E. (2016). Aligning research and the current practice of performance management. *Industrial and Organizational Psychology, 9*(2), 253–260.

London, M., & Mone, E.M. (2014). Performance management: Processes that reflect and shape organizational culture and climate. In B. Schneider & K.M. Barbera (Eds.), *The Oxford handbook of organizational climate and culture* (pp. 79–100). Oxford: Oxford University Press.

Lynch, R.L., & Cross, K.F. (1991). *Measure up!: The essential guide to measuring business performance*. Mandarin.

Mouzas, S. (2006). Efficiency versus effectiveness in business networks. *Journal of Business Research, 59*(10–11), 1124–1132.

Neely, A., Kennerley, M., & Adams, C. (2007). Performance measurement frameworks: A review. *Business Performance Measurement*, 143–162.

O'Leary, R.S., & Pulakos, E.D. (2017). Defining and measuring results of workplace behavior. In *Handbook of Employee Selection* (pp. 509–529). Routledge.

Pulakos, E.D. (2009). *Performance management: A new approach for driving business results*. John Wiley & Sons.

Pulakos, E.D., Mueller-Hanson, R., & Arad, S. (2019). The evolution of performance management: Searching for value. *Annual Review of Organizational Psychology and Organizational Behavior, 6*(1), 249–271.

Robbins, S.P. (2000). *Managing today*. Prentice Hall.

6 Managing Customer Relationships During Uncertainty

A Case of B2B Firms

Mikko Mäntyneva

Introduction

In business-to-business markets, robust customer relationships are vital for suppliers because often only a few major customers may generate a large share of a supplier's revenue. However, the business customer is not necessarily an end-user and may rely on their supplier to be able to deliver the goods further in the supply chain. The COVID-19 pandemic and related lockdown created an economic breakdown and major uncertainty in markets (Rapaccini et al., 2020). Altig et al. (2020) and Baker et al. (2020) have studied different indicators of economic uncertainty. They conclude that all indicators point out major uncertainty jumps in reaction to the COVID-19 pandemic. Bloom (2014) and Baker et al. (2016) conclude that rising economic uncertainty makes both firms and consumers cautious.

The increased uncertainty around market and customer demand as well as suppliers' ability to deliver creates major challenges for managing business-to-business customer relationships (Sheth, 2020). Mora Cortez and Johnston (2020) assert that COVID-19 is having disastrous effects for most business-to-business firms in different countries. A drastic drop in demand reduces sales, which is expected to provoke both inter-organizational and intra-organizational tension.

Rapaccini et al. (2020) argue that customer demand and industry activity and confidence have collapsed due to the COVID-19 pandemic. In many markets, customer demand is collapsing and supply chains are being interrupted as countries increasingly lock down and close their borders. Donthu and Gustafsson (2020) argue that it does not look like any country would be unaffected by COVID-19 and its severe economic consequences. Although it is difficult to foresee developments in the new future, managers should be able to navigate their firms through unpredictable and uncertain situations.

This article focuses on researching what kinds of uncertainties related to customer relationship management arose due to the COVID-19 pandemic and how these uncertainties could be counteracted within business-to-business buyer–supplier relationships. This paper contributes

DOI: 10.4324/9781003125648-6

to the body of knowledge on managing customer relationships during global market turmoil due to a pandemic. Major uncertainty on customer relationships and market demand has increased the importance of managing customer relationships because the sales to the customers create the firm's revenue and potential drop in revenue is about to create financial problems and even bankruptcies. While managing business-to-business customer relationships even individual major customers may create negative outcomes to the selling firm. Therefore, managing of those customer relationships is very important during economic uncertainty.

Theoretical Framework

The theoretical framework of this paper consists of three inter-related topics: customer relationship management in the business-to-business context, managing uncertainty in customer relationships, and counteracting identified uncertainties.

Managing Business-to-Business Customer Relationships

The main focus of this article is on managing customer relationships during uncertainty. Sheth (2020) maintains that COVID-19 has clearly demonstrated the fragility of firms and customer relationships. In the business-to-business context, the end-user is not that clear as is the case with consumers. The selling firm is acting as a supplier and the buying firm as a buyer. However, the buying firm may or may not be an end-user of the sold products.

Ellram and Krause (2014) conclude that buyer–supplier relationships respond differently to an economic downturn. This is due to varying degrees of bounded rationality. From the perspective of managing business-to-business customer relationships, economic downturns may cause vulnerabilities in these relationships. According to Ellram and Krause (2014), the distress is taking place also in strategic, long-term buyer–supplier relationships in different industries. This happens even if there is social capital bonding in these relationships.

Palmatier et al. (2013) argue that the dynamic components of relational constructs have a major role in driving performance. In practice, this means that the rate and direction of change in commitment are important while understanding relationships. This is called "commitment velocity". The rapid drop in demand that resulted due to COVID-19 is one example of an input that can adapt to commitment velocity. If the commitment rapidly drops and reverses from mutual partnership toward internal survival, this can be expected to also affect the volume of orders by buying firms. In the case where one customer's demand drops and this drop of demand is characteristic of the overall market due to the economic conditions, this without doubt will affect the supplying firm's economic performance.

Habel et al. (2020) argue based on positive decision theory that customers' probability of purchasing offerings from industrial suppliers is about to decrease due to the COVID-19 pandemic. This seems to be the case especially for high-priced offerings. However, they assert that different countries can be differentiated between dimensions of uncertainty avoidance and long-term orientation. In practice, this means that long-term orientation supports long-term supplier–buyer relationships. It seems that uncertainty avoidance in markets shifts the risk to other parties. This could be interpreted so that if a buying firm is uncertain about its own demand due to perceived uncertainty of the orders of its own customers it is likely to try to shift the risk to another counterpart, i.e., the supplying firm.

Other researchers have also identified a need of business-to-business firms to adapt to COVID-19. Obal and Gao (2020) have created a relationship audit template to assist business-to-business firms to adapt to the COVID-19 crisis and position themselves more strategically. In this way, the emergence of a crisis may create opportunities to challenge existing assumptions about the firm's buyer–supplier relationships.

Supplier Relationships and the Goals of the Purchasing Company

Guan et al. (2020) imply that China's lockdown in the early phases of the pandemic affected global supply chains. This has created difficulties in adapting sourcing strategies for many firms. Veronesi (2014) argues that business-to-business integration improves supply chain performance. However, during COVID-19 it may be that optimized supply chains with just-in-time demands for deliveries have not worked while the supplier has not been able to supply due to lockdown.

The selling company often has more interest in maintaining and developing the customer relationship than the customer firm itself. From the customer's perspective, the setup is often that there are several alternative supplier companies. The customer company strives to develop its own operations by managing its supplier relationships. In principle, development work can focus on, for example, logistics, delivery times, and warehousing, and it often has a significant impact on the customer company's operational activities. The acquisition price and working capital management are also important, especially with regard to the products to be stored.

In the business-to-business context, supplier relationship management can be seen as a mirror image of customer relationship management. One of the goals of supplier relationship management and, thus, supply chain management is to optimize procurement and delivery-related processes and reduce the turnaround time of the process, starting with the order and ending with delivery. From the end-customer's perspective, suppliers' capabilities reflect also the customers' capabilities and competitiveness.

The potential layoffs of suppliers have a negative effect on their capabilities (Ellram & Krause, 2014).

Often, a procurement operation has a major impact on the profitability of the buying. From a customer relationship management perspective, the key is to clarify whether profitability comes from the buying company's ability to negotiate lower prices and, thus, lower the profitability of the selling company, or whether potential cost savings can be achieved by other means like mutual operational excellence.

When choosing strategic supplier partners, suppliers whose goals are in line with the buyer company are often preferred. Purchasing organizations often want longer-term development cooperation in terms of products, processes and quality. This perspective allows for the creation of mutual added value. The purchase price of a single product is not everything. Material costs as well as the need for additional services and pricing also have an impact on how suppliers are selected.

The interest of the buying company is not equally divided among suppliers. Buyers are keen to focus on those supplier companies whose products or services sell a large proportion of total purchases. Due to the high volume, the supplier relationship also has a significant impact on the purchasing costs of the buying firm. Supplier relationships for high-volume products also have a significant operational and quality-related risk perspective. To reduce uncertainty, the purchasing company often seeks to ensure that delivery practices and forms of cooperation do not impede or risk its own delivery capacity.

Some large international companies have organized their own purchasing activities globally. In this case, global procurement is at its best a coordinated and integrated activity from the perspective of suppliers, processes, materials and technologies. The main motivation for global procurement is the potential cost savings. Another aspect is to identify potential suppliers, increase competition between suppliers and, thus, reduce procurement costs. In large organizations, global sourcing is a well-orchestrated function that implements both sourcing contractor practices and supplier performance evaluation in a globally consistent manner.

Key issues in global procurement are related to cross-cultural differences, logistical needs, and risks. To manage risks, the purchasing company can audit global purchasing activities from a process perspective. The key objective is to identify the risks that may affect the intended and realized benefits. Once potential risks have been identified, the means will be put in place to reduce or eliminate them.

The selling company may expect a high level of commitment and loyalty from its customer company, but the buying company may seek to diversify its risk or not to commit too much to a particular supplier. In many industries, negotiating power has shifted more to the customer. For example, the number of customers may decrease after the maturity stage of a particular industry due to the consolidation trend resulting from corporate acquisitions. In this context, suppliers are competing with each other for their own declining share of the market with fewer and fewer customers. Often, large corporate customers sense their own bargaining power. At the same time, they strive to select suppliers who are able to increase their own competitiveness and support the development of both products and processes.

From the perspective of a customer-oriented approach, it is also important to interpret the mindset of the customer firm's organization. How does an organization perceive the importance of its own supplier relationships to the firm's own business and operations?

Coopetition

Business relationships are often considered as mutual rivalry between buyer and seller on terms and prices. Even if customer relationship management is practiced, from the selling firm's perspective, it is possible that the supplier and their customer may combine their resources to fight against a crisis (Preikschas et al., 2017). This way, the cooperating partners can achieve mutually beneficial goals that could not otherwise be achieved alone.

Crick and Crick (2020) have covered coopetition and collaborative business-to-business marketing strategies during the COVID-19 pandemic. They conclude that coopetition may be a viable business-to-business marketing strategy. Those coopetition activities relate to both cooperative and competitive forces. In practice, this means that with competitors it is appropriate to collaborate. Time will tell whether coopetition strategies are relevant post-COVID-19 or whether they are temporary and terminated.

Even if coopetition shows promise during economically difficult times, there is still the matter of trust between competitors. One risk is open information-sharing in the event that a supplier company assumes a business relationship is confidential and thereby shares confidential information. While from the customer's point of view that information may be relevant, it may also be passed on through the customer to competitors of the selling company. Le Roy and Czakon (2016) assert that it is difficult to develop trusting relationships between direct rivals. Lascaux (2020) considers coopetition to allow a multilevel view. In practice, this means that coopetition and related trust can be considered in interpersonal, intergroup, inter-organizational, and inter-network settings.

Managing Uncertainty in Business-to-Business Customer Relationships

Uncertainty is a natural part of life for organizations and their employees. Simon (2013) argues that uncertainty should be reduced. From a management perspective, the COVID-19 pandemic is causing uncertainty about the future of their firms and economy as a whole. Toma et al. (2013) conclude on the difference between the concepts of risk and uncertainty that most risks can be anticipated and measured with varying degrees of probability. However, uncertainty is a more subjective and multidimensional concept, which is more difficult to measure. Sharma et al. (2020) argue that risk as a concept is related to an uncertain event or condition associated with doing business that may have a negative effect on the firm. The uncertainty is related to the lack of probabilities of the forthcoming events that may affect the firm.

Even if both concepts are relevant, this paper focuses more on managing uncertainty rather than quantifying risk probabilities. Sharma et al. (2020) imply that firms manage uncertainty either by reducing risk (risk management) or coping (strategic management). This is in line with Sniazhko (2019), who asserts that when a firm intends to cope with uncertainty, they adapt their strategy to deal with different kinds of uncertainty. Because the required adaptation timeframe to COVID-19 has been so rapid, it can be considered that firms have had to modify their operations to cope with uncertainty also on the tactical level.

Here, the discussion on managing uncertainties is mainly focused on business-to-business customer relationships. Certo et al. (2008) differentiate between exogenous and endogenous sources of uncertainty. In this article, uncertainties related to customer relationships can be divided into five subcategories: uncertainty regarding demand; financial uncertainty; uncertainty regarding ability to deliver; uncertainty regarding continuity; and customer interaction-related uncertainty.

Uncertainty Regarding Demand

COVID-19 decreased market demand across many markets and the related uncertainty makes it difficult to estimate future demand. In some specific markets, there has been a rise in market demand; however, these markets are an exception to this trend. The economy as a whole has contracted and the duration of the pandemic makes it difficult to estimate market demand and its development in the foreseeable future. Selling firms are projecting their future financial success by predicting the development of their revenue. As an indication of this difficulty to estimate, many publicly quoted companies are not providing monthly or quarterly projections about the development of their revenue.

As well as uncertainty about the general market demand, there is also uncertainty on the demand of individual customers. When it comes to predictability, it can be assumed that customer relationships always involve some sort of uncertainty. While estimating and budgeting future sales, professionals involved with sales management and account management encounter difficulties when estimating the amount and timing of sales volumes and prices. In the case of major external disturbances, like a global pandemic, it is assumed that uncertainty and, thus, difficulty related to predictability increase.

On a firm level, such predictability is important. However, in the case where the predictability on an individual customer level is difficult, it can be assumed that the aggregated sales forecasts include lots of uncertainty. In major business-to-business customer relationships, individual customers may generate a major portion of the firm's sales. However, if these customers cancel or postpone their orders from the selling firm, this could cause a major decrease in the firm's overall revenue. A typical reason for canceling or postponing orders is the radically reduced visibility of demand of the customer firm's customers due to the pandemic.

In a normal economic environment, it may be in the interest of the buying company to support the seller's ability to anticipate future purchase volumes. The rationale behind this is that while indicating its own purchases accurately, the buying firm also ensures the supplier's ability to supply the required goods or services without delays.

From a pricing perspective, it may be that during normal economic conditions there exist more tactical actions regarding customers' buying intentions. By keeping the seller uncertain about the continuity of orders, the purchasing company seeks to obtain more favorable purchase terms in the form of pricing and payment.

Financial Uncertainty

Financial uncertainty relates to levels of revenue and profitability. The cash flow perspective is also an important part of financial uncertainty. While the financial obligations of the selling firm remain, it is important that customers are able and willing to pay their bills. Often it is a reality that a few major customers account for a significant part of the company's revenue. Therefore, these major customers pose a concentrated risk with respect to the company's entire customer base. The profitability of even large customers is not self-evident: if the price level is too low and there are significant costs for both customer care and development, then the customer will turn out to be unprofitable in both the short and long term. Managing financial uncertainty and related risks can be implemented by managing the customer portfolio as a whole (Groening et al., 2014). However, their approach is more on a stable economic setting rather than in a specific setting created by a global pandemic.

Uncertainty Regarding Ability to Deliver

Hallikas et al. (2002) argue that a networked economy brings new risks and uncertainties for firms. This is due to interdependency among different firms. This increases uncertainty regarding the firm's ability to deliver to its own customers in the case where suppliers are not able to deliver or there are major delays. Manuj and Mentzer (2008) argue that global supply chains, which have large numbers of links interconnecting wide company networks, are more risky than domestic supply chains. Supply chain-related processes are often highly optimized with an objective to receive just-in-time deliveries. One financial rationale for this is that firms intend to minimize their allocated capital for warehousing goods. From a customer relationship management perspective, the potential uncertainty of customer's doubt about a firm's ability to deliver creates problems as they consider re-routing supplies in order to manage their own risks. The root cause of a firm's inability to deliver in time may be its suppliers' or subcontractors' inability to deliver in time.

Uncertainty Regarding the Continuity of Customer Relationships

Customer relationships, if maintained, are a valuable asset for the selling firm. Long-term orientation and continuity are important for managing customer relationships. This will ensure the existence of the business relationship and accumulation of the firm's sales. Even if in the normal economic environment there could be a preference to buy from a certain supplier, it may be that major market uncertainty forces the buying firm to prioritize its own survival. In practice, this means that the continuity of long-time buyer–supplier relationships may be challenged.

Palmatier et al. (2007) assert that developing strong bonds between the supplier and the customer creates a shared interest between these two parties. In a normal market situation, it is important from the perspective of the continuity of customer relationships to create strong bonds between the selling company and the customer company. These bonds can be divided into, for example, social, economic and structural bonds. It would also be desirable for these ties to be more numerous and strong. On the other hand, it is not self-evident that the buying firm has an interest in supporting the strengthening of these bonds.

The customer firm's commitment to the supplier firm is by no means self-evident. An example of this is the efforts of customer companies to reduce the number of supplier companies. The effort to reduce the number of supplier companies does not usually mean that the company has only one supplier in a given product or service area. Several customer firms want to maintain the competitive situation between alternative providers. From the perspective of its own supplier relationship risk management, the customer company also has an interest in maintaining more supplier relationships, for example, to obtain delivery security and a certain price level, as well as ideas to support the development of operations.

Customer Interaction-Related Uncertainty

Engaging people is important because it is practically a business between people even if the customer is a company. Hartmann and Lussier (2020) assert that COVID-19 has had an immediate and severe impact on the business-to-business sales forces. The lockdowns have increased remote work drastically. In practice, this means that people are working more from their homes. This being the case, it is more difficult to make physical sales calls. Virtual meetings have become an everyday setting (Rapaccini et al., 2020). They assume increasing digital readiness due to the COVID-19 pandemic will allow firms to go forward with intelligent digital innovation and, thus, increase the efficiency and productivity of their operations.

In addition, already agreed meetings may be postponed; as the rationale for these sales-related meetings is to sell more, such postponements delay the realization of sales revenue. In many business-to-business-related interactions, it is not only the salesperson and a buyer who interact. Long-term buyer–supplier relationships have multiple connections between personnel of these firms. These have to interact properly so that the purchases and deliveries are made promptly. A specific case of customer interaction-related uncertainty is a potential management-level interaction between buying and selling firms.

It would be important to involve the functions and people involved in customer work and customer relationship management and development in the creation and implementation of a concept and operating method related to key customer management. The later an attempt is made to engage others in an already completed concept, the more difficult it may be for them to embrace and implement it.

COVID-19 has increased the number of temporary or permanent layoffs of personnel made by firms in order to decrease salary-related expenses. These layoffs have an impact on the availability of customer-specific knowledge. It can be assumed that this knowledge is not all codified in the firm's customer relationship management (CRM) systems. Lack of this knowledge is expected to increase uncertainty in customer interaction.

Counteracting Identified Uncertainties

The dramatic drop in demand in many markets has made firms have to fight for their existence. Sharma et al. (2020) indicate that in 2020, global trade is expected to fall drastically due to COVID-19. They have studied different coping strategies for managers adapting to rising market uncertainty. Weick and Sutcliffe (2007) propose that unexpected events test a firm's resilience.

Liesch et al. (2014) assert that larger firms are likely to have more resources to reduce potentially perceived risk due to an uncertainty in the firm's environment. On the other hand, it seems that smaller firms perceive greater risk in the environment (Claver et al., 2008). However, in order to adapt and even survive COVID-19-related challenges, firms' managements must recognize suitable countermeasures against the identified uncertainties. Sufficiently careful risk management supports the successful implementation of customer relationship management. Risk management should contribute to adapting to the challenges of operations and the operational environment. Too little preparation for potential risks exposes the customer relationship to potentially identifiable risks. On the other hand, overweighting risk management unnecessarily stiffens customer work and increases administrative tasks and additional assurance measures.

To cope with uncertainty, firms should be flexible and reactive to be able to cooperate, and control and avoid risks (Simangunsong et al., 2012). To reduce uncertainty, firms should gather information, collaborate proactively and communicate with suppliers and customers (Sharma et al., 2020).

It can be expected that customer relationships do not always evolve as planned. Almost every long-term buyer–supplier relationship is affected by some kind of difficulty and unexpected adversity in one form or another. For this reason, it is important for the selling firm to identify the problems most likely to be encountered in the management and development of customer relationships well in advance. During a crisis like a pandemic, the advancement of customer relationships is not necessarily a relevant objective when the focus is on maintenance and existence.

Identifying uncertainties and managing risks is a core part of customer relationship management. Customer and risk-related analyses are a natural part of managing customer relationships. This enables the identification of potential risks related to the customer relationship and the preparation for them in a timely manner. Customer-related risk management identifies and assesses potential customer-related risks in order to try to avoid them or to minimize their adverse effects in advance. However, if risks become realized, firms should counteract them so as to minimize the hazards. Figure 6.1 summarizes the discussed uncertainties and counteracting against them.

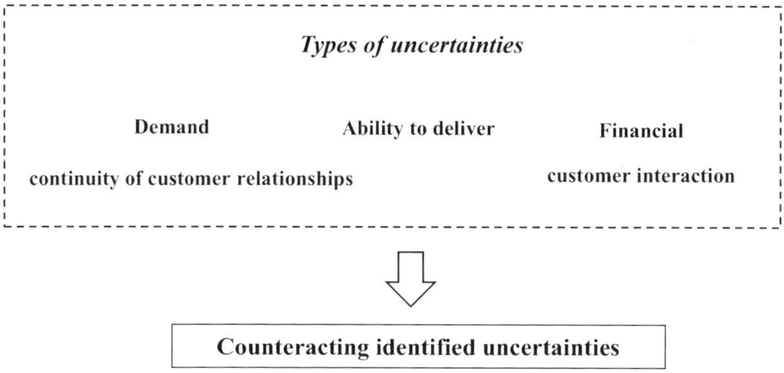

Figure 6.1 Conceptual framework on managing uncertainty in B2B customer relationships.

Empirical Research

This section focuses on the empirical research on managing uncertainty in business-to-business customer relationships. To collect empirical data two separate workshops were arranged in September 2020. Both of them were part of a two-day training which was arranged in two different cities in Finland. During both of these training programs the workshop was a separate entity. The participants of these workshops were key account management and sales management professionals. Individually each of them had business-to-business sales, sales management, or key account management-related work experience of several years to even several decades. They represented various industries and no specific industry segment was overly emphasized. The total number of workshop participants was 46. The intention of the workshops and an Internet survey that was sent to the participants was to identify relevant customer relationship management-related uncertainties the workshop participants had encountered during the COVID-19 pandemic. After identifying the uncertainties relevant solutions to counteract these uncertainties were co-created. This contributes by providing further knowledge on how customer relationships can be managed further during and after the pandemic.

The background was such that the first wave of COVID-19 had led to major changes in organizations starting in March 2020. People had worked remotely and during the data collection period it seemed the COVID-19 was not yet over. During the data collection period, it appeared that globally the rate of new infections was increasing. That probably positively motivated workshop participants to identify appropriate countermeasures for managing uncertainties in the business environment and customer relationships in particular. The workshops promoted genuine participation and were specifically designed to meet a pre-defined, but not predictable, purpose (Ørngreen & Levinsen, 2017).

Workshops as a Research Method

Cankurtarana and Beverland (2020) argue that COVID-19 represents a wicked problem that challenges established patterns of thinking. They propose that design thinking and problem-solving approaches may be one approach to new patterns of thinking. Ørngreen and Levinsen (2017) have studied workshops as a research methodology. They define a "workshop" as an arrangement where a group of people innovate in relation to a domain-specific issue. Workshops can be traced back to creative group problem-solving. Alternatively, workshops can be related to action research (Argyris & Schön, 1996; Reason & Bradbury, 2001) and design-based research (Cobb et al., 2003).

Workshops as a research methodology focus on domain-specific issues. During workshops, participants are motivated because they expect to achieve something related to their own interests (Ørngreen & Levinsen, 2017). Because the workshop is specifically designed to meet a research purpose, it can produce reliable and valid data about the domain in question (Darsø, 2001; Wakkary, 2007).

During the workshop, the researcher and participants worked together while the researcher was in control of the process. This is in line with the collaborative participation mode, which is an alternative when workshops are used as a research methodology (Ørngreen & Levinsen, 2017).

Identified Countermeasures, While Managing Customer Relationships

Workshops as a research methodology inspire new insight into the research domain in question (Ørngreen & Levinsen, 2017). However, they encourage using workshops in combination with other empirical approaches (mixed methods). This aspect was taken into account when developing a preliminary online survey for the participants.

The online survey comprised a short set of questions regarding how COVID-19 had affected their firms and what kinds of countermeasures they had taken. Fifty-four percent of participants replied to the survey prior to the workshop. This background information, documented in Table 6.1, reveals the main uncertainties and problem areas that arose in managing customer relationships due to COVID-19.

It seems that the main problems were difficulty in meeting customers face-to-face, postponement of customer orders, difficulty in anticipating the amount of customer orders, and large variations in orders. However, it seems that the firms' or subcontractors' ability to deliver orders was not much affected.

Table 6.1 Main uncertainties while managing customer relationships due to COVID-19

Type of uncertainty	*Percent*
Anticipating the amount of customer purchases	64%
Large variation in customer purchases	64%
Cancellation of orders	20%
Postponement of orders	68%
Delay in customer payments	32%
Supply difficulties of subcontractors	28%
Customer confidence in seller's ability to deliver	20%
Staff layoffs	32%
Remote working	60%
Customer encounters when physical appointments avoided	84%

When the respondents were asked what uncertainties and risks related to customer relationships and their management have been identified during the COVID-19 and what possible countermeasures have been taken, among others the following issues were mentioned:

- Bankruptcies and payment difficulties for customers unlikely to materialize until next year.
- Radical drop in volume.
- COVID-19 has modified the market and customer base as well as buying behavior.
- Postponement of major projects and orders.
- Customer payment difficulties.
- Delivery times for the product have been extended or are unreliable.
- Product availability problems with certain products.
- Awareness and identification of customer problems.
- Uncertainty in customer purchases, smaller orders.
- Fluctuations in purchase volume.
- Number of face-to-face meetings has decreased and they are conducted online.

The online survey results were verified by the workshop participants during both of the workshops. The reporting in Table 6.1 summarizes the data of the two separate online surveys participants responded to before the workshops. During the two separate workshops, many ideas for countermeasures against recognized uncertainties were identified. The outcomes of the two different workshops complement each other. However, there were no major differences between the two workshops when it comes to the suggested countermeasures for each identified uncertainty. The key findings are documented in Table 6.2.

Managerial Implications

Based on the previous discussion and empirical findings, it is important to draw managerial implications. Managing uncertainty is related to reducing the probability of undesirable outcomes and their impact on the firm's business (Figueira-de-Lemos & Hadjikhani, 2014). While managing customer relationship-related uncertainties and risks, the following aspects should be taken into account:

The Identification of Uncertainties and Risks Should Be Based on Objectivity

Attitudes toward risk vary between organizations and individuals. Some are risk-averse in nature or practice while others even see the risks as opportunities to be taken. In the analysis of risk identification, it is necessary to emphasize sufficient objectivity; the identification of risk must not

Table 6.2 Measures of counteracting identified uncertainties due to COVID-19

Identified uncertainty	*Suggested countermeasures*
Anticipating the amount of customer purchases	Constant and regular contact.
Large variation in customer purchases	Increased agility. Direct contact with customers to gain visibility.
Cancellation of orders	Modification of cancellation conditions. Ability to scale own activities.
Postponement of orders	Communicating to customers how potential postponements affect delivery times.
Delay in customer payments	Customer lists are monitored more actively through various alert lists.
Supply difficulties of subcontractors	Tighter monitoring and closer cooperation with suppliers.
Customer confidence in seller's ability to deliver	Customer will be informed and assured before placing an order. Discussion of obligations with customers. Fixing contract terms.
Staff layoffs	Finding new, value-creating work for employees
Remote working	Internal and external interaction by utilizing information and communications technology (ICT).
Customer encounters when physical appointments avoided	Utilizing online meeting technologies like Microsoft Teams and Zoom.

depend on who performs the analysis. Objectivity can be enhanced by various checklists to ensure the risks are related to, for example, customer continuity and profitability, or to individuals.

The Organization Should Follow Its Own Risk Management Practices

Large organizations in particular may have established fairly thorough risk management practices. For example, larger and older firms tend to have more resources that may help reduce the perceived risk due in an uncertain environment (Liesch et al., 2014). However, the risk of a long-term pandemic and its effects on operations and customer relationships has been considered to have very low probability. Nevertheless, when uncertainty rapidly grows and risks realize themselves, proper countermeasures should be taken.

According to Claver et al. (2008) family-owned firms perceive greater risk than non-family-owned firms. In most economies, family-owned firms constitute a large majority of all firms. However, there are many smaller and other firms that have not yet had time or the willingness to invest in risk management guidelines related to their customer relationship management.

Even if the pandemic as a risk has not been recognized in a firm's risk management guidelines, it is important to activate relevant countermeasures to lower the negative impact of increased uncertainty.

The Risks Must Be Specified in Sufficient Detail

Sometimes the risks associated with the customer relationship are only superficially identified. In that case, the problem may be that concrete contingency plans in the form of possible remedial measures cannot be drawn up in sufficient detail in terms of risk preparedness. Therefore, it is important to cover different kinds of uncertainties and risks and, thus, identify potential countermeasures related to them.

Risk Management Should Include Setting Roles and Responsibilities

A firm's customer relationships involve significant financial and operational risks. Managing uncertainties and related risks is not only about documenting and preparing for them. It is important also that roles and responsibilities for managing customer relationships-related risks are set. Risk-reducing countermeasures are implemented involving the whole organization. Chesbrough (2020) encourages concentrating on managing innovation as part of recovery from the effects of the pandemic. He argues that openness to ideas is crucial in times of crisis. Being open to new ideas improves a firm's internal innovation activities and makes it possible to utilize others' knowledge.

A Cost–Benefit Analysis Related to Risk Management Should Be Performed

Even if the customer-related risk assessment identifies multiple risks, this does not mean that all of them should be managed. Although a certain amount of risk has to be taken, some risks may be transferable to other parties and some can be avoided with careful precautions. In situations where the risk is unlikely and where the potential harm from the risk is estimated as minor, it may not be advisable to take massive measures to avoid them. This results in conscious risk-taking.

Managing Uncertainty Involves Making Compromises

A concrete way to improve risk management in relation to the risks already identified is to try to outline their severity and the likelihood of their realization, which will be reduced by various precautions. While the outcomes of different uncertainties and related risks differentiate between each other there may be some kind of prioritization between different uncertainties and risks. This could be based, for example, on the estimated financial hazards of those risks. On the other hand, some uncertainties and risks are intertwined with each other and their combined outcomes can be difficult to estimate in practice.

In connection with the risk analysis, the aim is to find out the possible effects of the identified risks on the business as a whole, the continuity of the customer relationships, and profitability. In risk management, special attention should be paid to risks that are probable and have serious consequences.

Risk management is about making compromises. It is also important to consider the probability and impact of the identified risk. Risks that are seen as significant or even moderately large from the customer's point of view are, where possible, prevented by changing the planned procedures or minimizing the identified risk factors. In risk management, a proactive approach enables a quick response: when a risk materializes, it is already planned in advance how to act. It is natural that there are various risks associated with different customers and operating environments. Nevertheless, it is necessary that the risks specific to a particular customer are taken into account and prepared for. It is usually not even realistically possible to prepare for all potential risks.

While many larger companies may have departments for risk management, it could be considered what the optimal roles and responsibilities are while managing market demand and customer relationship-related uncertainties and related risks. On the one hand, a difficult situation due to the pandemic creates the need to improvise while interacting with customers; on the other hand, firm-level countermeasures against recognized uncertainties should be well orchestrated by management.

Conclusions

The COVID-19 pandemic has created different kinds of uncertainties to economies, markets and individual firms. On one hand, this kind of a major pandemic with severe economic outcomes should be a wake-up call to reassess existing approaches to managing typical buyer–supplier relationship-related uncertainties and risks.

Customer relationships are often exposed to significant operational and financial uncertainties and risks, and these as well as risks related to continuity and other issues need to be identified in order to prepare for them. The survey research conducted before the workshops revealed that practitioners of customer relationship management in a business-to-business setting were faced with major uncertainties and problems caused by difficulties in meeting customers face-to-face, postponement of customer orders, difficulty in anticipating the amount of customer orders, and the large variation related to them. During the workshops, findings related to the countermeasures against identified uncertainties were recognized and documented. The findings of the two workshop groups are rather similar and thus complement each other. The tone of discussion was somewhat more pessimistic in the other workshop group. They felt that even if the management of the selling firm recognizes that something should be done differently to counteract the identified uncertainties then it still remains dependent on what the customer decides to do. Persuasive communication may affect the customer. These findings can be applied while firms are trying to adapt to changes in customer buying behavior and interacting with the customers. The findings contribute to the body of knowledge on managing customer relationships in a business-to-business setting during a global pandemic.

While managing business-to-business customers, it is suggested to create approaches and procedures to identify uncertainties and manage related risks. It is hardly uncommon for the same uncertainties, related risks and problems to recur with other customers. Careful foresight and preparation reduce the number of customer relationship-related uncertainties and their adverse effects. Pandemics create uncertainty in customer relationships, and this requires adaptation and agility in the buyer–supplier relationship in order to meet the requirements of the new business environment.

Limitations

It can be considered that most empirical studies have their limitations. Ørngreen and Levinsen (2017) assert that workshops as a research methodology intend to create reliable and valid data about the domain in question. While writing this research paper, the COVID-19 pandemic was active and a potential vaccine or other remedy seemed relatively far away. It may be that, in retrospect, other research methods could be applied to complement the mixed methods used, consisting of workshops and an advance online survey for the workshop participants. This could inspire alternative approaches to data collection and analysis that would allow further study of the management of business-to-business customer relationships during uncertainty.

The empirical insights were collected during workshops from sales management and key account management professionals who had encountered the effects of COVID-19 on their customer relationships, customer interaction and everyday work. However, as a limitation, the data were collected in Finland, which on international comparison was not among the countries worst-affected by COVID-19. It could be that the uncertainties would be even more severe in the represented markets had the country been more seriously affected. This could provide opportunities to identify more uncertainties affecting business-to-business customer relationships and, thus, potential countermeasures against these uncertainties.

References

Altig, D., Baker, S., Barrero, J.M., Bloom, N., Bunn, P., Chen, S., Davis, S.J., Meyer, B., Mihaylov, E., Mizen, P., et al. (2020). Economic uncertainty before and during the COVID-19 pandemic. https://doi.org/10.1016/j.jpubeco.2020.104274.

Argyris, C., & Schön, D.A. (1996). *Organizational learning II: Theory, method and practice*, 2. Upper Saddle River, NJ: FT Press.

Baker, S.R., Bloom, N., & Davis, S.J. (2016). Measuring economic policy uncertainty. *The Quarterly Journal of Economics, 131*(4), 1593–1636.

Baker, S.R., Bloom, N., Davis, S.J., & Terry, S.J. (2020). COVID-Induced economic uncertainty (No. 26983). National Bureau of Economic Research. https://doi.org/10.3386/w26983.

Bloom, N. (2014). Fluctuations in uncertainty. *The Journal of Economic Perspectives: A Journal of the American Economic Association, 28*(2), 153–176. https://doi.org/10.1257/jep.28.2.153.

Cankurtaran, P., & Beverland, M. B. (2020). Using design thinking to respond to crises: B2B lessons from the 2020 COVID-19 pandemic. *Industrial Marketing Management, 88*, 255–260. https://doi.org/10.1016/j.indmarman.2020.05.030.

Certo, S.T., Connelly, B.L., & Tihanyi, L. (2008). Managers and their not-so rational decisions. *Business Horizons, 51*(2), 113–119. https://doi.org/10.1016/j.bushor.2007.11.002.

Chesbrough, H. (2020). To recover faster from Covid-19, open up: Managerial implications from an open innovation perspective. *Industrial Marketing Management*. https://doi.org/10.1016/j.indmarman.2020.04.010.

Claver, E., Rienda, L., & Quer, D. (2008). Family firms' risk perception: empirical evidence on the internationalization process. *Journal of Small Business and Enterprise Development, 15*(3), 457–471. https://doi.org/10.1108/14626000810892283.

Cobb, P., Confrey, J., DiSessa, A., Lehrer, R., & Schauble, L. (2003). Design experiments in educational research. *Educational Researcher, 32*(1), 9–13.

Crick, J.M., & Crick, D. (2020). Coopetition and COVID-19: Collaborative business-to-business marketing strategies in a pandemic crisis. *Industrial Marketing Management, 88*, 206–213. https://doi.org/10.1016/j.indmarman.2020.05.016.

Darsø, L. (2001). *Innovation in the making*. Samfundslitteratur.

Donthu, N., & Gustafsson, A. (2020). Effects of COVID-19 on business and research. *Journal of Business Research, 117*, 284–289. https://doi.org/10.1016/j.jbusres.2020.06.008.

Ellram, L.M., & Krause, D. (2014). Robust supplier relationships: Key lessons from the economic downturn. *Business Horizons, 57*(2), 203–213. https://doi.org/10.1016/j.bushor.2013.11.004.

Figueira-de-Lemos, F., & Hadjikhani, A. (2014). Internationalization processes in stable and unstable market conditions: Towards a model of commitment decisions in dynamic environments. *Journal of World Business, 49*(3), 332–349.

Groening, C., Yildirim, P., Mittal, V., & Tadikamalla, P. (2014). Hedging customer risk. *Customer Needs and Solutions, 1*(2), 105–116.

Guan, D., Wang, D., Hallegatte, S., Davis, S. J., Huo, J., Li, S., ... Gong, P. (2020). Global supply-chain effects of COVID-19 control measures. *Nature Human Behaviour, 4*(6), 577–587. https://doi.org/10.1038/s41562-020-0896-8.

Habel, J., Jarotschkin, V., Schmitz, B., Eggert, A., & Plötner, O. (2020). Industrial buying during the coronavirus pandemic: A cross-cultural study.

Industrial Marketing Management, 88, 195–205. https://doi.org/10.1016/j.indmarman.2020.05.015.

Hallikas, J., Virolainen, V.-M., & Tuominen, M. (2002). Understanding risk and uncertainty in supplier networks – a transaction cost approach. *International Journal of Production Research, 40*(15), 3519–3531. https://doi.org/10.1080/00207540210146512.

Hartmann, N.N., & Lussier, B. (2020). Managing the sales force through the unexpected exogenous COVID-19 crisis. *Industrial Marketing Management, 88*, 101–111. https://doi.org/10.1016/j.indmarman.2020.05.005.

Lascaux, A. (2020). Coopetition and trust: What we know, where to go next. *Industrial Marketing Management, 84*, 2–18. https://doi.org/10.1016/j.indmarman.2019.05.015.

Le Roy, F., & Czakon, W. (2016). Managing coopetition: the missing link between strategy and performance. *Industrial Marketing Management, 53*, 3–6. https://doi.org/10.1016/j.indmarman.2015.11.005.

Liesch, P.W., Welch, L.S., & Buckley, P.J. (2014). Risk and uncertainty in internationalisation and international entrepreneurship studies. In P.J. Buckley (Ed.), *The multinational enterprise and the emergence of the global factory* (pp. 52–77). Palgrave Macmillan UK. https://doi.org/10.1057/9781137402387_3.

Manuj, I., & Mentzer, J.T. (2008). Global supply chain risk management strategies. *International Journal of Physical Distribution & Logistics Management, 38*(3), 192–223. https://doi.org/10.1108/09600030810866986.

Mora Cortez, R., & Johnston, W.J. (2020). The Coronavirus crisis in B2B settings: Crisis uniqueness and managerial implications based on social exchange theory. *Industrial Marketing Management, 88*, 125–135. https://doi.org/10.1016/j.indmarman.2020.05.004.

Obal, M., & Gao, T. (2020). Managing business relationships during a pandemic: Conducting a relationship audit and developing a path forward. *Industrial Marketing Management, 88*, 247–254. https://doi.org/10.1016/j.indmarman.2020.05.025.

Ørngreen, R., & Levinsen, K. (2017). Workshops as a research methodology. *Electronic Journal of E-Learning, 15*(1), 70–81.

Palmatier, R.W., Houston, M.B., Dant, R.P., & Grewal, D. (2013). Relationship velocity: Toward a theory of relationship dynamics. *Journal of Marketing, 77*(1), 13–30. https://doi.org/10.1509/jm.11.0219.

Palmatier, R.W., Scheer, L.K., & Steenkamp, J.-B.E.M. (2007). Customer loyalty to whom? Managing the benefits and risks of salesperson-owned loyalty. *JMR, Journal of Marketing Research, 44*(2), 185–199. https://doi.org/10.1509/jmkr.44.2.185.

Preikschas, M.W., Cabanelas, P., Rüdiger, K., & Lampón, J. F. (2017). Value co-creation, dynamic capabilities and customer retention in industrial markets. *Journal of Business & Industrial Marketing, 32*(3), 409–420. https://doi.org/10.1108/JBIM-10-2014-0215.

Rapaccini, M., Saccani, N., Kowalkowski, C., Paiola, M., & Adrodegari, F. (2020). Navigating disruptive crises through service-led growth: The impact of COVID-19 on Italian manufacturing firms. *Industrial Marketing Management, 88*, 225–237. https://doi.org/10.1016/j.indmarman.2020.05.017.

Reason, P., & Bradbury, H. (2001). *Handbook of action research: Participative inquiry and practice*. Sage.

Sharma, P., Leung, T.Y., Kingshott, R.P.J., Davcik, N.S., & Cardinali, S. (2020). Managing uncertainty during a global pandemic: An international business perspective. *Journal of Business Research, 116*, 188–192. https://doi.org/10.1016/j.jbusres.2020.05.026.

Sheth, J. (2020). Business of business is more than business: Managing during the Covid crisis. *Industrial Marketing Management, 88*, 261–264. https://doi.org/10.1016/j.indmarman.2020.05.028.

Simangunsong, E., Hendry, L.C., & Stevenson, M. (2012). Supply-chain uncertainty: a review and theoretical foundation for future research. *International Journal of Production Research, 50*(16), 4493–4523. https://doi.org/10.1080/00207543.2011.613864.

Simon, H.A. (2013). *Administrative behavior* (4th edn.). Simon and Schuster.

Sniazhko, S. (2019). Uncertainty in decision-making: A review of the international business literature. *Cogent Business & Management, 6*(1), 1650692. https://doi.org/10.1080/23311975.2019.1650692.

Toma, S V., Alexa, I.-V., & Nistor, C. (2013). Methods of risk modeling in economic activities. Advances in Business-Related Scientific Research Conference 2013 in Rome (ABSRC 2013 Rome) October 2–4, 2013, Rome, Italy.

Veronesi, L. (2014). How B2B integration drives superior supply chain performance. www.gxs-gmbh.de/wp-content/uploads/How-B2B-Integration-Drives-Superior-Supply-Chain-Performance.pdf.

Wakkary, R. (2007). A participatory design understanding of interaction design. Science of design workshop, CHI 2007, San Jose, CA, USA.

Weick, K.E., & Sutcliffe, K.M. (2007). *Managing the unexpected: Assuring high performance in an age of complexity*. Jossey-Bass.

7 Manufacturing vs Services

The Pandemic Impact

Archana Choudhary and Manoj Gour Chintaluri

Introduction

Many consider the COVID-19 pandemic a "black swan" event – arriving without notice and causing severe and catastrophic damage to all. But the challenges it poses also stand to become a kind of new normal and a blessing in disguise necessitating the need for innovating business models in situations of constraints of consumption, physical movement and buying needs. History shows that innovative business models have emerged during difficult times and have helped companies to adapt and flourish after the crisis is over. If one looks at history, the year 1991 was a watershed moment in the history of India: with little or no resources left to address the balance of payment, the government had to pledge gold to get funds (Vikraman, 2017). This triggered a push-back scenario of India opening up the shores for FDI and participation in the country, much to the disdain of a set of organizations that thrived on the benefits of *Licence Raj* (an elaborate system of licenses and regulations that were required to set up and run businesses in India between 1947 and 1990) (Kotwal et al., 2011).

Another case in point is the adoption of electronic modes of payments in the country since 2016 post demonetization with challenges of currency circulation and regularization of the same within the realms of the economic cycle (Mittal & Kumar, 2018). Leveraging on the same, a new set of companies leveraged technology, the penetration of the Internet built on models that a soothsayer would dread to think a few years ago. Both e-commerce and payment modes have penetrated the backbone of Internet penetration and acted as a breather in these times of despair for certain strata of the population (Kumar & Ayodeji, 2021). Today it is but impossible if someone is not hooked on to the Internet unless they hail from very low population strata towns. At the end of 2019, India had around 636.73 million Internet subscribers and a teledensity of 90.10%, indicating the reach, and these adaptions at a consumer level are driving changes in the way the consumer market is taking shape (International Telecommunication Union, 2020).

The above pointers are no longer differentiators in the manufacturing and the services sector but basic requirements that are required

DOI: 10.4324/9781003125648-7

for survival and continuity with no possible outcome of incremental top lines but pure sustainability. The changes warranted might be unseen or unthought-of, and the need for embracing transformation is in all aspects of the business.

Initially, the COVID-19 pandemic was perceived to be a short-lived one and everyone thought that things would get back to normalcy after lockdowns. As time progressed, stakeholders have understood that they have to learn to live with a new guest now. Stakeholders of an organization started acknowledging it as a health and humanitarian calamity with the option of either adapting oneself to it or becoming extinct. Leaders are preparing themselves to face the "new normal" as normal isn't available anymore and "business as usual" even less, especially in the sector of hospitality, travel and tourism (www.accenture.com, 2020). The new reality is bringing with it a number of ambiguities, complexities and opportunities, with the need for people and organizations to think fast forward, be agile, adaptive and highly resilient. The scenario has thrown the well-conceived strategic plans, forecasting models and operations plan out of the window for both the manufacturing and the service sector. The reality seems to be tangential to reality. This leads to the question of whether new business models will arise in these industries to combat this situation.

While delivering the first quarterly earnings report in the era of COVID-19 to Wall Street, Microsoft's CEO Satya Nadella stated that the company has seen two years' worth of digital transformation in just two months, in varying areas like remote teamwork, customer service, security, and critical cloud infrastructure (www.microsoft.com, 2020). This shows the urgency sensed by many executives to increase digital capabilities to sustain resilience in unpredictable times. Changes are also taking place in the areas of education, office hours, banking, e-commerce, etc. Needless to say that all industries are affected, but the intensity of the impact will be felt more in the manufacturing and services sector with some likely to perform better than others, but a few things that will change forever is the overall customer's experience in the service industry and established norms of work and processes in the manufacturing sector. Both the industries need to come out of this in one of these four states: i.e., transformed, strong, reshaped, or uncertainty-handling (www.ey.com, 2020) so that they are equipped to tackle these challenges.

Impact on Markets During COVID-19

The COVID-19 outbreak has played havoc for many companies and well-known brands are facing bankruptcy as consumers are confined at home and economies have faced a swift and stark shutdown (Tucker, 2020). Famous companies listed under Fortune 500 such as Stein Mart, Virgin Atlantic, Lord & Taylor, Neiman Marcus, Hertz and J. Crew have filed for bankruptcy (www.fortune.com, 2020). The hospitality industry is severely affected as 80% of the hotel rooms in the United States were unoccupied during the months of March and April 2020 (Asmelash & Cooper, 2020). The tourism sector is badly affected and airlines have cut their workforce as a consequence of the extended lockdown. Even services involving human contacts like dining in restaurants, gyms, taxis, salons and beauty parlors and shopping complexes have been affected and have come to a standstill. Service providers catering to social gatherings like marriages, cultural functions, religious congregations, sporting events and the entertainment industry are facing a lot of financial turmoil. Expos, meetings and events scheduled in different venues, museums and galleries were called off due to abrupt lockdowns. This opened up a plethora of questions for the organizations to explore and answer. What do we do now? Why couldn't we see that coming? As a business entity and as an employer how do we come out of this situation? How do we revive our business and take care of our employees well-being (Asmelash & Cooper, 2020)? How to turn this adverse situation into an opportune one? How are the business entities and even nations using the pandemic situation to survive let alone thrive? While some businesses are dwindling, others are flourishing. The businesses which are doing well are using a virtual platform to deliver products and services like those related to food delivery, online education, online entertainment, online shopping and offering remote work solutions. There have been changes in the consumption pattern of consumers also. There is a lot of focus on takeaways, snacks, cleaning and sanitization products as people spend more time in their homes. Healthcare, medication, nutritional and immunity enhancement products are also doing well.

It has been assumed that markets are static, but the COVID-19 pandemic has falsified this notion and has demonstrated that markets can move rapidly as they are dynamic (Jaworski et al., 2000). Further, a market is not just a business entity but comprises a network of actors like customers, firms and public organizations operating with a set of established norms. The purpose of these organizations is to generate value as they consist of a dynamic ecosystem (Vargo & Lusch, 2011). The COVID-19 situation has given a unique opportunity to understand how markets are formed and how they vanish within a short period. An example which befits this is co-working spaces, from being the happening sector creating arbitrage to office spaces to oblivion as the home space competes with it.

Strategies to Combat COVID-19 Business Challenges

After a lot of frantic activities, some organizations have started pondering on the way forward to capture the opportunities COVID-19 has brought. Wade and Bjerkan (2020) suggest three generic strategies that can be taken by organizations in the manufacturing or the service industry to match the emerging market trends. These strategies can be utilized by the organizations which are proactive and show agility in adjusting their product/service portfolio and infrastructure, or discover a new path to the market (Wade & Bjerkan, 2020). These strategies are given below.

Offering the Same Products through Different Channels

This strategy talks about offering similar products and services through a digital platform (Kumar & Saurabh, 2020). This may be made possible through online delivery of physical products or technology-mediated delivery systems in the case of the services segment. For example, when Nike was forced to close its stores in China due to the pandemic, its offline business nosedived, but its online operations continued. Nike's staff members started engaging with Chinese customers by offering online workouts. As stores started reopening after the lockdown, Nike's digital business escalated even more, and now the company has a strategy to follow as the virus spreads its tentacles across the world (www.cnbc.com, 2020). Similarly, whereas many educational institutions temporarily shut down and waited for things to return to normalcy, there were others that quickly shifted to online teaching.

Offering Different Products through the Same Infrastructure

This strategy refers to organizations' responding to this situation by using existing infrastructure to manufacture different products or to cater to new types of services. Companies like Pernod Ricard (alcoholic beverages) and Moët Hennessy Louis Vuitton (LVMH perfumes) started producing hand sanitizers and General Motors and Ford started producing life-saving ventilators by modifying idle production lines to cater to their rising needs worldwide. In the service industry, Hilton in the UK (theguardian.com, 2020) and the Taj group of hotels (indianexpress.com, 2020) in India started offering their rooms to doctors, nurses and COVID-19 patients to address the need of the highly stressed health infrastructure.

Offering the Same Products through Different Infrastructure

Some companies needed to quickly expand their infrastructure to accelerate their production and/or delivery capacity. They did this by collaborating with external partners. For example, Amazon hired 100,000 new employees in the USA to meet the increased demand of online sales. It also collaborated with ride-booking company Lyft, whose demand for trips had plummeted dramatically. In turn, Lyft allowed its drivers to apply for jobs as delivery and warehouse workers so that they could earn extra income (cnbc.com, 2020). Similarly, McDonald's staff in Germany have been allowed to work at Aldi, a grocery shopping store for a limited period, i.e., till the restaurants open (retaildetail.eu, 2020).

A Brief about Manufacturing and the Services Industry

All economic activities comprise three sectors. These are the primary sector consisting of agriculture, fishing and mining, the secondary sector concerned with manufacturing, i.e., producing finished goods, and the tertiary sector, i.e., the service sector. Economies have a propensity to follow a developmental advance from a heavy dependence on primary, towards the progress of manufacturing and finally towards a service-based structure. At the maturity stage, resources are then shifted from the secondary to tertiary sectors (Rostow, 1960; Lewis, 1972). This is what the global economy has largely experienced; i.e., as the economy advances, more resources will be shifted from the agricultural sector to the industry sector, and then to the service sector. Subsequently, with the passage of time, enhanced communication of information, cost reduction, speed and reliability enhancement in the transportation of people, the service sector has become one of the most concerted international competitions in developed and developing economies. The consequential shrinkage of manufacturing in the developed economies might explain their growing dependence on the service sector. The service industry consists of providing services to businesses as well as to the final consumers. This sector consists of soft parts of the economy such as tourism, banking, insurance, education, retail and social services. In the service sector employment, people use time to hire and collaborate knowledge assets, and engage in the process to create effectiveness, productivity, performance enhancement potential and sustainability (Kumar & Vidhyalakshmi, 2012). The service industry may involve transportation, distribution and the sale of goods from a producer to a consumer, like wholesaling and retailing, providing services, such as tourism, entertainment etc. (www.pwc.in, 2020). It may take the form of goods being transformed for provision of a service, as in restaurants or in equipment repair. However, the focus of services is on "people interacting with people" and serving the customers rather than just transforming physical goods. The service sector in India accounted for more than half of India's GDP in 2019, courtesy of information technology, software and telecommunications. The manufacturing sector contributed 25% of GDP, followed by a whopping 50% by the services industry (www.statista.com, 2020). Close to 47% of India's working category are employed in both these sectors together (www2.deloitte.com, 2017).

Some Insights from the Manufacturing Sector

The authors have attempted to study the initiatives taken by a few organizations in the manufacturing and services sectors to minimize the impact of the pandemic and ensure business continuity. In this attempt, the authors have browsed published interviews, reports, circulars from distribution partners, websites and other secondary resources to get inputs. The COVID-19 responses of some of the companies are as given below:

Luminous

About the Company

Luminous is a leading organization producing various forms of electrical appliances, namely power backup solutions, electrical appliances and solar panel batteries for providing electricity to customers. The organization predominantly deals with products in categories that are sold to distributors, dealers and direct consumers. At the onset of the pandemic, the organization had foreseen the challenges of sustaining the team's impact on business and their future along with the organization's future. The organization was dealing with categories in renewable energy which require high levels of interaction and market development activity to get potential customers buying the products (www.luminousindia.com, 2020).

Initiatives at Luminous

Onboarding and Engaging

Luminous always had in-house training initiatives which were more of the classroom type and here was a scenario wherein this mode was completely stalled. To address the issue of flagging motivation and upgrading skills, Luminous initiated online training modules for its sales teams. They planned a structured approach as they had to address the issue of digital adaptability and acclimatization. A few days were dedicated to onboard employees on the tools and techniques of virtual training, making close to 600 employees digitally ready. The process involved multiple levels of interactions and frequency and, more importantly, it had to set the ball rolling. In a short period, Luminous created a virtual space for product, skill, knowledge transfer, and training. This led to a scenario of building the confidence of employees and channel partners giving a message that "we are here to stay and we care" (Shukla, 2020)

Adopting a New Business Model for the New Normal

Over a period of time as the restrictions relaxed, the task of bringing the channel partners back on track was difficult. The larger aspect was blockage of working capital funds at all levels, resulting in a choc-o-block condition. The organization came to the rescue of its vendor and channel partners by ensuring that their commitment to payments was addressed immediately and at the same time wherever required they staggered the receivables. For example, in the sales system, all pending scheme payouts which typically are linked to a volume delivery were unlocked and settled upfront, thereby driving similar behavior by their distributors with the retailers. It was an attempt to leverage the size and strengthen its financials among its channel partners and vendors at the time of need. One of the larger initiatives taken was to lighten the supply chain and give visibility to both the vendors and channel partners on inventory flow. Seemingly the organization moved away from a stock pressure model, which ensured a seamless flow of goods and finances. A few channel partners to whom we spoke were super thrilled by this initiative, elatedly mentioning that this may become a new operation model and may cost them some margin. However, this would change the entire gamut of operations. By reducing costs on stocking inventory, through reduced rentals of godowns, a channel partner could devote time to earning revenues rather than getting stuck in the myriad of operations.

Leveraging Digital to Augment the Reach

In the ensuing period, when a few markets in the country opened, the continued impact of the pandemic and after-effects were felt, demand was not improving, primarily on account of changing priorities at a consumer level on account of fear and social distancing. Luminous built in a model of digital collaterals to facilitate sales and encouraged digital participation at all levels. By this time the ecosystem in the country was aggressively adapting to the digital way of life and Luminous leveraged it effectively. The sales teams became true digital ambassadors of the organization and adapted small digital marketing campaigns. This was a surprise for competitors in the renewable industry and among the sales team, as Luminous could channelize an opportunity which hitherto they had experienced in better times.

Establishing a Deeper Connection with New Practices

When the lockdown was imposed, many companies were busy chasing sales and revenues, leading to pressure on the channel partners. However, Luminous demonstrated empathy by encouraging their teams to engage with their stakeholders from a well-being and concern perspective. This projected a different face of a business entity to channel partners. Additionally, they used the time efficiently to enhance the capability of employees by training them on the importance of using solar power for a sustainable environment and the whole ecosystem. All these initiatives were highly appreciated by the channel partners, fundamentally with the intent of "keeping the flock together". These activities ensured engagement with all the stakeholders, giving away to a new paradigm for Luminous. Some sources which cannot be revealed say that Luminous has exceeded their business results for the period. The pandemic has brought in a new paradigm that can set a precedent for the future, namely:

- Lighter and more efficient supply chain.
  - Efficient inventory leading to a reduction of the holding costs at all levels.
  - Improving receivables.
- Care for all – overriding the business results – indicating a long-term need of everyone required for well-being.
- Sharpening the ax – upskilling the entire chain of resources.
- Evolving a digital mode of driving business in areas of people interaction, business development, and supply chain visibility.

We are sure the initiatives at Luminous with a core thought of well-being of the ecosystem will go a long way in being a part of a new paradigm in conducting business. The period would have made Luminous realize that a manufacturing company could work remotely without hampering its efficiency. What started as a contingency plan helped the company in leading through the innovative ideas of connecting with customers through social media, e-commerce platforms, using technology in automation of work, giving time to employees for upskilling and value addition, helping them in evolving to a great extent (Shukla, 2020). This shows that the company adopted a proactive strategy to mitigate the effect of COVID-19 on their business by engaging different stakeholders through digital platforms and offering the same products through an online channel.

Pernod Ricard India (Pernod)

About the Company

Pernod Ricard India is one of the oldest and largest organizations in the world in the Alcobev categories. The portfolio boasts of brands that a connoisseur will vie for consuming and adding to their bar shelves.

The sector Pernod deals in in India is a unique maze of regulation and policies driven by states. A few expatriate executives in different forums have commented that the Alcobev industry in India is no less than Europe, with each state legislating its own rules and regulations. This industry also has been the backbone of revenues for respective state governments and a few states had opened up retailing stores the earliest in comparison to other trades. With the pandemic prevailing, operating in this scenario had its own set of challenges (www.pernod-ricard.com, 2020).

Early Actions – Pernod India

Organization leverage is an important play basis for its position, size, scale, and reach. Pernod India took advantage of the head-start. Unlike a lot of other organizations, Pernod India drove home the early indicators of the pandemic and initiated a business continuity plan with the employee at the core. They started restricting travel and addressing their employees on the potential impact of the virus in early January 2020. Guidelines were established for running the operations keeping in mind social distancing norms and other preventive measures to ensure the safety of their employees around February, way ahead of government guidelines. Crisis management committees were set up at locations to manage all COVID-related situations in early March. In the pre-lockdown stage, Pernod had implemented work from home on a rotational basis. An internal self-declaration mechanism was set up to monitor health status and movements, tech enablement was activated to empower them to work efficiently from home, a business continuity matrix was developed with critical contacts for escalation at all times and a key transition the organization was facilitating is the adoption of the new ways of working for their employees through extensive training and providing necessary work-from-home infrastructure support to ensure that this is a smooth process. The excerpts of the Indian CHRO were picked up by the authors from an interview published online (www.humanresourcesonline.net, 2020).

Asset Management

At Pernod, the embodiment of a value system identifies with the core of "employees" as a critical asset; the entire response system of the organization revolved around this asset. They extended support to employees on a psychological and emotional level through an employee engagement platform, Ananda. This inclusive approach generated significant positivity amongst the employees and helped them through these trying times. The organization also made a tie-up with doctors and hospitals in all locations, while employing a hotline for employees and families for COVID-related assistance.

Engagement Continuity

To address their bit of engagement of employees, Pernod built a continuous engagement model with a list of activities under the gamut of occupational, social, physical, intellectual, spiritual, environmental, financial and emotional dimensions. All eight pillars were directed to the holistic development of the employees at both a professional and personal level.

Remote sessions were conducted for employees with topics related to Yoga, leadership connections, self-care, parenting, learning webinars, and counseling to name a few. Virtual coffee sessions also acted as a hearing out to the employees and keeping them in a good mood. To capture the effectiveness of the initiatives, feedback of participants was taken and

99% responded that their overall experience had been positive. Nearly 96% reported that the activities were most appropriate to engage them and their families. The above data bear testimony to the experience that they provided to their employees during the work-from-home period.

Managing Fatigue

To assess the sentiment of extended working from home, Pernod conducted an organization-wide pulse survey to gauge the mood and morale. The findings indicated that the boundaries of work-time and personal-time were getting blurred, which sometimes led to employees working long or odd hours. These inputs helped Pernod develop action plans around employees taking a break from working life. It actively encouraged employees to have discussions over the phone instead of email so that the social interactions were also initiated and as a source of venting off the pressure. The HR teams were making continuous efforts to maintain defined working hours and not to schedule any meetings after 5 p.m. (www.humanresourcesonline.net, 2020).

Pernod initiated the e-commerce model to reach the consumers with the likes of Zomato or Swiggy acting as pure transporters in a few markets. It had realized that it cannot change its business model entirely as the licensed outlets and on-premise outlet licensing cannot change unless there is a legislation in the anvil for any specific state. The proactive actions of Pernod indicated that their strategy was to engage with employees and resorting to digitization of their products to ensure business continuity.

The CHRO closed the interview with a quote, "At Pernod Ricard India, we remain steadfast in our drive to ensure that employees are motivated and experience high morale during these unprecedented times" (www.humanresourcesonline.net, 2020).

Some Insights from the Services Sector

ITC Hotels

About the Hotels

ITC Hotels is India's third-largest hotel chain with over 100 hotels. It is based in Kolkata, West Bengal. It is part of the ITC Limited group of companies. ITC Hotels is regularly voted amongst the best employers in Asia in the hospitality sector. They are the world's largest LEED Platinum-rated chain of hotels. With the philosophy of envisioned responsible luxury since a decade back, ITC Hotels incorporated several best practices in its DNA that helped in setting a benchmark for responsible hospitality. Through these efforts, it has been successful in strengthening its "WeAssure" program (www.itchotels.in, 2020)

People First Initiative for Employees

Sanjay Bose, EVP and Head HR, ITC Ltd – Hotels Division said that

> People First is a way of life at ITC Hotels. The well being of our human capital is of utmost importance to us. Together, they add up to a phenomenal number of "experience years" which is such a significant asset for the organization. Covid-19 presents itself as a challenge. However, we have taken a large number of initiatives to ensure we ride smoothly over the tough times. Training, learning, and good mental health are some of our focus areas at this hour. We are in this together.
>
> (www.foodhospitality.in, 2020)

SALARIES BEFORE TIME

The employees were given salaries before the lockdown began to ensure that there was no delay in dues.

ENGAGEMENT CONVERSATIONS

Even after 3,600+ employees reached their homes, ITC made efforts to provide the necessary support to them. They were in constant touch with their employees through engaging conversations about the well-being of their associates and their family members.

MENTAL HEALTH – ONE-TO-ONE HELP

The company got associated with One-to-One Help to offer a holistic employee assistance service for the mental well-being of employees and their family members.

ENHANCED COMMUNICATION – SMS BLAST

All of their 7,000 employees were constantly contacted and two-way communication was maintained in the ensuing tough times.

COVID ADVISORIES

To avoid any inconsistency, miscommunication, or information lag, several advisories were shared with all units. These advisories dealt with employees' well-being, standardized responses, generation of awareness, and upholding ITC's culture of care and concern. This included a COVID-19 booklet, on-premises assistance, and an HR approach document for employees.

Employee Learning and Growth

ITC rolled out several online learning courses aimed at specific roles and levels through different platforms of e-learning. Through this initiative, employees completed over 36,000 courses through different e-learning platforms.

ITC Hotels also held several online sessions to induct its new employees and train them in functional as well as general management skills. The organization had also upgraded its digital infrastructure to organize training sessions for 53 management trainees.

Safe Distancing, Cleanliness and Hygiene Protocol for Customers

ITC hotel's "WeAssure" promised rigorous clinical levels of hygiene through NABH Accreditation and DNV-GL Business Assurance certification in progress. These conformed to the guidelines laid out by the World Health Organization (WHO) and the Indian Tourism ministry. The "new normal" protocol mandated thermal screening, social distancing and usage of masks at various levels of operations of the hotel. The usage of additional protective gear and disposable gloves during service as and wherever required was also implemented. The guidelines were followed for both hotel guests and associates. It further redefined hotel operations along the lines of safe distancing, contact-less services and well-being, offering all the guests an unparalleled comfort and tranquility.

Apart from this, all managers and associates were trained in the hygiene certification in all aspects of Food Safety and Standards Authority of India (FSSAI) regulatory guidelines, and norms of cleaning and disinfecting according to hospital standards.

ITC Limited Executive Director Mr. Nakul Anand said,

> ITC Hotels has been a trailblazer in sustainability – from pioneering the Clean Air initiative to making all its properties free of single-use plastic and pioneering the LEED initiative. As per USGBC, "built to LEED" or "LEED equivalency" doesn't exist – there is no substitute for the certification and we are glad to have pre-empted this a decade back. Our "Namaste" logo too embodies our commitment to Responsible Luxury – Silent yet powerful, Distant yet connected, Embodying within itself, Oneness, of the soul Service can and must always touch the heart.
>
> (bwhotelier.businessworld.in, 2020)

Contactless Services

Efforts were made to clean touchpoints in the public area multiple times daily with sanitizers and disinfectants to keep it at par with clinical hygiene levels. The sitting areas in the lobby and restaurants were rearranged to ensure safe distances. Several operational activities were digitalized, like the Guest Service Directory, restaurant menus, QR Friendly In-Room Dining menu and Check In & Check Out processes, thereby enabling contactless services. The advanced sanitization techniques deployed in guest services and baggage duly tagged as "Sanitagged" provided visitors with added reassurance.

Due diligence was given in maintaining distancing in guestrooms. The rooms were cleaned only when the guest was not in the room after asking for a time. These rooms followed strict cleanliness standards adhering to the highest clinical levels of hygiene. The rooms were sanitized after the departure of every guest and were kept vacant for the next 24 hours.

ITC Hotels with a state-of-the-art ISO 22000 Food Safety Management quality accredited Microbiology Labs had a systematic and preventive approach to food safety and cuisine hygiene. The food and beverage section had also been re-engineered for the "new normal". While the "Knock n Drop" time-saver dining service was an optional service, served to a guest in their room, without any contact with staff members, the Grab and Go breakfast scheme offered guests the choice of having breakfast in their room without human contact.

App-based Home Delivery

ITC Hotels also started an exclusive app for home delivery of foods in Mumbai, New Delhi and Chennai to cater to the escalating demand for home delivery and gourmet servings. With the responsible luxury initiative "WeAssure" program, a diner was assured of rigorous hygiene and safety protocols for pan-India home delivery of food. This step further instilled confidence in the customers to order directly via the brand platforms. The special take-away counter at all hotels was stocked with thermometers and hand sanitizers to ensure the health of local delivery agents.

Lavanderia, the Laundry Services

ITC Hotels recently started "Lavanderia" – a contactless laundry service with stringent norms of safety and hygiene at every step. City residents not staying in the hotel could also avail themselves of the same. It also offered the "Safe Car Promise" to its guests. The cars were driven by experienced chauffeurs who adhered to strict health norms through daily thermal temperature checks and compulsory use of medically approved face masks, gloves and hand sanitizers.

Apart from addressing two important aspects, i.e., employee anxiety and support, ITC's strategy of using its infrastructure for providing new services (i.e. app-based food delivery and laundry services) through a technology-mediated delivery system spoke volumes about its innovation that surely gave an impetus to its revenue generation.

Care Group of Hospitals

About the Hospital

The CARE Group of Hospitals is a chain of multispecialty health care providers. It has 14 hospitals under its umbrella serving six cities in five states of India. CARE Hospitals provides comprehensive care in 30 specialties in tertiary care and is the regional leader in South/Central India in tertiary care and the top five among the pan-Indian hospital chains.

CARE Hospitals provides cost-effective medical care true to its core purpose i.e., "To provide care that people trust", by adopting a service-oriented delivery model. It aims to deliver world-class and affordable services to all.

The number of patients visiting outpatient departments (OPD) at Hyderabad's Care Group of Hospitals has come down to 30% to 40% as compared to the pre-pandemic situation. However, the teleconsultation numbers have gone up (www.carehospitals.com, 20).

According to Dr. Raajiv Singhal, Group CEO, Care Group of Hospitals,

> Screening protocols and Flu clinic was operational and all patients were being screened. Any patient found to be symptomatic or those who self-declared were being guided to the emergency department. There was a substantial decrease in the overall numbers and our call center kept on encouraging patients for video consultation and were asked to visit the hospital only if the consultant recommended the same. Home delivery for medicines and home collection services were provided to the patients at no extra cost.
>
> The rosters were also designed to make sure that senior consultants were available regularly, to offer complete coverage across the span of the week. The staff were planned for alternate day shifts and were operating at 50% of the pre-COVID-19 strength.
>
> (www.healthcareradius.in, 2020)

OPD Services

All necessary guidelines for COVID-19 management issued by the national and state health authorities were followed for the smooth running of OPD operations during the lockdown. The hospital had reduced the OPD operations to the minimum and allowed only needy patients to meet the doctors. Some of the norms that were put in place in the OPD areas to ensure safety were:

STRICT GATE-KEEPING

A single entry-and-exit gate was earmarked to keep track of the flow of patients, staff and visitors.

SCREENING ZONE

All the patients, hospital staff and attendants had to go through three-level screening before entering the hospital. This included a face mask, thermal scan and hand sanitizer kept at the entrance. A trained nurse kept a record of the brief history of travel and contact details if any patient showed up with respiratory symptoms.

FLU CLINIC

There was a separate designated area reserved for patients showing flu symptoms for further examination and they were segregated from others to avoid mass contact. A universal screening tool was in place for them.

REGISTRATION DESK

There were glass partitions or screens at all registration desks to maintain distance with the visitor and patients.

SOCIAL DISTANCING

There were highlighted markings every six feet for every desk to maintain social distancing.

PERSONAL PROTECTIVE EQUIPMENT (PPE)

All doctors, nurses and other staff were provided PPE kits which included masks, gloves and bodywear, to ensure the safety and protection of all concerned.

Though a majority of health service providers used to follow all safety and occupation hazards even before the onset of COVID-19, the pandemic had given rise to new challenges of ensuring safety and zero contamination. From the hospital's perspective, there was a huge change in the model as these places were a hotspot of both virus spread and relief. The hospital also started providing online consultancy to both general and COVID-19-positive patients who were asymptomatic and quarantining at home after the lockdown was announced to cater to the needs of the patients as well as generate revenues. They used the strategy of providing new services by using the same infrastructure. Though the business started limping back to normalcy after Unlock 4.0, health experts were of the opinion that these initiatives should stay till the COVID-19 vaccine came, as there were mass health concerns. They also felt that health regulators will mandate the compliance of these norms, the cost of which had to be borne by the consumers, leading to a rise in health care costs (www.healthcareradius.in, 2020)

Findings and Discussion

Emerging Norms

On analysis of the approach, reactions and workways of the cases mentioned above, the following perspectives emerged:

- The underlying theme build-up by organizations revolved around employee well-being, addressing uncertainties, and continuity of business issues.
- While Topline was important, the approach to different stakeholders like vendors and channel partners was empathetic with an eye on the future. Possibly this approach is an indication of universal issues across industries and countries. This may act as a differentiator when the market normalizes. Whether this will lead to engaged stakeholders: only time will tell.
- New modes of delivery, thinning of the supply chain, leveraging digital communication modes, employee-assistance programs and new product/service offerings were observed in almost all organizations. However, these did not drastically alter revenue or business models. Adapting the new norms was the buzzword.

The New Paradigms

Digital Leverage

The country has witnessed aggressive Internet penetration in the past few months indicative of an adaptation across categories of people aided by smartphones, laptops and gadgets which act as an interplay between the customers and markets. The digital leverage is happening across the manufacturing and service sectors at large with the likes of manufacturing goods to the services sector, such as online classes in educational institutions. The cost-benefit ratio will drive organizations to aggressively adapt and build tools around digital space in all walks of business. There are seemingly new ways of doing business. While these were at play in the past also and acted as a differentiator, now they have become a necessity. The organizations and employees who are not adapting a massive digital platform to work shall perish.

Business Continuity Plans (BCP)

COVID-19 has exposed the likes of organizations that were practice-led and had poor BCP processes. While not much leeway would have happened in others, there is sensitivity and understanding in such organizations. A new paradigm will begin in future planning processes.

What needs to be seen is who will pay the cost of such a BCP plan: the organization or the consumer?

Empathy at Play

Care for more with a drive on empathy was demonstrated by organizations. Across all strata of society, the pandemic has created social boundaries. While progressive organizations have demonstrated care with a long-term view, time will demonstrate whether this will translate into engagement or loyalty. However, research has proven that addressing distress pays as uncertainty leads to stickiness.

Supply Chain Dynamics

While decreasing inventory and reducing flab will become the norm, the authors foresee a scenario of eluding margins for all players in the value chain. Primarily driven by cost-cutting through all possible ways to manage the gaps in delivery in the pandemic period, business, as usual, will have a time frame by the end of 2021.

Basic Requirements – B2B

The pandemic has built a consuming mindset of wait and watch. Priorities of a larger part of the population across levels are driven by this approach, which is validated by the slowdown in the economy. One should not be surprised if in the next 18 months products with value and addressing the requirement at a basic level shall be in larger demand. Discerning spends will give way to the decision driven by the first two to three levels of Maslow's hierarchy (Maslow, 1943).

Alter Processes

Continuous changes in the market place will put pressure on the organization that does not take steps for the changeover and builds their process to address the new paradigms they are operating in.

Deep Pockets

Some organizations with larger net worth and surplus funds have demonstrated their bit to absorb financial shock to ensure continuity and reliability built up among their stakeholders. Not all have moved in the same direction; the startups seemingly have been effected, with fund flows from investors taking a hit. The pandemic has brought to the fore the leverage a good balance sheet can give. However, layoffs and unemployment rates are heading northwards. The above cases have demonstrated the motto of keeping the flock together and living for another day.

Businesses have been hitting rock bottom since March 2020 and no solution is visible in the immediate future. We may see a new India Inc. with a core focus on:

- Driving consumption.
- New "home economies product/solutions" from an organization offering perspectives seemingly may take the lead to address the new work from home phenomenon.
- Cost reductions.
- Reduction of flab across processes and people.
- Reduction in the median salaries of senior and middle-level leadership positions with a built-in skew toward results.
- The frontline sales teams, shop floor workers, and the respective supervisors where a lot of action is expected. These roles may get extra attention and possible median salaries at this level may go up as the economy improves.
- Tactical inputs as strategic time frame will get reduced.

Conclusions

COVID-19 has given rise to mass safety and health concerns amidst disruptions all over the world. All organizations across the manufacturing and service sectors are feeling the heat. Apart from these challenges, the pandemic has also offered new opportunities to the organizations which are agile, swift and resilient. New strategies have given rise to new business models. While in the manufacturing sector there has been an increase in the automation and robotics, in the services sector the personalized touch has been replaced by digitalized engagement and technology-mediated services. In the manufacturing sector, whereas pre-COVID-19 the focus used to be on productivity and quality, now it also strives to deliver the products through digital platforms. In the services sector also, the focus on delivering the best services has shifted to delivering the services through technology-mediated platforms and complementing it with hospital-standard hygiene. However, in both the sectors, employees' welfare, upskilling and the shifting demands of the customers have been the prime concern and focal point of all initiatives. It can be inferred that organizations that have the agility to quickly adapt themselves to the changing environment have been able to cope with the challenges and could thus ensure the continuity of the business. However, it remains to be seen whether these organizations can internalize these innovative norms and practices that they have developed during this tumultuous phase or not. Answering these questions and responding strategically to the current crisis requires a high degree of creativity, an openness to challenging assumptions, swift action and a willingness to look beyond the obvious in addressing the threats – and embracing the new opportunities – created by COVID-19.

References

Asmelash, L., & Cooper, A. (2020). https://edition.cnn.com/2020/04/08/us/hotel-rooms-industry-coronavirus-trnd/index.htm on 20 October 2020.

International Telecommunication Union. (2020). www.itu.int/en/ITU-D/Statistics/Pages/publications/yb2019/ accessed on 25 October 2020.

Jaworski, B., Kohli, A.K., & Sahay, A. (2000). Market-driven versus driving markets. *Journal of the Academy of Marketing Science, 28*(1), 45–54.

Kotwal, A., Ramaswami, B., & Wadhwa, W. (2011). Economic liberalization and Indian economic growth: what's the evidence? *Journal of Economic Literature, 49*(4), 1152–1199. doi:10.1257/jel.49.4.1152.

Kumar, V., & Ayodeji, O.G. (2021). E-retail factors for customer activation and retention: An Empirical study from Indian e-commerce customers. *Journal of Retailing and Consumer Services*, 59C, 102399.

Kumar, V., & Mittal, S. (2020). Mobile marketing campaigns: Practices, challenges and opportunities. *International Journal of Business Innovation and Research (IJBIR), 21*(4), 523–539.

Kumar, V., & Vidhyalakshmi, P. (2012). Cloud computing for business sustainability. *Asia-Pacific Journal of Management Research and Innovation, 8*(4), 461–474

Lewis, W.A. (1972). Reflections on unlimited labor. In L.E. DiMarco (Ed.), *International economics and development* (Essay in Honor of Raoul Prebisch) (pp. 75–96). New York: Academic Press.

Maslow, A.H. (1943). A theory of human motivation. *Psychological Review, 50*(4), 370–396.

Mittal, S., & Kumar, V. (2018), Adoption of mobile wallets in India: An analysis. *IUP Journal of Information Technology, 14*(1), 42–57

Rostow, W.W. (1960). The five stages of growth – a summary. *The stages of economic growth: A non-communist manifesto* (pp. 4–16). Cambridge: Cambridge University Press.

Shukla, A. (2020). www.linkedin.com/posts/amit-shukla-624a9711_above-and-beyond-lockdown-story-by-mr-activity-6711571228051681280-yO7O accessed on 16 September 2020.

Tucker, H. (2020). Coronavirus bankruptcy tracker: These major companies are failing amid the shutdown. Forbes. www.forbes.com/sites/hanktucker/2020/05/03/coronavirus-bankruptcy-tracker-these-major-companies-are-failing-amid-theshutdown/#5649f95d3425.

Vargo, S.L., & Lusch, R.F. (2011). It's all B2B … and beyond: Toward a systems perspective of the market. *Industrial Marketing Management, 40*(2), 181–187. DOI: 10.1016/j.indmarman.2010.06.026.

Vikraman, S. (2017, April 5). The Indian Express Newspaper. Retrieved from https://indianexpress.com/article/explained/in-fact-how-govts-pledged-gold-to-pull-economy-back-from-the-brink/, accessed on 19 September 2020.

Wade, M., & Bjerkan, H. (2020, April 17). MIT Sloan management review. Retrieved from https://sloanreview.mit.edu/article/three-proactive-response-strategies-to-covid-19-business-challenges/, accessed on 25 October 2020.

Online Resources

www.accenture.com/us-en/services/consulting/coronavirus-industry-impact, accessed on 12 October 2020.

http://bwhotelier.businessworld.in/article/Safe-Distancing-Cleanliness-Hygiene-Protocol-sets-in-as-ITC-properties-re-open/03-08-2020-304453/.

https://carehospitals.com/about-care/, accessed on 12 September 2020.

https://cio.economictimes.indiatimes.com/news/corporate-news/we-saw-2-years-of-digital-transformation-in-2-months-satya-nadella/75471759, accessed on 17 September 2020.

www.cnbc.com/2020/09/14/amazon-to-hire-100000-more-workers-in-its-latest-job-spree-this-year.html, accessed on 22 September 2020.

www.cnbc.com/2020/09/23/nikes-ceo-says-digital-is-here-to-stay-e-com-business-fuels-sales.html/, accessed on 25 October 2020.

www2.deloitte.com/content/dam/Deloitte/in/Documents/industries/in-india-services-sector-ges-2017-noexp.pdf, accessed on 25 October 2020.

https://edition.cnn.com/2020/04/08/us/hotel-rooms-industry-coronavirus-trnd/index.html, accessed on 25 September 2020.

www.ey.com/en_be/strategy-transactions/how-scenario-planning-can-create-clarity-in-the-midst-of-uncertainty, accessed on 17 September 2020.

www.foodhospitality.in/latest-updates/the-well-being-of-our-human-capital-is-of-prime-importance-to-us-itc-hotels/420344/, accessed on 22 October 2020.

https://fortune.com/2020/08/04/companies-filing-bankruptcy-2020-due-to-covid-list-filed-chapter-11-coronavirus-pandemic/, accessed on 25 September 2020.

www.theguardian.com/world/2020/mar/19/hotel-chains-in-talks-to-turn-properties-into-nhs-hospitals-coronavirus, accessed on 22 September 2020.

www.healthcareradius.in/25966-safe-opd-management, accessed on 20 September 2020.

https://hospitality.economictimes.indiatimes.com/news/hotels/people-first-initiative-by-itc-hotels-focus-on-work-force/75162766, accessed on 22 September 2020.

www.humanresourcesonline.net/work-from-home-scenario-in-times-of-covid-shrikant-lonikar-chro-pernod-ricard-india /, accessed on 25 October 2020.

https://indianexpress.com/article/trending/trending-in-india/tata-group-opens-taj-hotels-to-doctors-and-nurses-on-covid-19-duty-6347094/, accessed on 23 September 2020.

www.luminousindia.com/about-us, accessed on 14 September 2020.

www.microsoft.com/en-us/microsoft-365/blog/2020/04/30/2-years-digital-transformation-2-months/, accessed on 25 September 2020.

www.itchotels.in/, accessed on 22 September 2020.

www.itchotels.in/content/dam/projects/hotelswebsite/itc-hotels/WeAssure, accessed on 22 September 2020.

www.pernod-ricard.com/en, accessed on 22 September 2020.

www.retaildetail.eu/en/news/food/aldi-employ-redundant-mcdonald%E2%80%99s-staff, accessed on 22 September 2020.

www.pwc.in/assets/pdfs/future-of-india/future-of-india-the-winning-leap.pdf, accessed on 10 October 2020.

www.statista.com/statistics/271329/distribution-of-gross-domestic-product-gdp-across-economic-sectors-in-india/, accessed on 29 September 2020.

8 Government Policies During Pandemic

Indonesian vs Sri Lankan Perspective

Hotniar Siringoringo and Ravindra Hewa Kuruppuge

Introduction

The WHO declared the COVID-19 virus a pandemic on 11 March 2020, as it had been transmitted in 114 countries. Today, no one country in the world is free from the COVID-19 pandemic. Different countries interpreted the COVID-19 threat in different ways. In addition to the China government, many countries followed the instruction of WHO to implement the lockdown (Kashyap & Raghuvanshi, 2020) such as Bangladesh (Haque, 2020), South Africa (de Villiers, 2020), India (Kumar et al., 2020), Spain, Iran, Italy (de Villiers, 2020), Denmark, Israel, Germany and the United States (de Villiers, 2020), etc. Contrarily, a few countries chose to implement another policy, such as Indonesia.

According to Argento et al. (2020), Finland and Norway seem to take the COVID-19 pandemic as a war, while Sweden considered it as an exceptionally difficult flu. The lockdown policy was meant to close the border, whether it is city lockdown or country lockdown. No entry or exit to or from the city or country. No matter lockdown or not lockdown policy, people's mobility was restricted. Schools and universities were closed and online learning was implemented. Stores and shopping malls were closed. People gathering for all purposes were forbidden. Business is not running as usual. Firing occurs, a cut of salary was taken by a few companies, etc.

No matter the policy implemented, the COVID-19 spread was getting wider. On the other hand, the policy implemented and the pandemic caused a significant impact on economies over the world (Baker et al., 2020; de Villiers et al., 2020; MacIntyre, 2020; Shigemura et al., 2020). Due to the COVID-19 pandemic, the South African government according to de Villiers et al. (2020) has had to increase its borrowings. Meanwhile, the future tax take is forecast to be significantly reduced. Increasing borrowing and a decrease in national revenue will lead to severely constrained public expenditure for many years to come.

Indonesia and Sri Lanka are different in terms of many aspects such as geography, population number and culture, including approaches in

DOI: 10.4324/9781003125648-8

preventing the spread of COVID-19 and the impact of policy implemented on the economy and business activities, etc. Thus, it is interesting to discuss the policy chosen by both governments in combatting COVID-19, the impact of the policy implemented toward the nation's economy and business activities, and the economic policy that was undertaken to stretch the economy. Thus, the next section addresses matters related to the government policies related to economy and business during the pandemic from Indonesian and Sri Lankan perspectives.

Indonesian Perspective

DKI Jakarta is the capital of Indonesia and the most populous city. There are 16,704 citizens for every 1 km^2. DKI Jakarta is the most infected since the first transmission in Indonesia. DKI Jakarta is a reflection of various policies and their impacts on Indonesia. In this respect, we discuss DKI Jakarta exclusively in some parts of this section.

The Policies Implemented to Combat the COVID-19 Pandemic

The pandemic affected a large population (at the beginning, not all provinces in Indonesia), caused very high economic cost, extreme uncertainty, and critical communication problems (Boin and Lagadec, 2000), and directed the government to respond with four political-administrative approaches (Ansell et al., 2010), i.e. coping with uncertainty, providing surge capacity, organizing a response and communicating with the public. The first action taken by the government was the establishment of the National Task Force, called "Satgas Covid-19". On 13 March 2019, President Joko Widodo issued Presidential Decree number 7 the Year 2020 related to "Satgas Covid-19" for the acceleration of COVID-19 handling in Indonesia, which was led by Doni Monardo.

Doni Monardo is Head of the National Disaster Management Authority. Every day the public relations of the "Satgas Covid-19" reported the conditions through national television. The reportage was not only about the COVID-19 statistics in Indonesia (nationally and locally), but also advice and directions to always maintain cleanliness (wash hands with soap and water flow, use a hand sanitizer if necessary), do not leave the house unless it is urgent (always use a mask and bring a hand sanitizer when leaving the house), do not make or approach a crowd, no gathering (even if it's family), and so on. The government actively promotes social and physical distancing.

As the number of infected people increased sharply, the President of Indonesia on 13 March 2020 issued Presidential Decree number 12 the Year 2020 that sets out COVID-19 as a national disaster. With this decree, the local and central government collaborates tightly in overcoming the pandemic. This decree was followed by the government and all the ministry's regulations.

The government of Indonesia did not follow other countries in implementing lockdown. But the local government implemented social restrictions on a large scale, called "PSBB". The first local government that implemented PSBB was DKI Jakarta on 10 April 2020, then followed by other local governments. Up to 18 April 2020, two provincial governments (DKI Jakarta and West Sumatera) and 16 districts and cities implemented PSBB. The implementation of PSBB was regulated in government regulation number 21 the Year 2020. To be able to implement PSBB, the local government must get approval from the Ministry of Health.

Every cycle of the PSBB is two weeks. During the "PSBB", all shopping malls, offices, schools, universities and others were closed except food and beverage, pharmacy and similar industries. Also allowed to be operated during the PSBB is the distribution of basic needs. These restrictions are regulated by the respective local governments. In Jakarta, the Governor issued Regulation number 33/2020 concerning the Implementation of PSBB. All outside activities are prohibited except 11 sectors that are considered very important to support citizen life. The 11 sectors are health, foodstuffs, energy, communication and information technology, finance, logistics, hospitality, construction, public, and industry, which are designated as national vital objects, and daily necessities.

Responding to the implementation of PSBB, The Ministry of Transportation confirmed the flight closure policy applied in the area implementing PSBB or the red zone for the spread of the coronavirus. This closure will run from 24 April to 31 May 2020, for commercial and charter flights during the prohibition period for going home. Although The Ministry of Transportation at the beginning confirmed that the flight closure policy had no impact on international flights to and from Indonesia, practically there are no commercial flights due to restrictions from other countries. Finally, The Ministry of Transportation announced the closure policy of international flights since 24 April. Although a few countries are already open for tourists, the Indonesian government is still reviewing the opening of commercial international flights. But for pilgrim traveling, the first group of umrah departed Indonesia from Soekarno-Hatta airport on 1 November 2020.

The most suffering of this pandemic is in DKI Jakarta, so thus it has the longest of PSBB implementation among provinces, districts, and cities which implemented it. The first PSBB implementation was 10 April–4 June 2020. In line with the president's announcement to enter the new normal in June 2020, the local government of DKI Jakarta announced the new normal phase. Offices open, shopping malls open, and other economic activities are also open, but with new rituals: always use a mask, check body temperature, always wash hands, and avoid crowds. But because the number of infected people increased, on 14 September 2020 PSBB was again implemented in Province DKI Jakarta up to 11October 2020.

The Impact of the Policies on the Nation's Economy

This pandemic along with the policy applied influences the economy. Firing occurs everywhere. There are more and more poor people due to firing or business bankruptcy. Companies reduce production or even stop the business due to demand decreasing, supply chain disruption, etc. Due to travel restrictions globally, procurement and transportation of raw material are hampered. Following this, the distribution of the final product is also obstructed due to travel restrictions.

The tourism business suffers a lot because traveling is restricted. Domestic and international travel has been restricted only for very essential matters. The United Nations World Tourism Organization (UNWTO) reported that the 100% travel restrictions on global destinations in 2020 had the hardest hit on the tourism industry. Aside from the travel restriction, public places and tourist destinations are also closed to visitors. This situation has forced the tourism business (all related business to tourism) to close temporarily or indefinitely.

Only one month after the announcement of the first infected, on 7 April 2020, The Ministry of Labor announced that 39,977 companies in the formal sector were laying off their workers, in total 1,010,579 (Rizal, 2020). Almost two months later, on 27 May 2020, data from The Ministry of Labor show the total laying off workers reached 1,792,108 (Rahmadi, 2021).

Thus, the government must support them. The government needs urgently a big budget not only to support the citizen's economy but also to handle the pandemic. At the beginning of the pandemic, in March 2020, President Joko Widodo announced nine policies (Ihsanuddin, 2020) to maintain national economic growth. Four of these policies are discussed here, like those related to overcoming the impact of the pandemic on the citizen economy. First, the president ordered all ministers, regional governors and mayors to cut spending plans that are not priority expenditures, such as official travel expenses, regular yearly expenditure, etc.

The second policy was outlined in Presidential Instruction (Inpres) Number 4 of 2020, refocusing activities, budget reallocation, and procurement of goods and services in the context of the acceleration of handling coronavirus disease 2019. The third policy was the president's order to all the ministries and regional government to guarantee the availability of basic commodities, followed by ensuring that the purchasing power of the people, especially the lower classes, is maintained.

The fourth policy is social security, which is related to the basic food card program for the needy during a sixth month period. Citizens categorized below the poverty line received this card. This program was implemented in stages from April along with other policies. To run this program, the government has budgeted IDR 4.56 trillion. This budget was also used to support the hospitals and build new systems to treat infected people and handle the dead ones.

The impact on the economy is depicted in national economic growth. During the PSBB, although it was not locked down, economic activities greatly decreased, and thus economic growth. According to BPS (2020a), the economic growth in the first quarter of 2020 was 2.97%, and experienced a contraction –2.41% compared to the last quarter of 2019 and –1.26% compared to the first quarter of 2019. It is worse in the second quarter of 2020 (BPS, 2020b). It decreased by –5.32% compared to the second quarter of the year 2019. The contraction is 4.19% compared to the first quarter year of 2020. This situation makes sense because government spending increases at a time when revenue decreases.

In June 2020, the president announced the beginning of the new normal phase nationally. This policy was taken due to the economic impact of the PSBB. After the new normal phase, starting from June as the president announces it, the economic activities started again. The result of this new normal is the increase in economic growth. The economic growth increases in the third quarter of 2020 compared to the second quarter of 2020 as much as 5.5% (BPS, 2020c), but still decreased compared to the third quarter of the year 2019, i.e. –3.49%. On another side, the spread of the COVID-19 is increasingly widespread. The number of infected and dead people increased day by day.

Economic Policies

The pandemic along with the policies taken to combat it affects the economy. The government immediately formulated policies to reduce the negative effect on the economy. As mentioned above, the President issued nine policies to overcome the economic impact of the pandemic (Ihsanuddin, 2020). We have discussed four policies above as those implemented to overcome the impact of the pandemic on the citizen's economy. The five other policies discussed here as are intended to revive the nation's economy.

The fifth policy is related to labor-intensive industries. The president ordered respective ministries (such as the Ministry of Public Works and Public Housing, the Ministry of Transportation, the Ministry of Agriculture and the Ministry of Maritime Affairs and Fisheries) and regional governments to reproduce and multiply labor-intensive industries with daily payment. Along with that, the President ordered the respective ministries and regional governments to implement high adherence to health protocols such as social and physical distancing, wearing masks, cleaning hands with soap, etc. This policy is risky but it is very much needed to cope with the decrease of economic growth.

Sixth, the president has accelerated the implementation of pre-employment cards to anticipate workers who are laid off, workers who lose their income, and micro-entrepreneurs who lose their market and turnover. It is hoped that the affected communities can improve their competence and quality through pre-employment card training. This year, the government has allocated IDR 10 trillion for pre-work cards.

The government is also aware of the burden of income tax imposed on workers in processing industries. Therefore, the government launched the seventh policy, i.e. the government takes over the payment of employees' income tax in manufacturing industries. The allocation for this policy is IDR 8.6 trillion. The eighth policy is intended to support micro, small and medium enterprises (MSMEs). These MSMEs play a very vital role in the Indonesian economy (Subagyo et al., 2020). In this policy, the Financial Services Authority (OJK) provides credit relaxation to MSMEs with assets under IDR 10 billion. The relaxation was in the form of lowering interest rates and postponing installment costs for a year, from both the banking and non-bank financial industries. In addition, a year-long installment suspension also applies to motorcycle taxis, taxi drivers and fishermen who have vehicle installments.

In order to stimulate the real estate business, the President issued the ninth policy. With this policy, low-income people who carry subsidized housing loans will be given a stimulus. The government provides an interest subsidy up to a 10-year installment period. If the interest rate is above 5%, the government will pay the difference. In addition, there is also assistance in providing down-payment subsidies for subsidized housing loans, with a prepared budget allocation of IDR 1.5 trillion.

The pandemic seems likely to continue to the year 2021. The government should get ready for that. The government of Indonesia announced four economic policy plans to be implemented in the 2021 (Santoso, 2020). Those four economic policies are accelerating national economic recovery due to the COVID-19 pandemic; encouraging structural reforms to increase productivity, innovation and economic competitiveness; accelerating the economic transformation to the digital era, and utilization and anticipation of demographic changes. The president also announced the next year's deficit is set up at 5.5% of gross domestic product (GDP), due to a relaxation policy of more than 3% of GDP, parallel with maintaining prudence, credibility and fiscal sustainability. The government projected national revenue is IDR 1,776.4 trillion and spending is Rp. 2,747.5 trillion.

Sri Lankan Perspective

Sri Lanka is a small island country which is located on the southern coast of India in South Asia. The Democratic Socialist Republic of Sri Lanka is considered as a lower-middle-income country consisting of a population of 21.8 million with US$ 3852 GDP per capita in 2019 (World Bank, 2020).

Sri Lanka has implemented three types of policies to address the COVID-19 outbreak and its impact. Those policies were mainly based on border control and health sector policies, fiscal measures, and monetary and financial sector measures with capital flow management. The border control and health sector policies have been implemented to limit the spread of the pandemic, while the other policies address the government and the Central Bank to provide relief to businesses and individuals affected by the pandemic.

The Policy Chosen by the Sri Lankan Government in Combatting COVID-19

In Sri Lanka, the first COVID-19 case was reported in January 2020; this was a female Chinese tourist who has fully recovered and returned to China (KPMG, 2020). The first wave in Sri Lanka began with a Sri Lankan tour guide reporting COVID-19 positive on 10 March 2020 and cases have increased rapidly thereafter till today. Sri Lanka's second wave of the COVID-19 outbreak caused severe damage compared to the first wave, with the highest number of cases reported in the Western Province (the province where the capital city is located) in the country. The second wave of the outbreak mainly consisted of the two clusters of the garment factory and a fish market in Colombo (The capital city) in October 2020. When the second wave was reported in Sri Lanka in October, there were only 3,396 cases with just 13 deaths reported in relation to COVID (the first wave). But, with the second wave of COVID-19, Sri Lanka faced a greater difficulty of moving the country (WHO, 2020).

Considering the prevailing situation of the country, the Sri Lanka government implemented the following to overcome the problems in the country. In relation to the border control and health sector policies:

1 The government of Sri Lanka has implemented a presidential task force to fight against the pandemic which impacted vulnerably on the whole society and economy. As the first step of the task force, they have mainly emphasized the disastrous consequences of behaving in irresponsible manners and the importance of the cooperation of everyone in the quarantine process with the aim of protecting all the nation of Sri Lanka.
2 The Disaster Management Centre has been formed in Sri Lanka for handling emergency situations. Thus, this Centre uses government funds and resources to help people in disasters. Although the Sri Lankan government has announced the COVID-19 pandemic as an emergency period in the country, the funds in the Disaster Management Centre have been used to ensure the well-being of individuals. Further, the Presidential Task Force announced a hotline (117) for the public to obtain or notify any details regarding the Coronavirus situation.
3 The director-general of health services and the Defense Ministry contributed to the COVID-19 prevention body. At the start of the

first wave of COVID-19, the decisions were carried out by the presidential task force. The most prominent decisions were in establishing and maintaining a quarantine center in Sri Lanka for locals and foreigners.

4 Sri Lanka as a small island has taken several initial steps such as to disinfect public transport, studies of China's success, directives to minimize public gathering, experimenting with the possibility of continuing services provided by the school and university studies through the Internet for educational and service purposes, guiding people on the quarantine process, social distancing and the terminal at the airport and working from home. It also modified 12 major government hospitals to treat suspected or confirmed cases of COVID-19. Several measures have been taken to avoid large gatherings such as cinema halls, sports events, international conferences, and religious gatherings, and all the education centers from pre-schools to universities have been closed, all the inbound passenger flights to the country are suspended and an island-wide curfew has been imposed.

The Impact of the Policies on the Nation's Economy

With the spreading of the COVID-19 outbreak within Sri Lanka, the government has implemented public health measures, movement restrictions, nationwide curfews, travel bans and border closures to tackle the pandemic, which has a huge impact on people's lives, families and communities and national economies and global trade (Weekly Report of Health Ministry, 2020). However, these policies may not ensure the economic benefits of the country with the availability of the excess cash in the system. The reduction of interest rates will make it difficult to attract foreign investors to the bond market, which will generate unnecessary complications as well.

As per the policies implemented by the Sri Lankan government, many of the pros and cons have been identified in society as well as in the economy. The main sectors which have suffered a bad influence with the policy implemented were tourism, environment, education, entertainment and the economy in general. The COVID-19 outbreak severely affected the tourism sector in Sri Lanka as a result of the policies such as travel bans, airport closures, restrictions on travel and transport, and curfews.

The Sri Lankan economy is composed of the main sectors of agriculture, industry and services. All the sectors show growth during 2019 with the growth of agriculture sector at 0.6 percent, industry sector at 2.7% and the services sector at 2.3% in 2019 with higher growth in the wholesale and retail trade, telecommunication and IT (Annual Report of Central Bank of Sri Lanka, 2019). The Sri Lankan economy has a large portion of trade, investments, agreements and tourism with China. China's decline with the COVID-19 outbreak has significantly impacted

Sri Lanka's economy as well. Thus, construction and trade have declined in the Sri Lankan economy.

The sectors like apparel, manufacturing, agriculture, tourism and the retail and consumer sector, with small and medium-scale enterprises, have been worst affected by the COVID-19 outbreak (KPMG, 2020). Also, individuals in Sri Lanka have become jobless. The impact of COVID-19 on economies is a challenge for every economy in the world. Simply, there are too many responses to face the COVID-19 outbreak with the rate of infection and immunity, policy response, demand-supply dynamics and the reaction of firms.

As a result of the government's order to close schools, private tuition classes, and tutorials and universities, the Sri Lankan education system moved to another chapter with more concern for the Internet-based education, which has both positive and negative results for students. The ban imposed on public gatherings, film theaters, national parks, zoological gardens and botanical gardens in Sri Lanka has triggered a lay-off of workers and had a high impact on the income of the country.

The Sri Lankan domestic rupee value has been depreciated against the US dollar as a result of severe challenges faced by the country. Also, several companies in Sri Lanka such as John Keells Holdings, Sri Lankan Airlines and Brandix Lanka have reduced their employees' salaries by 5% to 35%. There was a fall in investor sentiment globally, which will be more challenging to Sri Lanka with a negative impact on attracting foreign direct investments during 2020.

The closing down of airports, travel bans and the quick spread of the coronavirus across the world has a high impact on both domestic and foreign demand by virtually becoming zero. The recovery of the sector is dependent on how fast the COVID-19 outbreak will be controlled and reopening borders internally and externally. The United Nations World Tourism Organization (UNWTO) reported that the 100% travel restrictions on global destinations in 2020 had the hardest hit on the tourism industry, compared to the other trades. The tourism sector has collapsed during the pandemic situation due to policies such as social distancing, the closing of airports, curfews and lockdown within the country. The tourism industry is composed of many other economic sectors such as hotels, community-level operations, education, financial, agriculture, travel and transportation, construction, real estate, retail, etc.

The tourism sector in Sri Lanka played a key role within the country as the country's economy heavily depends on the service sector, and the GDP contribution of the tourism sector in 2019 was 12.5%. As the tourism sector is one of the prominent sectors in Sri Lanka, it is more significant to have proper policies and procedures to achieve the growth of the tourism sector in Sri Lanka. According to The Sri Lanka Tourist Development Authority (SLTDA) data, tourist arrivals fell by over 30% during the first quarter of 2020, compared to 2019, as Sri Lanka closed its borders for non-essential passenger travel and domestic travel restrictions, which still have an impact on the survival of the tourism industry (Weekly Report of Health Ministry, 2020).

Apparel and textile are one of the highest contributors to Sri Lankan export revenues. As shown in the PMI data as of February 2020 in CBSL, "New Orders" and "Employment" have reduced drastically within the manufacturing of textile and wearing apparel sector with the decrease in global demand. The disruptions in the raw material imports with supply-side disruptions had an impact on the industry in an unfavorable manner. Thus, the industries showed a decline in manufacturing in the short term (PWC Global Survey, 2020).

The apparel and textile industry in Sri Lanka has the highest GDP contribution of the industry sector in the Sri Lankan economy. The raw materials have been delayed as a result of the pandemic situation around the globe. Further, China is the largest supplier of raw materials for Sri Lanka. Many of the European and US buyers canceled orders due to the decrease in demand for textiles. The garment factories have been negatively impacted by the pandemic situation due to the lack of supply, labor shortages, lack of demand and temporary closures. It is more important for the apparel industry to be secure within the pandemic situation, which has a major and severe impact on factories.

All the above conditions affect the Sri Lankan economic growth. The economic growth in the first quarter declined sharply to negative (–1.8%) according to CBSL. In the second quarter, the economic growth was still negative (i.e. –1.7%). However, in the third quarter, Sri Lanka has enjoyed positive growth (i.e. 1.5%).

The banking sector is the backbone of any economy and the downturn of the economy will directly affect the banks. The profitability and asset quality of the banks become more challenging with the operating conditions and the performance of the banking sector. A six-month debt moratorium and other financial measures imposed by the Sri Lankan government impact positively towards the individuals and businesses, but for the banks the non-performing loans will be increasing in 2020. As per the Fitch Ratings, the outlook for Sri Lanka's banking sector is negative for 2020 (PWC Global Survey, 2020).

However, with the loan and debt moratorium measures and other measures imposed on the banking sector, it is expected that the profitability of the banking sector will further decline (Faculty of Humanities and Social Sciences, 2020). The main parties who worked for the betterment of society were the public health doctors and inspectors. The general public violate the rules like maintaining proper hygiene methods and self-quarantine methods to safeguard themselves from the disease as it takes some time for the public to get in line with the situation.

As a result, the Sri Lankan economy experienced an unprecedented economic breakdown and unemployment within a short period of time and also the collapse of market share during the COVID-19 outbreak. The number of poor people increased. The government needs to issue a policy to handle this situation. Several extraordinary regulatory measures have been introduced to provide some relief to the businesses which are affected by the COVID-19 crisis by the Monetary Board of the Central Bank of Sri Lanka (CBSL, 2020). Low-income people and the most vulnerably affected persons have been offered a material benefit of the Rs. 5,000 by the Sri Lankan government in the second week of April. This allowance has also been offered to the 119,300 disabled persons, 160,675 farmers who are registered under the Farmers' Insurance Scheme, 39,170 kidney patients, 416,764 senior citizens and 2,398,994 Samurdhi recipients.

Further, handling the impact of policies on the citizen economy, in relation to financial sector measures with capital flow management, The Presidential Office of Sri Lanka announced the following steps:

1. To extend all the fund settlements on the income and VAT taxes, renewal fees of the driving license, water and electricity bill payments, assessment taxes, and bank cheques valued less than Rs. 15,000, and repayment of all credit cards below the limit Rs. 50,000 until 30 April, 2020.
2. Offer a moratorium for the period of six months on the leasing loan installments (three-wheelers), and the public and private sector employees' loans.
3. Loans with a value less than Rs.1 million obtained on personal banks and leasing companies have been given a three-month moratorium.
4. To offer an allowance of Rs. 20,000 on the month of March to the graduates selected for employment.
5. To increase the Agrahara Insurance benefits by 100% for all the employees who are engaged in controlling the spread of the pandemic situation in the country.
6. The interest rate of credit cards of value up to Rs. 50,000.00 which has been spent locally has been reduced up to 15% and the minimum monthly charge of the credit cards has decreased by 50%.
7. Offer full-time banking services to the customers when the curfew of the country has been removed.
8. To release food and essentials such as fertilizers, medicines and fuel by the Sri Lanka Ports Customs without any disruptions.
9. Samurdhi Bank Associations are advised to offer interest-free loans of Rs. 10,000 to Samurdhi recipients and Samurdhi cardholders.
10. Samurdhi Authority advised to offer nutritional food items such as rice, lentils, onions and also food cards to low-income families immediately.
11. A special bank account has been opened at the Bank of Ceylon for collecting funds with the aim of preventing the spread of the COVID-19 pandemic within the country and also for providing the necessary health and relief facilities for the public. Thus, the President's Fund has deposited Rs. 100 million.

Economic Policies

The governments around the world have imposed health measures to save people in their countries. They have imposed travel restrictions, social distancing, travel bans, curfews, closure of airports, etc. Despite those restrictions positively affecting public health, they have created an adverse impact on businesses communities and households. Where Sri Lanka is concerned, each and every sector, including travel and tourism, construction, banking and finance, was severely affected by the COVID-19 outbreak. Further, the pandemic has caused economic shocks in industries such as tourism, aviation, automotive, constructions, manufacturing including textiles and garments, and marginally affected sectors have been identified as agriculture, e-commerce, telecommunications, pharmaceuticals and medical service (Faculty of Humanities and Social Sciences, 2020).

As a result, the Sri Lankan economy experienced an unprecedented economic breakdown and unemployment within a short period of time and also the collapse of market share during the COVID-19 outbreak. Several extraordinary regulatory measures have been introduced to provide some relief to the businesses which are affected by the COVID-19 crisis by the Monetary Board of the Central Bank of Sri Lanka (Quarterly Report of Central Bank of Sri Lanka, 2020). Further, the Sri Lankan government has taken a number of policy responses and relief measures to keep the situation under control.

The CBSL has released a monetary policy review and it has decided to maintain policy interest rates to be secure from the halted stock market activities with the closing of the Colombo Stock Exchange with the pandemic situation in the country. Further, the Governor of CBSL requested the financial institutions face the challenges during the pandemic to build a strong economy within the country.

The Sri Lankan Government has introduced stimulus packages to prevent a financial crisis of SMEs, reduced the key policy interest rates and offered a debt moratorium on the repayment of loans, introduced several measures to ease the pressure on the exchange rate to counteract the financial markets; in addition government also provided working capital loan for COVID-19-hit businesses and individuals. A temporary deferment of amounts of money due to leases was also applied by the leasing firms. Moreover, a special relief fund was set up by the President in Sri Lanka to face the pandemic situation in 2020 (CBSL, 2020).
The President of Sri Lanka also issued the policy related to:

1 The tourism sector, garment sector, and SME sector in Sri Lanka have been given a six-month debt moratorium by the Central Bank of Sri Lanka.
2 Bank of Ceylon, People's Bank, National Savings Bank, Sri Lanka Insurance Cooperation, Employee Provident Fund and Employee's

Trust Fund have been invested in treasury bonds with the aim of stabilizing the money market at a 7% interest rate.

3 To remove the local taxes and the charges of Lanka Sathosa and Co-operative shops.

In relation to monetary measures, the Central Bank of Sri Lanka has reduced the key policy interest rates such as Standing Deposit Facility Rate (SDFR) and Standing Lending Facility Rate (SLFR), by 100 basis points across three cuts. The Statutory Reserve Ratio (SRR) on all rupee deposit liabilities of licensed commercial banks (LCBs) was reduced by 1.00 percentage point, which helps in injecting permanent liquidity of around Rs. 65 billion to the market. Across the financial sector, several measures have been implemented on businesses and individuals. The debt moratorium, investment-purpose loans and working capital loans at concessional rates have been announced for the tourism, plantation, IT and apparel sectors, related logistics providers, and small- and medium-scale enterprises.

Another key initiative for the businesses is the introduction of the "Saubagya Covid-19 Renaissance Facility", which provides working capital for adversely affected businesses to revive their activities. The New Comprehensive Rural Credit Scheme facility offers loans for farmers in Sri Lanka (CBSL, 2020). The government of Sri Lanka has announced several relief measures for businesses and individuals during March 2020 such as tax concessions, concessions for businesses engaged in the tourism, apparel and wholesale and retail trade sectors, the introduction of maximum retail prices for selected essential food items and certain medical items, and a cash grant of Rs. 5,000 payments for low-income and vulnerable families, and doubling the Agrahara insurance benefits for health, police and civil defense employees, and all government servants engaged in controlling the spread of the COVID-19 outbreak.

The government has implemented a relief package for the most vulnerable sectors in the economy via the COVID-19 pandemic. As stated by the Faculty of Humanities and Social Sciences (2020) monetary policies of Sri Lanka have been adjusted by the Central Bank as it is the main regulatory authority of the financial sector. The Central Bank of Sri Lanka (CBSL) has introduced an LKR 50 billion refinancing facility to help affected sectors of the economy, such as small and medium-term enterprises (SMEs), tourism, export-import-related businesses and self-employment. They offered a six-month debt moratorium and provisions for non-performing loans (NPLs) obtained by the individuals and businesses.

The Central Bank also further took actions to reduce the policy rates, allowing excess cash into the system. Further, the CBSL also introduced a new credit scheme on 16 June 2020 based on the provisions in Section 83 of the Monetary Law Act No. 58 of 1949. The President of Sri Lanka directed the Governor of Central Bank of Sri Lanka, the secretaries of the ministries, chief secretaries of provincial councils and the heads of the banks, financial institutions and leasing companies to offer relief packages with the following measures during the first wave of the COVID-19 (Presidential office, 2020).

The policies were implemented to mitigate the economic impacts on the nation's economy. The measures to reduce interest rates were aimed to enhance market liquidity and finance the government, which may support the economic activity in the context of a low-inflation environment. The CBSL provided reduced and concessional interest rates with the aim of ample liquidity. The Sri Lankan banking system had offered support to the individuals who are facing difficulties during the pandemic era by offering large liquidity injections to the economy.

These liquidity injections have been in the money market without absorption by the Central Bank. The lowest level of the policy interest rates and the Statutory Reserve Ratio has been seen in the country for the first time in Sri Lankan history. At the same time, the Bank rates also have been reduced to the lowest level. These lower interest rates reduce the burden on borrowers in the economy. The CBSL has provided the financing requirements of the government to overcome the financial barriers faced during stressful situations in the country with low revenue and increased expenditure.

They offer funds to the government to secure the payments for the population to provide health and public services efficiently. The CBSL has taken more risk with the situation and by timely intervention helped reverse the large depreciation observed until mid-April with the lockdown policy. It has helped to maintain the stable prices of essential domestic goods by maintaining exchange rates. With the decline of foreign exchange earnings, it has created an environment for domestic producers to develop with the benefit of low interest rates.

The CBSL took several measures to ensure a smooth flow of currency required by the economy during the lockdown which has allowed the general public to fulfill their currency needs through bank branches and ATMs. At the same time, the public has been offered several electronic modes of payments to enhance convenience in transactions. The CBSL has provided a series of extraordinary measures during the COVID-19 pandemic to support the economy. Thus, Sri Lanka was able to overcome the unprecedented difficulties during the pandemic with the support of all the stakeholders of the economy, such as the CBSL, government, financial institutions, businesses and the general public. Sri Lanka's economy was a success in the short term, as per the successful implementation of policies.

Conclusion

The COVID-19 pandemic has created the "new normal" situation in the world. Irrespective of the wealth, size and abilities of countries, almost all countries are suffering from the pandemic. However, the successes of measurements taken to combat the pandemic by diverse countries were not consistent with each other. Accordingly, this chapter is reserved to identify policy responses by both Indonesia and Sri Lanka towards preventing COVID-19. The overview more focuses on the policy chosen by those two governments in combatting COVID-19, the result of the policy implementation, and the impact on the nation's economy. The chapter has mainly used secondary data such as various reviews, journal articles and reports from WTCC, UNWTO, UNCTAD and the World Bank. Further, news articles and web pages also were reviewed for the purpose.

When Indonesian and Sri Lankan perspectives combatting against COVID-19 are taken into consideration, it is clear that diverse strategies are used in the case of health, economic and social aspects. Although the COVID-19 transmission in Sri Lanka is less than in Indonesia, the Sri Lanka government implemented lockdown, whilst Indonesia partly implemented lockdown. These different policies taken by both governments in combatting the transmission of COVID-19 impacted the economy differently.

Although both countries have suffered enough economically due to COVID-19, the economic growth of Sri Lanka is worse. The economic growth of both countries was decreased, but the decline in Sri Lanka was sharper. In the first quarter of 2020, the economic growth of Sri Lanka was –1.8% whilst Indonesia was yet positive, 2.97%. But in the second quarter, the economic growth of both countries was negative, –1.7% for Sri Lanka and –5.32% for Indonesia. In the third quarter, the economic growth of both countries inversely compared to the first quarter of 2020. Sri Lanka enjoyed positive growth while Indonesia still had negative growth. Sri Lanka experienced 1.5% growth and Indonesia experienced –3.49%.

Sri Lanka suffered harder than Indonesia economically in the first quarter because the Sri Lankan government implemented a lockdown policy following other countries globally since the first detected transmission in March 2020, while Indonesia has never implemented a lockdown, but the social restrictions on a large scale (PSBB) began in April 2020 in several cities. However, virus transmission in Indonesia has never been decreased or flat until today.

However, the researchers could provide an overview based on available information, that the pandemic has created a "new normal situation" enabling almost all countries in the globe to rise against COVID-19 with possible strategies. Even though Indonesia and Sri Lanka could not avoid the bad impact totally in their countries, good control has been created to protect the people and properties of each country. In this case, the role played by each government of these countries is remarkable.

References

Annual Report of Central Bank of Sri Lanka (2019). Colombo, Sri Lanka: Central Bank of Sri Lanka.

Ansell, C., Boin, A., & Keller, A. (2010). Managing transboundary crises: Identifying the building blocks of an effective response system. *Journal of Contingencies and Crisis Management, 18*(4), 195–207.

Argento, D., Karbøe, K., & Vakkuri, J. (2020). Constructing certainty through public budgeting: Budgetary responses to the COVID-19 pandemic in Finland, Norway and Sweden. *Journal of Public Budgeting, Accounting & Financial Management,* 32(5), 875–887.

Baker, S., Bloom, N., Davis, S.J., Kost, K., Sammon, M., & Viratyosin, T. (2020). The unprecedented stock market reaction to COVID-19. *Covid Economics: Vetted and Real-Time Papers, 1*(3).

Biro Pusat Statistik. (BPS, 2020a). [Online] Available at: Ekonomi Indonesia triwulan I 2020 tumbuh 2.97 persen. Retrieved from www.bps.go.id/website/materi_ind/materiBrsInd-20200505115439.pdf [accessed November 30, 2020].

Biro Pusat Statistik. (2020b). Available at: Ekonomi Indonesia triwulan II 2020 turun 5.32 persen. Retrieved from www.bps.go.id/website/materi_ind/materiBrsInd-20200805114633.pdf [accessed November 30, 2020].

Biro Pusat Statistik. (2020c). Available at: Ekonomi Indonesia triwulan III tumbuh 5.05 persen (q-o-q). Retrieved from www.bps.go.id/pressrelease/2020/11/05/1738/ekonomi-indonesia-triwulan-iii-2020-tumbuh-5-05-persen--q-to-q-.html [accessed November 30, 2020].

Boin, A., & Lagadec, P. (2000). Preparing for the future: critical challenges in crisis management. *Journal of Contingencies and Crisis Management, 8*(4), 185–191.

CBSL Quarterly Report. (2020). Colombo, Sri Lanka: Central Bank of Sri Lanka.

de Villiers, C., Cerbone, D., & Van Zijl, W. (2020). The South African government's response to COVID-19. *Journal of Public Budgeting, Accounting & Financial Management.* DOI 10.1108/JPBAFM-07-2020-0120. Early cite.

Faculty of Humanities and Social Sciences. (2020). *COVID-19: The Socio-Economic Impact on Sri Lanka. Part-1: The Economic Impact of the COVID-19 Pandemic in Sri Lanka.* Matara: University of Ruhuna.

Haque, A. (2020). The COVID-19 pandemic and the public health challenges in Bangladesh: a commentary. *Journal of Health Research, 34*(6), 563–567.

Kashyap, A., & Raghuvanshi, J. (2020). A preliminary study on exploring the critical success factors for developing COVID-19 preventive strategy with an economy centric approach. *Management Research: Journal of the Iberoamerican Academy of Management, 18*(4), 357–377.

KPMG. (2020). [Online] Impact on COVID-19 on the Sri Lankan Economy. Available at: https://home.kpmg/lk/en/home/insights/2020/04/impact-on-COVID 19on the sri lankan-economy.html [accessed November 20, 2020].

Kumar, M.S., Maheshwari, V., Prabhu, J., Prasanna, M., Jayalakshmi, P., Suganya, P. Benjula Anbu Malar, M.B., & Jothikumar, R. (2020). Social economic impact of COVID-19 outbreak in India. *International Journal of Pervasive Computing and Communications. 16*(4), 309–319. DOI: 10.1108/IJPCC-06-2020-0053.

MacIntyre, C.R. (2020). On a knife's edge of a COVID-19 pandemic: is containment still possible? *Public Health Research and Practice, 30*(1), 3012000. DOI: 10.17061/phrp3012000.

Presidential office Statement. (2020). [Online] Available at: News Archive, Colombo, Sri Lanka. Retrieved from www.president.gov.lk/possibility-of-releasing-prisonerscharged-with-minor-offences-explored [accessed April 30, 2020].

PWC Global Survey on COVID-19. (2020). PricewaterhouseCoopers (Private) Limited, Liability Company incorporated in Sri Lanka, Sri Lanka.

Rahmadi, I.F. (2021). Teachers' technology integration and distance learning adoption amidst the Covid-19 crisis: A reflection for the optimistic future. *Turkish Online Journal of Distance Education, 22*(2), article 2.

Rizal, J.G. (2020). [Online] Available at: Pandemi Covid-19, Apa Saja Dampak pada Sektor Ketenagakerjaan Indonesia? Retrieved from www.kompas.com/tren/read/2020/08/11/102500165/pandemi-covid-19-apa-saja-dampak-pada-sektor-ketenagakerjaan-indonesia-?page=all [accessed December 5, 2020].

Santoso, Y.I. (2020). [Online] Available at: Jokowi sampaikan 4 rancangan kebijakan ekonomi Indonesia pada APBN 2021. Retrieved from https://nasional.kontan.co.id/news/jokowi-sampaikan-4-rancangan-kebijakan-ekonomi-indonesia-pada-apbn-2021 [accessed December 10, 2020].

Shigemura, J., Ursano, R.J., Morganstein, J.C., Kurosawa, M., & Benedek, D.M. (2020). Public responses to the novel 2019 coronavirus (2019-nCoV) in Japan: Mental health consequences and target populations. *Psychiatry and Clinical Neuroscience, 74*(4), 281–282.

Subagyo, Kumar, V., & Ernestivita, G. (2020). Entrepreneurial parameters and performance of MSMEs in East Java Province of Indonesia. *International Journal of Business Innovation and Research (IJBIR), 23*(2), 267–282.

Weekly Report of Health Ministry. (2020). Colombo, Sri Lanka: Epidemiology Unit in Ministry of Health (MOH).

World Bank. (2020). [Online] Available at: World Bank Predicts Sharpest Decline of Remittances in Recent History. Retrieved from www.worldbank.org/en/news/pressrelease/2020/04/22/world-bank-predicts-sharpest-decline-of-remittances-in-recent-history [accessed December 14, 2020].

World Health Organization (WHO). (2020). [Online] Available at: Coronavirus (COVID-19). Retrieved from https://covid19.who.int [accessed November 25, 2020].

9 Bailouts and Government Support During Pandemic

Mohit Rewari and Vibha Kalra

Introduction

The year 2020 had its own share in disturbing events like the US-China trade war, the US presidential elections and Brexit. All this slowed down the economic growth globally, therefore the IMF projected a modest global growth of 3.4%.[1] As soon as we entered the year 2020, COVID-19, the great pandemic, brought with it fear, uncertainty and rapid erosion of wealth, which changed the outlook abruptly and further pulled back expected global growth numbers. The IMF downgraded its growth estimations for the global economy to –4.4% (October 2020)[2] from 3.4% (January 2020).[3] The impact was brutal and pervasive. OECD (The Organization for Economic Co-operation and Development)[4] also revised its global economic outlook estimates for the year 2020 from 2.9% to 2.4% with a caveat that it may go down further if the pandemic is not tackled efficiently.[5] The tourism industry was affected a lot, as there was a stop on tourists, who usually spend billions annually. There was massive cancellation of flights, hotel bookings and local and international events.[6] Global supply chains were impacted as the world's largest manufacturer and exporter China lost the status (Ozili & Arun, 2020). Its impact on the global food system has rendered the poorest of the poor as most vulnerable.[7] As at 16 January 2021, the total global cases of COVID-19 were 94.34 million out of which 67.37 million have recovered and been discharged and around 2.01 million lost their lives to the pandemic.[8] The number of deaths is concentrated in a few countries.

The international manufacturing hub (China) is being accused of having spread this virus.[9] A series of lockdowns, mandating social isolation and restrictions, significantly disrupted businesses and communities across the globe (Ozili & Arun, 2020). It brought the global economy to a halt, pushing the world into recession.[10] The serious long-term financial ramifications of this black swan event have generated an urgent need for states' interventions, to recapitalize their economic systems. All governments almost immediately sprang into action and ordered stay-at-home policies and closed all facilities except essential items. Different countries adopted varied degrees of lockdown. The crisis has forced

DOI: 10.4324/9781003125648-9

governments across the globe to follow austerity measures. Governments in different parts of the world are charting out plans for economic recovery. Government intervention is sought at this critical juncture by almost all the economies of the world. To mitigate the impact of this pandemic, policy makers of almost all countries relied on scaling up the government spending with huge financial stimuli. Bailout and support packages were announced to keep the system afloat across different parts of the world, thus it became an issue of concern for economies big and small internationally. The primary reason for a government's support at times of crisis is the government's ownership of resources and ability to mobilize them. The volume and instruments of this support were different for different economies. Some economies substantially increased investment in infrastructure and public health to combat the crisis. Special assistance has been provided to industry with the intention of boosting employment opportunities and demand for economic revival. Some economies looked upon it as the only way to stay afloat and others took it as an opportunity to implement bold and forward-looking reforms, to build a more sustainable, green and resilient economy. Different economies have different thrust areas and have designed and implemented their economic support accordingly. Economies have resorted to various initiatives like tax rebates, loan moratoriums, liquidity support, equity infusion, direct benefit transfers etc.

The UK government introduced the corona-virus Job Retention Scheme (JRS), a package of policy measures.

> This allows companies to reduce the hours of workers to zero without laying them off, removing the costs of searching and re-hiring workers later on. It is estimated that the scheme will cost $60 billion for the 8-months duration of the scheme.
>
> (Brewer & Tasseva, 2020)

The impact of these initiatives is to be seen. This economic restructuring and lessons learnt during this pandemic would enable economies to stand strong against any financial crises in future. The subject of the current study is bailout packages announced in four severely affected economies from COVID-19: the United States, India, France and Germany, shortlisted from the top ten economies of the world. One-fourth of the world's population live in these countries, which have been forced to be locked inside due to the pandemic and economic activities have been closed. There is a need to focus research and action on building sustainability and strengthened resilience into the future recovery along with mitigating the impact of the pandemic.

The Twin Crises

The magnitude of economic distress caused by the pandemic can be assessed from the fact that right at its onset "more people lost their jobs over four weeks in March and April than did so during the entire 2008–09 financial crisis".[11] According to Kimberly Chriscaden, Communications Officer, World Health Organization, "tens of millions of people are at risk of falling into extreme poverty". More than 3 billion people are at risk of losing their livelihoods where for most of them loss of jobs also means loss of food. The food security of all these people is under threat.[12] The global supply chain has been impacted by the restrictions imposed on travel: border closures, factory closures and slowdown in the services industries. Stay-at-home enforcements and massive layoffs have had a terrible impact on demand. Slowdown in demand and supply together has created "an uncertainty affecting both consumer and producer confidence negatively" (Ahmed, 2020).

It actually blew the world economy mainly due to two reasons which unfortunately attacked the health and economy simultaneously. First, the only way to contain the virus was social distancing, which implied shutdown of all economic units except for those engaged in essential services. Second, the incredible rate at which the virus spread caused uncertainty that led to "flight to safety in consumption and investment among consumers, investors and international trade partners" (Ozili & Arun, 2020).

Human history has been a testimony to a number of significant crises, some of them being economic in nature and some relating to health, among others. COVID-19 is essentially a health crisis that became an economic crisis. However, it was the quick transformation of health crises into economic crises that made COVID-19 so dreadful. The twin health and economic crises exposed entities that were economically and politically sensitive to extreme liquidity needs and myriad market conditions (Farhi & Tairole, 2012). A virus that apparently was unbelievable at first changed our life like never before. The pandemic put forth unimaginable challenges for the world and is yet far from over.

Role of Government in Crises

There is a need for ample resources and coordination among economic entities to pull an economy out of recession. "Given the scale, scope, and complexities of crises as well as the adverse impact on socially vulnerable populations, it is unsurprising that citizens, media, and policymakers alike turn to governments to take a leading role in response, recovery, and even mitigation and preparedness of efforts" to combat crisis (Haeffele & Storr, 2020). Crises cause loss of infrastructure, displacement of population, shortage of essential items etc., which leads to uncertainty about the future of crisis survivors. After a crisis there is a need to rebuild, so that the economy can be taken back to at least the previous normal. Rebuilding can be approached in two ways. It could be done by the people who suffered the loss, known as the bottom-up approach. Such approaches are effective at smaller scales but when the scale is large and destruction is widespread the citizens often turn to government to take charge. This is called the top-down approach. Business draws resources from society and produces goods and services for society. They are mutually interdependent and in times of crisis the government has to come to their rescue (Sheth, 2020). Because the government has the resources, ability to mobilize them and coordinate efforts, it makes sense for the government to lead the campaign to recovery, but government intervention has its own set of limitations. The government takes time to assess the need, plan to use resources to satisfy that need and execute the plans for recovery. This invites criticism of the government and delays the recovery process (Haeffele & Storr, 2020).

The pandemic has impacted all spheres of life across the globe. Governments all around faced the tough challenge of maintaining stability of the economy and ensuring health and safety of its citizens. Only a stable and effective government can initiate sensible and timely government support measures that can be instrumental in bringing the economy back on track.

The governments across the globe were expected to take prompt action even with limited knowledge about the impact of the pandemic. The government played the critical role of assessing the impact and taking the measures; all this happened almost in real time in this pandemic. In addition to it the government in developing countries like India had the herculean task of creating a healthcare infrastructure to take care of the huge population. Ahmed (2020) recommends that

> there is need for coordinated action by all countries in implementing medical protocol of curtailing the spread and a fiscal response targeted at the productive sectors to fast-track kick-starting of the economies. This will require more palliative measures to consumers and bailout to businesses.
>
> (Ahmed, 2020)

"In the COVID-19 crisis food security, public health, and employment and labor issues, in particular workers' health and safety converge".[13] The government may adopt a three-step recovery process of respond, recover and thrive to combat this pandemic. It is also suggested that challenges may be addressed on three fronts, namely health, economy and business of government.[14]

Health, Environment and Economy

Crises can be natural, man-made, or more often than not a combination of them. Every country/community is vulnerable to crises even though the magnitude may vary because of the economic or social status. Whether economies fail or flourish through the crisis depends on their response to the crisis. Economic crises often lead to recession but the social impact is often ignored. Health and economy have a very significant relationship. Richer countries have healthier people; it could be attributed to their capability of taking strong initiatives like banning tobacco in the interests of better health of people. The health of people also affects the economic growth, in the sense that if the people are not healthy they cannot contribute according to their full potential in nation-building.[15] COVID-19 has impacted the health of the people and it has also taken away the opportunities for employment. So that is a double whammy for the economy. The economy is also closely linked with the environment. All economies striving for development and sustenance draw their very existence from the resources offered by the environment. Any deterioration in environmental quality is passed on to the resources that in turn delay the much sought-after economic growth[16]. It is acknowledged that development, job creation, education should not be at the expense of environment. So, there is inherent connectedness between health, environment and economy.

Every country is putting up a fight with this pandemic to save the health of its people and economy. While it is important to take care of the issues at hand, it is prudent to ponder over the indications of the environment and the challenges making way for mankind in the long run. The pandemic and measures taken to tackle the pandemic have affected efforts being undertaken for Sustainable Development Goals 2030. SDG 2030 is in fact an attempt to restore the environment and prevent such crises in future or at least minimize their impact (Srivastava et al., 2020).

Whenever there has been a crisis of this sort it has pushed the economy into slowdown and sometimes into recession. Generally the economic impact of recession is highlighted but the social aspects are ignored. In fact, governments adopt measures that target economic revival and ignore health and environment. This has severely impacted the health of the people and environment in the past.[17] "The pandemic has reinforced the connectivity between health, environment and the economy" (Srivastava et al., 2020).

To come out of the present crises it is important to adopt an integrated approach that focuses on health, environment and economic recovery. The previous attempts at recovery (2008, 2011 etc.) were isolated approaches to pull up growth and employment figures. The present economic stimulus must focus not only on economic recovery but also cover social aspects like health of the population and environment. Such a stimulus would then enable the economy to mitigate not only the economic aspects of recession but also the social impacts of recession.[18] Governments are not ignoring the social aspects of the pandemic altogether. The peculiar nature of the disease has forced them to be sensitive toward these aspects.

This pandemic has been a disruptive phenomenon that has lent an opportunity to restart the economies. All measures taken at this time have long-term implications for the economy. The current pandemic is being touted as the great reset.[19] It is being considered as an opportunity to undertake tasks that have been lying dormant for a long time. On one hand the crisis brought everything to a halt; on the other it gave an opportunity to make reforms and modify various systems in the economy. Some countries like the UK and Spain improved their public healthcare system. It was also an opportunity to fix some other lacunas in public infrastructure like education and transportation systems and even the economic system and the financial system with the planned stimulus package (Ozili & Arun, 2020). This implies the attempts at development must not be restricted to the pre-COVID levels: the countries must try to reopen, rebuild and recreate the economy capable of surpassing the previous levels. To achieve these objectives the governments are going all out for bailouts and other support mechanisms.

Bailout and Government Support

Bailout is an important tool of government support or intervention. Merriam-Webster defines bailout as "a rescue from financial distress". "Bailout is a general term for extending financial support to a company or a country facing a potential bankruptcy threat".[20] Bailouts are a form of state intervention into the economy with significant redistributive effects. Primarily a bailout is given to support an industry or a business that potentially affects millions of lives and is going through a prolonged financial crisis so acute that it may cause bankruptcy. Commonly loans, cash, bonds and stock purchases are used as instruments of bailout. Sometimes even direct subsidies are provided to the parties concerned.[21] As they say there are no free lunches in the world, and the economist community repeatedly runs a disclaimer about the moral hazards and welfare-reducing effects of bailout. The stimulus is financed by taxpayers' money that would have been otherwise utilized to work on the infrastructure and environmental conservation and is now being utilized to bail out the industry, so it is the taxpayer who is financing the bailout. Internationally it is being argued whether it is justified to give money to big companies that would use it to pay salaries to their top management, who have absolutely no issues in affording a decently luxurious life and pay dividends to shareholders, whereas for some the crisis has raised doubts on sustenance. Having said that the big businesses houses are run not just by the top management, there are so many at the bottom of the pyramid as well; the bailouts are for them to carry on with dignity in their life. It should be ensured that taxpayers' money is going to finance their existence and top-level management does not make merry at the expense of the people at the bottom level (Giuliani, 2020).

There are repercussions for the businesses and industries as well. Owners, promoters and other stakeholders (customers, lenders and suppliers) have to become aggressive risk-takers in financial transactions. The organizational structure has to be reorganized with inputs from the government; they may even shuffle the management. Restrictions may be enforced on payment of dividends and salaries for executives, otherwise they have to adhere to stricter regulations and supervision by the government. Bailouts have several merits to their credit as well, like surety of survival of the distressed entity even under most troubled waters that may save a total economic collapse as well if the industry is too big to fail.[22] In the past many governments have bailed out different industries and even companies of national significance. The US history of bailouts goes back to the Panic of 1792. The government rolled out huge bailouts in the years 1989 and 2008 to save the financial industry. Even corporate giants like Lockheed aircraft corporation, Chrysler, General Motors and the airline industry were bailed out by the US government. Before the pandemic the US bailout of 2008 to recover from the financial crisis was the biggest bailout ever.[23] The essence of the bailout was the troubled asset relief program (TARP), which was originally limited to USD 700 billion, later reduced to half a trillion USD.[24]

Bailouts are not just economic decisions but are also political moves. In democracy voters are an important entity. Studies suggest policy responses to economic crises impact voters' assessment of the government. However, it is difficult to understand the isolated impact of a particular policy or event on the citizens' actions. It is difficult to find whether voters are able to credit the government for their response to economically stressful events. Financial crisis in the economy may not necessarily create dissatisfaction with the government amongst the voters. The voters appreciate and reward actions taken by the government in times like these. Bailouts add to government performance and such policies do not go unnoticed in the public eye and sometimes save the state from the punishment for an adverse economy (Larsen et al., 2020). The voters regard the government's ability to handle crises.

> Although there is a strong link between the popularity of the government and the propensity to vote for a government party, we do not show that specific government policies in an economic crisis are a guarantee for good reelection prospects. Thus, we are not able to shed light on how voters weigh different policies in relation to other factors that will matter for their vote choice.

This suggests that voters incorporate economic policies like bailout in assessing the performance of a government rather than basing the verdict on an adverse economy (Larsen et al., 2019).

Bailout, Government Support and the Pandemic

Because this is an unprecedented situation in the recent history there are no guidelines to come out of this situation, there is no ideal way in which the governments should act. The pandemic caught the world off guard. There were no policy prescriptions or pretested models to address the outbreak. There was widespread uncertainty relating to the nature, mutation, impact, remedy and outcome of the pandemic. The impact of

COVID-19 on heath and the economy is uncertain. In fact the measures taken to get the economy out of this situation will also have a long-term irreversible effect on various economies. Medical science and economics both have been exposed to extreme conditions from where the concept of normalcy has changed (Ahmed, 2020).

Governments pumped money into the economies to support the households, stop job loss and keep businesses afloat. Various measure including tax benefits, direct money transfers, economic stimulus and a number of social welfare measures have been taken to support the economies. The restrictions imposed by the governments to contain the spread of disease led to temporary or permanent shutdown of many small businesses. Many businesses could not work at their full capacity; in response governments have intervened in the form of bailout and other support measures. "Government support for business during the current crisis has had broadly three phases: rescue, recovery and restructure" (Haeffele & Storr, 2020).

"Difficult economic conditions call for public policy to help financial institutions weather the shock" (Farhi & Tairole, 2012). The government intervened with stimulus policy packages primarily to save the businesses from permanent economic damage and retain the human and intangible capital with them. The crisis led to broken supply chains and decreased demand. Massive layoffs and unemployment led to loss of income and killed demand and contracted GDP. Fiscal stimulus by government will reverse this cycle and kick-start the economy. Economies have announced stimuli ranging from around 6% to 14% of their respective GDPs.

The literature suggests that liberal economies resist extensive government support while interventionist governments follow a proactive approach in extending support to the economy. Orientation of political parties also affects government support and bailout (Grossman & Wall, 2014). "Traditionally, conservative parties are assumed to have closer ties with the banking sector and financial interests, while left governments should be concerned about the redistributive effects of bank rescues" (cf. Cioffi & Höpner, 2006). Ivanović et al. (2020) recommended that fiscal authorities worldwide wish to accelerate the economy and that is the primary reason behind any support package but a fiscal stimulus has negative impacts as well. Therefore these policy measures should be used very judiciously and future fiscal policy must be "more selective, tailor-made and focused on the critical economic sectors and activities" (Zdravković, 2020). The crisis demands an integrated long-term and short-term planning.

> COVID-19 has pushed the world into such deep realms of darkness that only visionary leadership and meticulous planning can pull it out. Fears of unprecedented recession and financial collapse are obvious. Strategic planning targeting short term problems and long term contingencies is needed to bring the economies back on track.
>
> (Nicola, et al., 2020)

Short-term focus has been and will continue to be on preventing the spread and making sure people are not starving as it would lead to more deaths than the disease itself. When the crisis commenced the medium-term goal was to expand the healthcare infrastructure; as the pandemic progressed the aim became to integrate the economic interventions and healthcare infrastructure. The long-term plans target sustainable development and more sensitivity towards the natural environment.[25] A snapshot of the bailout packages by four major economies is presented in Table 9.1.

Detail of the Relief Package

India

General Information

1. Total population 1.38 billion.
2. GDP of $2.83 trillion.
3. Well known for textile, precious stones, information technology and pharmaceuticals.
4. Literacy rate of 77.8%.
5. Progressive tax structure which increases the tax with taxable income.
6. Level of unemployment: around 8% in 2020.
7. Immediate fiscal impulse of $280 bn.

Main Orientations Recovery Plan

- Direct benefit, make in India, healthcare, digital transformation and self-reliance.

Tax Measures – Direct and Indirect

Tax measures and reliefs in response to COVID-19:

- $6.5 bn liquidity through 25% reduction tax deduction at source for the pending period of FY 20–21.
- Immediate tax relief granted to businesses, non-profit charitable organizations and non-corporate businesses and activities with the immediate release of pending income tax refunds.

Employment and Economy-Related Measures

- $39 bn uncollateralized loan with 100% credit guarantee.
- $2.6 bn of subordinate debt for micro, small and medium enterprises which have been severely affected and an equity infusion $6.5 bn for high-potential MSMEs with growth and future prospects.

Table 9.1 A snapshot of the bailout packages

Parameters		*India*	*United States*	*France*	*Germany*
		Immediate fiscal impulse of $280 bn	*Immediate fiscal impulse of $1,940 bn and a total of $2.7 trillion*	*€137 bn package, in addition to €430 bn public spending*	*Total volume of €130 bn and a total of €750 bn*
Tax measures	**Tax rate cuts and tax deferrals**	25% reduction in tax deduction at source and GST deferrals	Around $500 bn of deferrals	Corporate taxes lowered and exemptions given to employees	€20 bn of tax cuts and €246 bn tax deferrals
Economic and employment generation measures	**Support to financial system**	$10 bn to support the economy	More than $500 bn to provide loans to kick start the economy	France Relance to support the economy with investment and €30 bn in green initiatives	Support given by developing a solidarity fund comprising of 3 major pillars
	Support to MSMEs	$9.3 bn to support the small enterprises	Around $350 bn for pay protection and retaining employees	Support for training, credit guarantees and vocational trainings	Benefit of more than €50 bn for small firms
	Support to start-ups	$20 bn under Digital India	Extended support to tech start-ups	Package for increasing the employability of youth	€2 bn assistance to finance the tech start-ups
	Agriculture	$20 bn focusing on farmers and agriculture market	$13 bn focusing on farmers	Major emphasis on tourism and green initiatives	
	Loan moratorium	For 6 months and extendable up to 2 years	$25 bn specifically to pay rents	Extended schemes have been announced	Huge deferrals have been given

Social security measures	**Direct benefit transfers**	$22.6 bn relief package (Pradhan Mantri GaribKalyan Scheme)	$600 bn relief package with child allowances		
	Healthcare	$2 bn package for healthcare preparedness	$117 bn in strengthening the infrastructure	€8 bn in strengthening the national health system	€20 bn assistance in improving the healthcare system
Additional measures	**Credit guarantee scheme**	$6 bn package for NBFCs	$560 bn with major package to airlines	€315 billion in guarantees for bank loans to businesses and credit insurance	Extended credit guarantees of up to €400 bn covering debt securities

- $3.9 bn for liquidity infusion for microfinance institutions, housing finance companies and non-banking finance companies.
- $5.9 bn grant for credit guarantee scheme for non-banking finance companies.[26]
- Corpus of $60 bn to provide direct assistance for MSMEs.
- Creation of a corpus of $1 trillion to create a modern and green infrastructure India for smart cities, sanitization and water distribution, modern freight corridors and clean energy.
- $20 bn funding to expedite Digital India initiatives, tech start-ups and high-speed Internet facility.[27]
- $11 bn for liquidity infusion for power distribution companies to clear their liabilities.[28]
- $13.34 bn agriculture infrastructure fund, to support the post-harvest agriculture infrastructure and credit guarantee for small and medium farmers. The fund to be used to strengthen the supply chain and capacity-building in agriculture, aquaculture and setting of export-based food-processing units[29]
- With a boost of $9 bn, extended the CLSS scheme in the housing sector for middle-income groups up to March 2021.[30]

Social Welfare and Additional Measures

- Contribution for EPF contribution for employers and employees to be reduced from 12% to 10% for 3 months; this reduction in contribution benefitted around 43 million employees and employers of around 65 million establishments facing financial crisis during the pandemic.[31]
- A credit fund of $26 bn to provide concessional loans, covering 25 million farmers including fishermen.[32]
- $2 bn package for healthcare preparedness and emergency response. The healthcare relief package to be used in improving the healthcare facilities, treatment of COVID patients, procurement of PPE kits and setting up of isolation wards with all necessary equipment.[33]
- $22.6 bn relief package under the Pradhan Mantri Garib Kalyan Scheme for free grain including $4.8 bn for direct benefit transfers to 160 million people including women, poor senior citizens and farmers.[34]
- $2 bn animal husbandry infrastructure fund to support dairy processing and establishing export-based units.[35]
- $11.3 bn allocated to the world's largest employment guarantee scheme, under MGNREGS, which mandates at least 100 days of employment guarantee for at least one person in every rural family.[36]

United States

General Information

1 Total population 328.46 million.
2 GDP of $21.92 trillion.
3 Well known for construction, retail, technology and healthcare.
4 Around 7 million engineers and scientists.
5 Literacy rate of 99%.
6 Progressive tax structure which increases the tax with taxable income.
7 Level of unemployment: around 6.7% in 2020.
8 Immediate fiscal impulse of $1,940 bn.

Main Orientations Recovery Plan

- Sustainable economic recovery, green infrastructure and jobs, aviation.

Tax Measures – Direct and Indirect

Tax measures and reliefs in response to COVID-19:

- Around $492 bn tax deferrals for employers and suspension of $69 bn student loans.[37]
- $560 bn for guarantee measures including $500 bn for distressed companies, mainly in airlines, and $60 bn for the economic injury loan disaster program.[38]

Employment and Economy-Related Measures

- $320 bn for the pay protection of employees working in small businesses which are severely affected and struggling to pay salaries. The loans have been made available at a much cheaper rates of 1%, which can also be waived if the firms don't fire their employees.[39]
- $19 bn for payment of sick leave, $10 bn for employee retention, and $45 bn for the tax deferral of employees on payroll.[40]
- A pool of $500 bn for extending loans, credit guarantees to industries severely affected by the crisis, additional $17 bn in loans and loan guarantees for unspecified "businesses critical to maintaining national security".[41]
- $50 bn in tax credit for retaining employees on wages during crisis.[42]
- $32 bn in grant for the airline industry and supporting the employees for wages and additional benefits in the form of loan guarantees. This grant includes $25 bn for passenger airlines, $4 bn for cargo airlines.[43]

- $13 bn grant to support agricultural producers and farmers for assisting the losses suffered by livestock/poultry growers, producers of renewable fuels and small food-processing units due to the current pandemic.[44]

Social Welfare and Additional Measures

- Around $600 bn in direct payments in the following form:
  - a direct benefit of $1,200 per married couple having an annual income up to $75,000
  - b an additional support of $500 per child with social security number.[45]
- $117 bn for upgrading the hospitals and veterans' health care and additional $100 bn for emergency measures including free corona testing, unemployment insurance.[46]
- $16 bn for pharmaceutical and medical supplies, creating a stockpile of COVID medicines and other necessary medicines.[47]
- $35 bn for a digitalized technology-based Medicaid fund, to expand the telehealth coverage and quarantine-related cost.[48]
- $8.3 bn to contain the pandemic outbreak and $3 billion in research for vaccines.
- $25 bn to provide a moratorium for the families to pay their rentals.
- $13 bn for the Supplemental Nutrition Assistance Program.
- $7 bn to expand the broadband services to help students' families and employees working from home.[49]

France

General Information

1. Total population 67 million.
2. GDP of $2.92 trillion.
3. Best European energy network and cheapest electricity.
4. More than 1 million engineers.
5. 47% of 25- to 34-year-olds in France hold a higher education diploma.
6. Lower corporate tax.
7. Level of unemployment: around 7.1% in 2020.
8. Immediate fiscal impulse of €124 bn.

Main Orientations Recovery Plan

- Green energy, competitiveness and territorial solidarity.

Tax Measures – Direct and Indirect

Tax measures and reliefs in response to COVID-19:

- Payment of taxes postponed for three months from March to June without any penalty.[50]
- For supporting and strengthening the SMEs, corporate tax has been lowered by 28% in 2020 and to be 25% by 2025.
- Estimated exemption of €3 bn for SMEs operating in severely affected sectors like tourism, hospitality, event management during the lockdown period.
- Exemptions in direct taxes for employees till the end of declared health emergency up to a limit of €7,500 per year.
- Postponement of payments of bills for SMEs and canceling the rents for the period of administrative lockdown.
- Advanced reimbursement of tax credits and VAT claims for three months, giving a relief of €23 billion.
- Permanent reduction of production taxes €20 billion for the period 2021–2022 €10 billion per year.
- Reduced tax on COVID protection items.

Employment and Economy-Related Measures

- Grants of €6.7 billion for hiring young people.
- More than 2 lakh people to be trained on digital technology, green transition and relocation of production.
- Deferrals of social security contributions if the activities of the business have been hit badly due to health emergencies and administrative closures and are currently unable to pay the contributions.
- In the case of the suspension of employment contract, the compensatory indemnity must not be less than 70% of the gross remuneration, which may be increased to 100% if training is provided.
- The employees cannot be hired below hourly payment rates of €8.03.
- The payment hours for the business have also been limited to 1,607 hrs per employee per year.
- Worst affected sectors like tourism, aviation, events, hotels etc. will continue to benefit from a 100% reimbursement of employee compensation.
  - Announcement of a massive €100 bn investment plan "France Relance" to support the economic activities in the country.[51]
  - Corporate loan moratorium of €180 bn deferred by six months.[52]
  - Expenditure of over €30 bn for supporting green financing, developing green infrastructure projects and green technologies.
  - €1.2 bn to finance investments for de-carbonization.

- Supporting strategic companies by initiating a credit line of €20 billion.
- Fund of €500 million for small industrial units with not more than 250 employees suffering from credit crisis.
- €11 bn for investments in key technologies and to be increased to €20 bn, with focus on conglomerate industries and digital transformation of small and medium industries.
- €36 bn toward investing in employability skills of youth and territorial solidarity. Under this many supportive steps to be taken:
  a vocational training, incentives to be given to youth
  b boosting the demand by supporting the purchasing power of low-income groups
  c digital and financial inclusion for territorial solidarity.
- Additional emergency reserves of €2.5 bn for unforeseen expenditures.
- €15 bn for supporting the R&D of small industries, increasing competitiveness and export guarantees.
- Solidarity Fund of €6 bn to strengthen small firms.[53]
- €3.9 bn to support digital and tech start-ups in the country.
- Setting-up of a repayable advance fund of €500 million for insubstantial SMEs that immediately need finance to stand.
- €21.5 bn for reimbursement of state tax credits.[54]

Social Welfare and Additional Measures

- €8 bn for national health system including expenditure for necessary medical equipment, masks and allowances with compensation of frontline healthcare personnel.[55]
- €3.5 bn for upgrading and greening the supply chain of the aeronautics sector.[56]
- Supportive measures for businesses by the financial institutions include:
  a credit repayments are allowed to be deferred up to six months
  b removal of additional charges or monetary penalties for extensions of credits.
- Extension of insurance period by one year
- Credit guarantees and mediation facilities for companies of all sectors facing difficulties with banking partners.
- €9.3 bn to support the tourism industry in the country.[57]

Germany

General Information

1 Total population 83 million.
2 GDP of $4.32 trillion.

3 Well known for automobiles, machines, chemicals, and food processing.
4 Around 2 million engineers.
5 Literacy rate of 99%.
6 Progressive tax structure which increases the tax with taxable income.
7 Level of unemployment: around 5.9% in 2020.
8 Immediate fiscal impulse of $1,940 bn.

Main Orientations Recovery Plan

- Sustainable economic recovery, green infrastructure and jobs, climate-friendly transport and export-based industries.

Tax Measures – Direct and Indirect

Tax measures and reliefs in response to COVID-19:

- €20 billion for reduction in indirect taxes/VAT tax rate which have been slashed from 19% to 16%.[58]
- Tax deferrals and reduction of tax prepayments up to €50.7 bn at state and local levels.
- €246 bn tax deferrals for industries including direct, indirect taxes and social contributions.[59]

Employment and Economy-Related Measures

- €23.5 bn as compensation for decreased working hours during the administrative lockdown.
- €18 bn as direct compensation to microenterprises and other distressed businesses.[60]
- €4.4 bn to invest in upgrading the digital infrastructure of the country with boosting the investment in artificial intelligence and next-generation IT technologies.[61]
- A three-pillar Economic Stabilization Fund consisting of:
  a 1st pillar comprising €100 bn for recapitalization to stabilize the firms[62]
  b 2nd pillar comprising extended credit guarantees of up to €400 bn covering debt securities under the Economic Stabilization Fund for extending the credit guarantees to manage the liquidity crisis covering all eligible debt securities for a period of maximum 5 years.
  c 3rd pillar comprising €100 bn for additional loans, if needed.
- €30 bn for expansion of credit guarantee activities to support the agriculture sector.
- €50 bn for direct benefits to approximately 3 million small business owners, having up to 10 employees. The grant includes remission of

up to €9000 for a span of 12 weeks for small businesses having a maximum of 5 employees and €15,000 for those having a maximum of 10 employees.[63]
- €6.0 bn to invest in developing eco-friendly infrastructure, grants for e-vehicles and climate-friendly fuel supplies for the shipping and aviation sector.[64]
- €2 bn assistance package to finance the tech start-ups and small businesses during the COVID crisis, to ensure the growth of innovative enterprises.[65]
- €25 bn to reinitiate the activities of companies which had suffered losses.[66]

Social Welfare and Additional Measures

- €7.7 bn social welfare payments, supporting low-income families to receive allowances like child allowance as additional income support.
- €18.9 bn for health-sector expenditure, financing for purchase of COVID safety equipment, raising awareness among the public and increasing the emergency capacity of the hospitals.
- Full reimbursement of social security contribution to all employers.[67]
- €5.3 bn to protect the income of employees to stabilize their contribution to the social guarantee scheme to reduce the ambiguity about the future.[68]
- €4.3 bn grant in Children's Bonus fund which includes one-time payment of €300 per child to be reimbursed to all eligible families.
- €5.2 bn for additional expenditures for lawful health insurance.[69]
- €3.7 bn for COVID safety measures and procurement of COVID protection kits, face masks and financing for swift working for development of corona vaccine.[70]

Conclusion

The world was eagerly waiting for the vaccines to arrive and bring back the earlier normal. However, now when the wait for the vaccine is over, there are many questions surrounding them (Ahmed, 2020). Jordan et al. (2020) concluded that that real GDP per capita and the real rate of return on assets show long-term impacts after pandemics and wars. Wars destroy capital, pulling up the rate of return for decades, which slows down recovery. In the case of pandemics capital is preserved, the real rate of return may remain negative for a long period but the economic recovery is much faster than in the case of wars. The supply, demand and confidence could be the most severely affected aspects of the economy in this pandemic. The pandemic has not only impacted the health of the people it has raised questions on achieving sustainable development. Countries have given a boost to their economies by giving appropriate relief packages. Many ways have been adopted by countries to pump money into their economic systems as per their requirement and attributes. Social welfare measures and supporting the industries have been the most common measures by which relief has been provided. Still the countries are supporting their industries and hoping for the economies to recover soon.

Notes

1 www.imf.org/en/Publications/WEO/Issues/2020/01/20/weo-update-january2020#:~:text=Global%20growth%20is%20projected%20to,World%20Economic%20Outlook%20(WEO)) (Last accessed on 28 November, 2020)
2 www.imf.org/en/Publications/WEO/Issues/2020/06/24/WEOUpdateJune2020 (Last accessed on 28 November, 2020)
3 www.imf.org/en/Publications/WEO/Issues/2020/01/20/weo-update-january2020#:~:text=Global%20growth%20is%20projected%20to,World%20Economic%20Outlook%20 WEO (Last accessed on 28 November, 2020)
4 www.oecd.org/about/ (Last accessed on 28 November, 2020)
5 www.oecd.org/berlin/publikationen/Interim-Economic-Assessment-2-March-2020.pdf (Last accessed on 28 November, 2020)
6 http://everythingexperiential.businessworld.in/article/Top-15-events-that-got-cancelled-postponed-due-to-COVID-19-scare/09-03-2020-185803/ (Last accessed on 28 November, 2020)
7 www.thelancet.com/journals/lanplh/article/PIIS2542-5196(20)30168-6/fulltexthttps://doi.org/10.1016/S2542-5196(20)30168-6) (Last accessed on 28 November, 2020)
8 www.worldometers.info/coronavirus/ (Last accessed on 28 November, 2020)
9 www.forbes.com/sites/kenrapoza/2020/03/01/coronavirus-could-be-the-end-of-china-as-global-manufacturing-hub/?sh=1eb43db95298 (Last accessed on 28 November, 2020)
10 www.worldbank.org/en/news/press-release/2020/06/08/covid-19-to-plunge-global-economy-into-worst-recession-since-world-war-ii (Last accessed on 28 November, 2020)
11 www.bloomberg.com/news/features/2020-04-30/bailout-isn-t-enough-for-economy-to-recover-from-coronavirus (Last accessed on 10 December, 2020)
12 www.who.int/news/item/13-10-2020-impact-of-covid-19-on-people's-livelihoods-their-health-and-our-food-systems (Last accessed on 10 December, 2020)
13 www.who.int/news/item/13-10-2020-impact-of-covid-19-on-people's-livelihoods-their-health-and-our-food-systems (Last accessed on 10 December, 2020)
14 www2.deloitte.com/us/en/insights/economy/covid-19/governments-respond-to-covid-19.html (Last accessed on 10 December, 2020)
15 https://oecdobserver.org/news/archivestory.php/aid/1241/Health_and_the_economy:_A_vital_relationship_.html#:~:text=Health%20performance%20and%20economic%20performance,healthier%20populations%20for%20a%20start.&text=National%20income%20has%20a%20direct,and%20public%20spending%2C%20for%20instance (Last accessed on 10 December, 2020)

16 www.oecd.org/economy/greeneco/global-forum-on-environment-2016.htm#:~:text=The%20links%20between%20the%20economy,sink%20for%20emissions%20and%20waste.&text=Poor%20environmental%20quality%20in%20turn,due%20to%20health%20impacts%2C%20etc. (Last accessed on 10 December, 2020)
17 www.nature.com/articles/s41893-020-0563-0 (Last accessed on 18 December, 2020)
18 www.nature.com/articles/s41893-020-0563-0 (Last accessed on 18 December, 2020)
19 www.weforum.org/agenda/2020/06/todays-bailouts-tomorrows-economies-covid-19-coronavirus-economy-crisis-pandemic-great-reset-government-stimulus/ (Last accessed on 18 December, 2020)
20 https://economictimes.indiatimes.com/definition/bailout#:~:text=Definition%3A%20Bailout%20is%20a%20general,greater%20government%20oversee%20and%20regulations (Last accessed on 18 December, 2020)
21 https://economictimes.indiatimes.com/definition/bailout#:~:text=Definition%3A%20Bailout%20is%20a%20general,greater%20government%20oversee%20and%20regulations (Last accessed on 18 December, 2020)
22 https://economictimes.indiatimes.com/definition/bailout (Last accessed on 22 December, 2020)
23 www.bbc.com/news/world-us-canada-52815357 (Last accessed on 22 December, 2020)
24 www.washingtonpost.com/politics/2019/03/18/did-wall-street-get-trillion-dollar-bailout-during-financial-crisis/ (Last accessed on 22 December, 2020)
25 www.theindiaforum.in/article/twin-crises-covid-19-and-how-resolve-them (Last accessed on 22 December, 2020)
26 https://home.kpmg/xx/en/home/insights/2020/04/india-government-and-institution-measures-in-response-to-covid.html (Last accessed on 22 December, 2020)
27 www.adlittle.com/sites/default/files/reports/adl_india_surmounting_covid-19.pdf (Last accessed on 22 December, 2020)
28 https://economictimes.indiatimes.com/industry/energy/power/rs-90000-crore-package-to-provide-only-temporary-relief-to-discoms-indra/articleshow/76002245.cms?from=mdr (Last accessed on 22 December, 2020)
29 www.hindustantimes.com/india-news/govt-to-create-rs-1-lakh-crore-agri-infrastructure-fund-for-marginalized-farmers-fm/story-NHzXbkxLRQjFzmO1nl3vOI.html (Last accessed on 22 December, 2020)
30 https://bfsi.economictimes.indiatimes.com/news/policy/rs-70000-crore-boost-to-housing-sector-with-clss-extended-up-to-march-2021-fm-nirmala-sitharaman/75741650 (Last accessed on 22 December, 2020)
31 https://ebizfiling.com/blog/epf-contribution-reduced-from-12-to-10-for-three-months/ (Last accessed on 22 December, 2020)
32 https://pib.gov.in/PressReleasePage.aspx?PRID=1665849 (Last accessed on 26 December, 2020)
33 https://pib.gov.in/PressReleseDetailm.aspx?PRID=1623601 (Last accessed on 26 December, 2020)
34 www.ineteconomics.org/perspectives/blog/indian-economic-policy-stimulus-deficits-and-privatization (Last accessed on 26 December, 2020)

35 https://agritimes.co.in/policy-research/india-pumps-inr-150-000-crore-on-agriculture-infra-allied-sectors (Last accessed on 26 December, 2020)
36 https://nrega.nic.in/netnrega/circular_new.aspx (Last accessed on 26 December, 2021)
37 www.cnbc.com/2020/03/25/coronavirus-stimulus-bill-updates-whats-in-the-2-trillion-relief-plan.html (Last accessed on 26 December, 2020)
38 www.nytimes.com/2020/03/25/us/politics/coronavirus-senate-deal.html?action=click&module=RelatedLinks&pgtype=Article (Last accessed on 26 December, 2020)
39 www.bloomberg.com/news/articles/2020-04-21/senate-passes-484-billion-interim-economic-stimulus-package (Last accessed on 26 December, 2020)
40 www.crfb.org/blogs/2-4-trillion-fiscal-relief-out-door (Last accessed on 26 December, 2020)
41 www.cnbc.com/2020/03/25/coronavirus-stimulus-bill-updates-whats-in-the-2-trillion-relief-plan.html (Last accessed on 2 January, 2021)
42 www.nytimes.com/aponline/2020/03/25/business/ap-us-virus-outbreak-congress.html
43 (https://edition.cnn.com/2020/03/25/politics/stimulus-package-details-coronavirus/index.html). (Last accessed on 2 January, 2021)
44 www.natlawreview.com/article/federal-covid-relief-bill-passed-congress-december-2020 (Last accessed on 2 January, 2021)
45 www.nytimes.com/2020/03/25/us/politics/coronavirus-senate-deal.html?action=click&module=RelatedLinks&pgtype=Article (Last accessed on 2 January, 2021)
46 www.bruegel.org/publications/datasets/covid-national-dataset/#usa (Last accessed on 2 January, 2021)
47 www.cnbc.com/2020/03/23/trump-fed-congress-government-efforts-to-contain-coronavirus-economic-impact.html (Last accessed on 2 January, 2021)
48 www.cbpp.org/blog/medicaid-funding-boost-for-states-cant-wait (Last accessed on 6 January, 2021)
49 www.natlawreview.com/article/federal-covid-relief-bill-passed-congress-december-2020 (Last accessed on 6 January, 2021)
50 Report on Policy measures taken against the spread and impact of the coronavirus – 20 August 2020 by European Commission Directorate General Economic and Financial Affairs (Last accessed on 6 January, 2021)
51 www.diplomatie.gouv.fr/en/french-foreign-policy/economic-diplomacy-foreign-trade/promoting-france-s-attractiveness/france-relance-recovery-plan-building-the-france-of-2030/ (Last accessed on 6 January, 2021)
52 www.economie.gouv.fr/files/files/PDF/2020/Coronavirus-MINEFI-10032020.pdf (Last accessed on 6 January, 2021)
53 www.assemblee-nationale.fr/dyn/15/textes/l15b3074_projet-loi.pdf (Last accessed on 6 January, 2021)
54 https://ec.europa.eu/info/sites/info/files/2020-€pean-semester-stability-programme-france_fr.pdf (Last accessed on 6 January, 2021)
55 www.senat.fr/rap/l19-385/l19-3851.pdf (Last accessed on 6 January, 2021)
56 https://minefi.hosting.augure.com/Augure_Minefi/r/ContenuEnLigne/Download?id=94C9F4D9-0CB4-4D85-9026-7801E5E7F1E7&filename=2196%20DP%20-%20Plan%20de%20soutien%20%C3%A0%20l%27a%C3%A9ronautique.pdf (Last accessed on 11 January, 2021)

57 www.economie.gouv.fr/covid19-soutien-entreprises/plan-soutien-secteur-tourisme (Last accessed on 11 January, 2021)
58 www.bundesfinanzministerium.de/Content/DE/Standardartikel/Themen/Schlaglichter/Konjunkturpaket/2020-06-03eckpunktepapier.pdf?__blob=publicationFile&v=9 (Last accessed on 11 January, 2021)
59 https://ec.europa.eu/info/sites/info/files/2020-€pean-stability-programme-germany_en.pdf (Last accessed on 14 January, 2021)
60 www.bundesfinanzministerium.de/Content/DE/Gesetzestexte/Gesetze_Gesetzesvorhaben/Abteilungen/Abteilung_II/19_Legislaturperiode/2020-06-16-Zweites-Nachtragshaushaltsgesetz2020/2-Regierungsentwurf.pdf?__blob=publicationFile&v=2 (Last accessed on 14 January, 2021)
61 www.bundesfinanzministerium.de/Content/DE/Standardartikel/Themen/Schlaglichter/Konjunkturpaket/2020-06-03-eckpunktepapier.pdf?__blob=publicationFile&v=23 (Last accessed on 14 January, 2021)
62 www.bmwi.de/Redaktion/EN/Pressemitteilungen/2020/20200327-altmaier-unprecedented-support-programme-for-employees-and-enterprises.html (Last accessed on 14 January, 2021)
63 www.bundesfinanzministerium.de/Content/DE/Standardartikel/Themen/Schlaglichter/Konjunkturpaket/2020-06-03eckpunktepapier.pdf?__blob=publicationFile&v=9 (Last accessed on 14 January, 2021)
64 www.bundesfinanzministerium.de/Content/DE/Standardartikel/Themen/Schlaglichter/Konjunkturpaket/2020-06-03-eckpunktepapier.pdf?__blob=publicationFile&v=19 (Last accessed on 15 January, 2021)
65 www.bmwi.de/Redaktion/EN/Pressemitteilungen/2020/20200401-customised-support-for-new-businesses-affected-by-the-coronavirus-crisis.html%0b%0b (Last accessed on 15 January, 2021)
66 www.bundesfinanzministerium.de/Content/DE/Standardartikel/Themen/Schlaglichter/Konjunkturpaket/2020-06-03-eckpunktepapier.pdf?__blob=publicationFile&v=14 (Last accessed on 15 January, 2021)
67 https://home.kpmg/xx/en/home/insights/2020/04/germany-government-and-institution-measures-in-response-to-covid.html (Last accessed on 15 January, 2021)
68 www.bundesfinanzministerium.de/Content/DE/Standardartikel/Themen/Schlaglichter/Konjunkturpaket/2020-06-03-eckpunktepapier.pdf?__blob=publicationFile&v=10 (Last accessed on 17 January, 2021)
69 www.bundesfinanzministerium.de/Content/DE/FAQ/2020-03-13-Corona-FAQ.html (Last accessed on 17 January, 2021)
70 www.bundesfinanzministerium.de/Content/DE/FAQ/2020-03-13-Corona-FAQ.html%0b%0b (Last accessed on 17 January, 2021)

References

Ahmed, B.A. (2020). *Impact of Covid-19 Pandemic on Global Economy.* Retrieved from https://mpra.ub.uni-muenchen.de/103753/1/MPRA_paper_103753.pdf.

Brewer, M., & Tasseva, I. (2020). Did the UK policy response to Covid-19 protect household incomes? Available at SSRN 3628464.

Cioffi, J.W., & Höpner, M. (2006). The political paradox of finance capitalism: Interests, preferences, and center-left party politics in corporate governance reform. *Politics & Society, 34*(4), 463–502.

Farhi, E., & Tirole, J. (2012). Collective moral hazard, maturity mismatch, and systemic bailouts. *American Economic Review, 102*(1), 60–93.

Giuliani, E. (2020). Piketty, Thunberg, or Marx? Shifting ideologies in the COVID-19 bailout conditionality debate. *Journal of International Business Policy*, 3, 443–450.https://doi.org/10.1057/s42214-020-00072-8.

Grossman, E., & Woll, C. (2014). Saving the banks: The political economy of bailouts. *Comparative Political Studies, 47*(4), 574–600.

Haeffele, S., & Storr, V.H. (2020). Government responses to crisis. *Mercatus Studies in Political and Social Economy*, https://doi.org/10.1007/978-3-030-39309-0_1.

Ivanović, M., Mirjana, Đ., Aleksandar, K., Filip, M., Kristina, N., Tamara, P., ... & Bojan, T. (2020). Serbian citizens' opinion on the COVID-19 epidemic. *South Eastern European Journal of Public Health (SEEJPH)*. Available online at www.seejph.com/index.php/seejph/article/view/3459/3585. Accessed April 28, 2021.

Jordan, R. E., Adab, P., & Cheng, K. (2020). Covid-19: risk factors for severe disease and death. Available on line at www.bmj.com/content/368/bmj.m1198. long Accessed April 28, 2021.

Larsen, E.H., Klemmensen, R., & Klitgaard, M.B. (2019). Bailout or bust? Government evaluations in the wake of a bailout. *European Political Science Review, 11*, 231–246. doi:10.1017/S1755773919000092.

Nicola, M., Alsafi, Z., Sohrabi, C., Kerwan, A., Al-Jabir, A., Iosifidis, C., ... Agha, R. (2020). The socio-economic implications of the coronavirus pandemic (COVID-19): A review. *International Journal of Surgery, 78*, 185–193. 10.1016/j.ijsu.2020.04.018.

Ozili, P.K., & Arun, T. (2020). Spillover of COVID-19: Impact on the global economy. Available at SSRN 3562570.

Sheth, J. (2020). Business of business is more than business: Managing during the Covid crisis. *Industrial Marketing Management, 88*, 261–264. https://doi.org/10.1016/j.indmarman.2020.05.028.

Srivastava, A., Sharma, R.K., & Suresh, A. (2020). Impact of Covid-19 on sustainable development goals. *International Journal of Advanced Science and Technology, 29*(9s), 4968–4972.

Zdravković, A. (2020). Do growth expectations match up with fiscal bailout and containment measures in the time of covid-19? http://ebooks.ien.bg.ac.rs/1491/.

10 Triple Bottom Line During Pandemic

Akanksha Jain, Priyam Mendiratta and Smita Kashiramka

Introduction

"The social responsibility of business is to increase profits" was an article authored by Friedman in 1970, where it was asserted that shareholders are only concerned with a single bottom line of profit, within the rules of the game relating to society and environment (Deodhar, 2016). Profitability as the sole objective of business is perceived to be too narrow a concept, focusing only on the shareholders and not the stakeholders. The Triple Bottom Line approach has been in place for quite some time now. In order to be successful in these changing times, a paradigm shift toward new metrics of stakeholder value by going beyond the traditional single bottom line of profitability is obligatory. The concept was brought forward in the late 1990s by John Elkington where he proposed that financial health is not the sole measure of a company's performance (Elkington, 1998a). Rather, it is imperative to look at a bigger picture by taking into account the social and environmental performance. It is an accounting framework where the ultimate success of a firm is judged on its contributions toward three parameters: people, planet and profit. These are popularly referred to as the 3Ps. The idea is to gauge corporations' commitment level to sustainability and corporate social responsibility. The three pillars of TBL, people, profit and planet, known as 3Ps, evoke the holistic approach of achieving sustainability with value creation of all stakeholders instead of only shareholders of the organization. The approach of Triple Bottom Line can be seen akin to the definition of sustainability, which integrates social, environmental and economic responsibilities (Gimenez et al., 2012). The triple bottom line reporting by companies allows them to be more transparent in their functioning and accountable to their stakeholders by turning the stipulated code of conduct into practice (Morland, 2006). Profit is considered to be a perfect substitute for measurement of economic prosperity of an organization in economic terms. However, planet and people are qualitative dimensions which can be gauged only through the impact created. The idea of TBL has further infused concepts like the Global Reporting Initiative and the Dow Jones Sustainability Index, while bringing out a change in

DOI: 10.4324/9781003125648-10

corporate accounting and stakeholder engagement (Elkington, 2018). To ensure such a strategy of transition toward sustainability, the role of complements and long-term partnerships would be crucial (Elkington, 1998b).

- ***Profit*** – It is an inherent quantitative measure of a corporate's financial performance. It is an indicator of a firm's operational outcome, available for dividend distribution (Littleton, 1928). The focus is on the economic value created by an organization which is measured in terms of profits earned on a year-on-year basis. Profit is indicative of real economic benefit as it is earned over and above the total costs. Traditionally, this aspect has been the sole point of emphasis of the business houses to create shareholder wealth, because of which it is the utmost important element of TBL approach.
- ***People*** – This is inclusive of all the individuals or groups of individuals related to a business, that is, employees, suppliers of raw materials, customers and community at large (Norman & MacDonald, 2004). It pertains to the fact that the company has a social structure in a manner in which interests of labor, employees, corporate and other stakeholders are protected. The "people" aspect covers fair and non-exploitative business practices towards employees and even the community in which a business operates. The increasing emphasis on the protection of stakeholders' interests and laws like the Minimum Wages Act put corporates in a position to act responsibly towards employees, suppliers, consumers and the entire society. It provokes the idea of social equity whereby a company needs to give back to the society from which it extracts resources for business activities.
- ***Planet*** – This element of TBL is concerned with the environmental impact that an organization has. A company adopting the TBL approach endeavors to reduce its ecological footprint by sticking to sustainable environmental practices during the entire business process (McWilliams et al., 2016), right from procurement of raw materials to ultimate disposal of waste material. With the enactment of various environmental laws and increasing consumer awareness, it has become important for a corporate to adopt nature-friendly practices to sustain it in the long run (Lata & Gupta, 2020). Tracking of environmental impact and running the business sustainably lie at the core of this aspect so that the planet doesn't feel the brunt as a result of the business line. The concept of natural capital which involves natural wealth (the one supporting ecosystem) is relatively complex and still in the evolving stage despite the introduction of several measures (Elkington, 1998b).

Figure 10.1 is a visual representation of the concept which invokes the idea of striking a balance between the three components, that is reaping

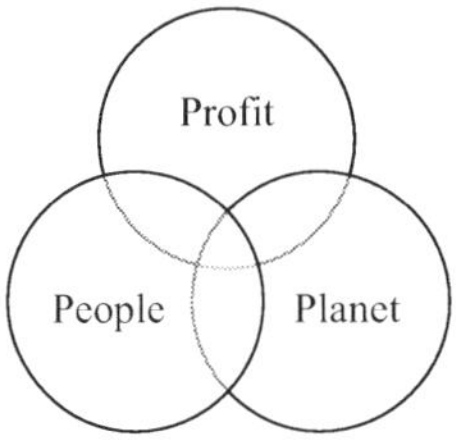

Figure 10.1 Constituents of TBL.
(Source: Authors' compilation)

profits but not at the cost of other elements and bringing them together in an integrated manner.

Despite the concept being coined for over 25 years, it has gained attention in recent years due to rising consumers' interests towards companies that align with their beliefs at an aggregate level. Companies like Puma have pioneered the Environmental Profit and Loss approach. More recently, Boston Consulting Group (BCG) has come up with the Total Societal impact framework (Elkington, 2018). According to the Wall Street Journal, companies which are strong ESG (environmental, social, governance) performers have better sustained the after-effects of the virus, in contrast to their peers devoid of a strong ESG thrust.

> Environmental, social and governance investing was growing in popularity before the virus began to circulate, as investors flocked to companies that have taken steps to manage nonfinancial risks related to matters such as climate change, board diversity or human rights issues in the supply chain. But the pandemic has demonstrated on a large scale the importance of other factors that are paramount to ESG investors. Among them: disaster preparedness, continuity planning and employee treatment through benefits such as paid sick leave as companies direct employees to work from home.
>
> (ERM, 2020)

The trend in the corporate governance which had led to "triple bottom level thinking" was further fueled by the emergence of a new category/form of organizations called certified B corporations in the early twenty-first century. They are such enterprises which have been identified as creating value for their stakeholders other than shareholders by making amendments to their corporate charter. The certification is granted on the basis of extent of value creation and fulfillment of fiduciary duties by a corporate toward all its stakeholders by a non-profit organization named B Labs. Since 2007, there has been an exponential increase in the number of firms earning this certification, which is indeed an indication of organization's inclination toward a level of commitment and success of its shareholders as well as other stakeholders. Only the business enterprises which aid in furthering the Triple Bottom Line concept on the lines of how the practices of such organizations create value for the people in general and the immediate environment form a part of these new-age firms. The primary motivation leading to the emergence of B Corps is that organizations should be perceived as "good" and "green", as the concept of measuring the performance of any firm solely on the basis of short-term profits is seen as a faulty concept:

> Certified B Corporations are social enterprises verified by B Lab, a non-profit organization (https://bcorporation.net/about-b-lab). B Lab certifies companies based on how they create value for non-shareholding stakeholders, such as their employees, the local community, and the environment. Once a firm crosses a certain performance threshold on these dimensions, it makes amendments to its corporate charter to incorporate the interests of all stakeholders into the fiduciary duties of directors and officers. These steps demonstrate that a firm is following a fundamentally different governance philosophy than a traditional shareholder-focused corporation.
>
> (Harvard Business Review, 2016)

Since the advent of the concept of Triple Bottom Line, companies have been trying to balance between social, economic and environmental aspects simultaneously. The implementation of various acts in India like the Environment Protection Act (1986), Consumer Protection Act (1986) (now it is replaced by Consumer Protection Act, 2019), Minimum Wages Act (1948), Corporate Social Responsibility (CSR) rules under Companies Act, 2013 and many other such legislations have altogether evoked a corporate's attention toward all the stakeholders, thereby replicating the idea of stakeholder theory. There are many global-level initiatives aimed at environment protection like United Nations Framework on Climate Change Convention, Kyoto Protocol, Vienna Convention for Protection of Ozone Layer amongst others. In the United States, the Sarbanes Oxley Act of 2002, Consumer Protection Act of 2010 has gained prevalence in this regard while in the European Union, corporate governance attracts CSR Directive 2014 which invokes self-commitment to the policy (Leyens, 2018). In the normal course of business, a company's efforts are equally targeted toward the 3Ps of the TBL approach that give equal and due importance toward all the aspects.

The pandemic has left the entire world in shatters and completely changed the way of carrying out business activities. Not only the business, there has also been a drastic shift in doing almost anything. It is in this time period that the focus of business houses in terms of 3Ps has undergone a change. The entire COVID-19 scenario has emphasized the fact "People before profit". The corporations have been constantly trying their level best to maintain safety and health of the employees and community, in general. The profit motive has shrunk to a certain extent. The priority is "People" (Reuters Events, 2020). Undoubtedly, profit is the essence of any business but people's importance is bigger than any other thing.

Entwining Triple Bottom Line and Corporate Social Responsibility

CSR "is context-specific organizational actions and policies that take into account stakeholders' expectations and the triple bottom line of economic, social, and environmental performance" (Aguinis, 2011). Moravcikova et al. (2015) define CSR as triple bottom line itself. Marrewijk (2003) suggested CSR as the intermediate goal of businesses, under which they aim to manage the three pillars of triple bottom line, in order to achieve the ultimate objective of corporate sustainability. Therefore, TBL can be assumed to be a path or the basic foundation leading to the final goal of sustainability. So far, CSR reporting has been mandatory while CSR spending has been voluntary for countries like Australia, France, Norway and Sweden, to name a few. However in the context of the Indian landscape, with the advent of Companies Act 2013, this voluntary act has been made mandatory in terms of both reporting and spending for specific corporates (Deodhar, 2016), making India an exception. This mandate applies to corporates with thresholds of INR 5 crore, INR 500 crore and INR 1,000 crore as net profit before tax, net worth and turnover, respectively, in a particular financial year. The firms, whether holding, subsidiary or foreign with a branch in India, falling under this threshold are required to spend a minimum of 2% of the average net profits of the preceding three financial years. Socially responsible firms do not limit themselves to using resources merely for earning profits. Instead, they use CSR as a way to integrate and collaborate economic, ecological and social goals within the ambit of company's operations. In recent times, CSR is used as a yardstick to measure company's commitment and looked at as way of growing reputation amongst all stakeholders. What can be argued is that the activities performed under CSR do not bear a direct linkage to further a corporate's profit or performance, but make a direct contribution to the two key aspects of TBL – people and planet. An increased adoption of CSR-related disclosures in the annual reports of firms advocates a rising awareness of the social and environmental concerns of the stakeholders (Tate et al., 2010).

As per Invest India's report (Invest India, 2020), till financial year 2019, the areas which received the maximum CSR funding are education, health and rural development. This fulfills the "people" aspect of TBL.

Following this, another domain receiving a sizable funding is environment sustainability, taking care of the 'planet' aspect. Further, to encourage and support the companies towards making their contribution, any expenditure incurred out of the CSR funds for COVID-19

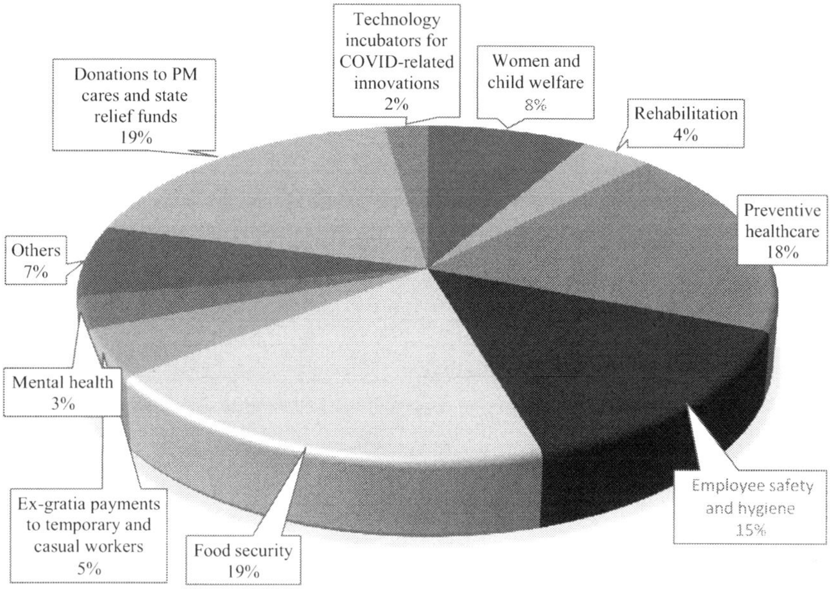

Figure 10.2 Key areas receiving COVID-related CSR in India.
(Data Source: Invest India Report, 2020)

would be considered an eligible CSR activity in India (The Hindu, 2020). The key areas receiving the CSR fund to combat Covid-19 pandemic has been presented in Figure 10.2.

Not only monetarily, companies are also practicing CSR by spreading awareness. These companies include Mc Donald's, Coca-Cola, Audi, Volkswagen, among others, which are big names and have a far-reaching audience, surpassing geographical boundaries. For instance (Economic Times, 2020a), Mc Donald's bifurcated the "M" into "n-n", sending a message to practice social distancing. Audi followed suit, where the four entangled rings in its logo are separated into four separate rings. A similar strategy is adopted by Volkswagen. Apart from playing with the logos, the companies also played with the advertisement slogans. Through their changed slogans, Nike urged the people to play indoors to play for the world and Pizza Hut stressed eating pizza at home. Thus, as a part of their non-monetary CSR practice, these companies duly fulfilled the framework on TBL. Amul, an Indian dairy brand, floated a contemporary advertisement with the popular girl mascot washing her hands and telling people rather to be clean than sorry. Through the medium of a web series, Netflix used subtitles to encourage people to wash hands (Livemint, 2020a). Continuing the trend, BBDO, an advertising agency headquartered in New York, urged the people to "Be a Chicken", a term associated with being afraid of something; their advertisements spreading the message "Chicken is the new brave" and "Beat the virus, Have no guts. Be a chicken. Be safe" (Financial Express, 2020).

Economic Aspect of TBL

In common parlance, profit is the traditional financial gain covered under the domain of corporate accounting. Profit acts as the core motivator behind operating a business and is the key to sustenance in the long run. Profit as an aspect has undergone various changes.

Earlier profit maximization used to be the sole objective of businesses. This notion was criticized by many on various parameters. It was believed that since organizations function in a society, utilizing the resources available in its external environment, they owe an obligation to pay back. This narrow approach was substituted with a broader concept of wealth maximization, which takes into account all stakeholders including the three pillars of TBL approach. The approach of wealth maximization has been in practice for quite a long time. However, the current pandemic has questioned its relevance.

The profit aspect seems to be merely changed to "survival". Amidst the uncertain global environment around pandemic, it has become challenging for all the businesses, whether big or small, to keep financial wheels running due to the brunt of less revenue and economic slump. Such impact has been more brutal for small businesses and start-ups due to scarce reserves and low margins to manage abrupt slumps (Economic Times, 2020b). The testing times have forced organizations to take a step back, re-look their way of management, re-visit business plans and even modify their entire business models, if the need be.

To support the operations, companies need to invest in tools to enable personnel to work remotely and collaborate virtually, assess current bandwidth to support remote work, perform periodic network stress testing and identify workarounds for critical tasks that are not executable from home. It is worth noting that while remote working is a viable option for the service sector, it is not so for manufacturing firms, thus resulting in critical implications for product supply chains (EY, 2020).

The major three phases of a company to survive and grow include (McKinsey, 2020):

- Safeguarding all stakeholders (specifically, employees and customers) and viability of business.
- Reorientation of business to plan for recovery.
- Repositioning of the business.

Revenue growth management, which means deriving sustainable, profitable growth through a range of strategies, has a key role to play in these phases. It is imperative for the corporates to analyze and develop a pragmatic approach to bring about a systematic change in the operations of their companies along with a change in their financial structure in such a manner that they survive at very low or negligible profits yet have sufficient funds to retain the employees so that the people's well-being is assured amidst the health crisis. To quote an example (Bloomberg Quint, 2020), Arcelor Mittal is a leading global giant in steel-making and mining with steel manufacturing facilities in 18 countries. With the net loss of approximately USD 559 million for the quarter ended June '20, the company is actively working on cost-reduction techniques to shield its profitability layer in an uncertain environment around pace of recovery. The steel industry has a fixed-cost-dominated structure which in turn intensifies the need for action to appropriately position the fixed-cost base. The company has taken steps toward adaptation of production levels to market demands, increasing production to lower the fixed cost per unit and developing options in order to operate on a leaner cost structure. Following the pandemic, the company announced layoffs of an unspecified number of jobs in its South Africa operations as a part of restructuring to curtail costs. This exemplifies the brunt to sustain profits even by big industry giants in a situation of global pandemic.

Though the economic activities all around the globe are facing a hard-hitting time, there is an ample bundle of opportunities to reshape the existing models of business and sustainability in the long run. In practice, the "profit" aspect seems to be dwindling with survival of business remaining the key factor. However, this is partially true as the pandemic has paved the way for an opportune time to grab the market for a shift in existing demands towards sanitizer, PPE kits, face masks, disinfectants. Online education has altogether created a bigger market for laptops, smartphones, online educational platforms. While most of the companies have been struggling for survival in the uncertain period, the edtech start-up White Hat Jr is riding on benefit of ever-increasing growth due to a shift towards the online mode of teaching for all levels of students. The key area of the company is online coding. BYJU's 300$ million acquisition of White Hat Jr and accelerated espousal of technology are the catalyst towards edtech's extraordinary growth. This demonstrates one of the opportunities that can be leveraged upon in these difficult times (Livemint, 2020b).

Keeping in mind the safety and preferences of consumers, many businesses have done away with the traditional brick and mortar model and made a transition toward the online model of operations, thereby cutting fixed costs while improving customer experience/response. In a situation of pandemic when the normal economic activities are hampered, the government steps up to support domestic industries to become self-reliant, creating room for ample business prospects. Deutsche Post DHL group is the world's leading logistics company, based in Germany. Despite the disruption in economic activities due to COVID-19, the company was able to increase its revenue by 3.1% and operating profits by 18.6% in the quarter ending June' 2020 as compared with the same quarter in the previous year. The extraordinary performance in the times of crisis reveals the resilience and robust position of Deutsche Post DHL group. The increasing profits could be attributed to a number of factors: wide geographic footprint, inclusive portfolio of logistic solutions, maintenance of strong supply chains by ensuring availability of its own flights for smooth delivery, adaptability to the crisis by digital transformation and adjustment of capacities in a swift way to meet altered demand, focus on core business areas being some of the key factors. Optimization of the portfolio with increased efforts to manage costs and efficiency at the same time has led to improved performance even in an uncertain period of pandemic (Freight Week, 2020).

To keep the businesses running, many companies especially in the service sector have switched to the work-from-home model so that sustainability and continuity of business go hand in hand (Kumar & Vidhyalakshmi, 2012). One such example is that of Hindustan Coca Cola Beverages, which has introduced permanent work-from-home as an option for the employees whose physical presence is not required in the offices to carry out operations smoothly (Business Standard, 2020a). To facilitate the smooth transition for employees, the company will provide monetary support to install UPS and reimburse monthly wi-fi expenses. This support could be further extended for the purchase of tables, webcam, headphones and other necessities required by the employees.

Environment Aspect of TBL

With the changing times and growing consciousness toward the environment, having a good product is not enough for a successful business. It is essential to develop sustainable practices and adhere to corporate social responsibility. Most of the companies have gone green in their business practices to create a sustainable future. Over the last few decades, businesses all around the globe have changed their way of doing activities and even modified their business models to allow for green initiatives. Some prominent examples of such companies include IKEA, Nike, Hewlett Packard and Patagonia (The Environmental Magazine, 2020). The concerns of global warming and climate change had drawn attention from all the top leaders and businesses can play a major role by using their brand to draw the attention of the general public to environmental issues. Due to enforcement of many regulations and self-consciousness, corporates are constantly working toward reducing their carbon footprints and emission levels. The concept of carbon trading is very much prevalent in many countries (Gupta & Kumar, 2010). India's transition directly from BS IV norms to BS VI norms for vehicular emission is a depiction of the efforts toward reducing environmental pollution by the government. In the normal course of business, organizations have been persistently working toward sustainable practices along with focus on waste reduction and increased use of renewable sources to build upon a viable business which is not detrimental to the planet's health.

The rapid spread of COVID-19 worldwide had brought normal industrial activities, traffic to a standstill. In the initial time, all economies had imposed complete lockdown to combat the pandemic which in turn meant no human activities (except essential ones) or interference with nature. It could be seen as a momentary blessing in disguise from the perspective of the environment. Reports from all around the world had pointed to the fact that nature had been healing on various environmental parameters like the air quality index (AQI), water quality in rivers, wildlife, lower greenhouse gas emissions among others during the suspension of economic activities, which is indeed reflection of a positive sign toward restoration of the environment (Lokhandwala and Gautam, 2020). Corporates have unintentionally contributed toward improvement in the environment due to imposition of restrictions in activities for some time. This had not been a business strategy.

The concept of planetary health ideates a fine balance between human health and the ecological disruptions caused by the social structures. It is a demonstration of the fact that there is a two-way street in the sense that in addition to humans' impact on the planet, any disruption of the human-ecological balance has major implication for human health too (We Forum, 2020). This reality has been augmented and very well depicted by the COVID-19 pandemic. However, a new problem has been posed for the planet due to the onset of the pandemic. Due to the exorbitant production levels of disposable masks, PPE kits and other products due to the concerns for safety, waste generation (especially, plastic) is now a new hazardous problem for nature. Many countries have a system of waste recycling in place. As a result of the pandemic, countries like the USA have stopped activities in recycling centers to avoid the risk of spreading the virus while waste management has been restricted in many European countries (Zambrano-Monserrate et al., 2020). The famous city Dubai in UAE has been setting an excelling example for its peculiar CSR and sustainability model in giving acceleration to responsible business activities. There exists collaboration between stakeholders in public and private sectors to address key CSR issues in order to maximize social impact. The institutional and cultural setup is such that all businesses from small to large conglomerates contribute toward sustainable growth (Entrepreneur, 2020). The question of achieving sustainability still remains unanswered. The least businesses can do now is to ensure that the new production facilities that would be set up to meet changed consumer preferences are developed in a way that it is not deleterious for nature. The pandemic has led to the production of bio-medical waste (in the form of used PPE kites, disposable masks, discarded gloves and others) in large quantity whose proper disposal still poses a challenge. Ramky Enviro Engineers Ltd (REEL) has entered into an agreement with

Abu Dhabi's Waste Management Center called Tadweer to establish a waste treatment facility with a rotary incinerator which would aid in getting rid of COVID-19 medical waste (BusinessLine, 2020).

Social Aspect of TBL

Traditionally, businesses have focused on the financial aspect of "profitability", thus sidelining the key input responsible for generating such financial returns. However, taking into consideration the concept of "externalities" in the field of economics and "stakeholder theory" in the field of financial management, a need was felt to incorporate other aspects under the umbrella of a business operation, rather than just profits. With the advent of "triple bottom line", the "people" or "social" aspect got formal recognition in the business world. Going by the "people" perspective, the point in focus is the employees. The people aspect can be defined as the human capital of any operating concern, taking into account the latent knowledge and capabilities of the employees of a business. These resources serve as drivers of the operations of a business, and in turn get impacted by the outcome of such operations. However, the people part is not only restricted to the individuals on the payroll of a business concern, but also includes other interested parties like the customers, suppliers, investors and community members at large. Although the concept of Triple Bottom Line was first coined in 1994, the importance of people for a firm had started getting recognition under the area of "intellectual capital" in 1960s.

Prior to the novel coronavirus pandemic, all the three spheres of the Triple Bottom Line were assumed to be given equal theoretical importance, with profit still taking the front footing in practice. However, with the onset of the pandemic, the people aspect has assumed prime importance. Companies have already moved toward newer business models of working from home, staggered operations with employees being called on a rotational basis. The work-from-home model has not only made employees more technologically efficient but has also helped firms in cutting down their functional costs. The idea is to prevent layoffs and ensure financial security of the employees by different means like freezing fresh recruitment, promotions, increments, top executives taking pay cuts so that the remuneration of employees is ensured in the stint of crisis. It is imperative for the corporates to analyze and develop a pragmatic approach to bring about a systematic change in the operations of their companies along with a change in their financial structure in such a manner that they survive at very low or negligible profits yet have sufficient funds to retain the employees so that the people's well-being is ensured amidst the health crisis.

But naturally, people being the key inputs for any business, without their well-being profits cannot follow. Companies around the globe are responding to this need.

One of the largest North American organic breakfast and food snack companies popularly known as Nature's Path has been the first of its kind to install far-UVC downlights and sanitizing troffers in its facilities to ensure protection for team members against harmful pathogens (GlobeNewswire, 2020). The step was taken amid the pandemic for security of employees and facilitation of an uninterrupted food-supply chain.

Taking an example of the practices undertaken by Amazon, they have divided people into three broad groups, namely, employees, customers and the community at large.

> For the employees, we are granting a special one-time Thank You bonus totalling over $500 million. We expect to invest approximately $4 billion on COVID-related initiatives getting products to customers and keeping employees safe. We have made over 150 process updates, from enhanced cleaning and social distancing measures to new efforts like disinfectant spraying. Anyone diagnosed with COVID-19 will receive up to two weeks of paid time off, in addition to their other paid and unpaid time off options. Large COVID testing facilities have been built. Extra time off with full pay for those diagnosed with COVID-19 has been offered. Also, we have established a $25 million relief fund for employees facing financial hardship or quarantine. For the customers, we are providing free masks with enhanced cleaning to customers at all open Amazon physical retail stores and Whole Foods Market locations nationwide. Dedicated shopping hours have been framed to service customers who are 60 plus, those with disabilities and fall under the high risk category. We have enabled front-porch delivery where the delivery team will leave the item at your front door and you will not be required to sign for it. All delivery vehicles and equipment are disinfected each day, and delivery devices and mobile phones are disinfected after each delivery appointment. For the communities around the globe, we have launched a $20 million AWS Diagnostic Initiative to accelerate COVID-19 research. In Europe, we committed €21 million (almost $23 million USD) to support those most affected by the COVID-19 pandemic. Jeff Bezos, the founder of Amazon, has donated $100 million to Feeding America. The company hired 175,000 additional full- and part-time employees and is working with foodbanks in 25 cities across the country to deliver 6 million meals to underserved and vulnerable populations. Moreover, the company donated $5 million in Amazon devices globally to those in need, also donating 8,200 laptops to Seattle Public Schools students who do not have access to a device at home.
>
> (The Amazon Blog, 2020)

It can be implied that the ill-managed firms with lack of contingency funds are the worst sufferers who are left with no choice other than layoffs. Limiting to the Indian landscape, it is anticipated that about one-fourth of the start-ups would face a wipe-off, given the pandemic lasts for a long period (Economic Times, 2020c). This could be attributed to their reliabilance on immediate revenues to aid operations, paucity of contingency reserves and limited capital at their disposal. However, due to the shrinkage in revenues, in practice, the "profit" aspect seems to be dwindling, with survival of business remaining the key factor. As per a recent ILO survey spanning over eight countries from four continents (ilo.org, 2020), a harsh reality of the pandemic has come to the fore. Out of the 1,000 sample MSMEs, about 70% have shut down their operations. About half of the remaining have temporarily shut down owing to regulations imposed by the government and the other half have halted their operations due to a fall in orders, followed by a drop in revenues and cash crunch.

Thus, as it can be seen that at the present hour, companies are pro-actively engaged in addressing the needs of their workforce and the people at large. However, the problem is that every organization is not as big as Amazon, which has huge funds at its disposal and can earmark funds for charity. How medium and small enterprises thrive during the pandemic will be the prime challenge.

A number of Indian companies have contributed to support the initiatives during pandemic (Business Standard, 2020b), and a summary of these contributions has been compiled in Table 10.1. It is quite evident from Table 10.1 that the companies which are making contributions to society at large to fight the pandemic are all big names, with operations spanning over many decades. Thus, such companies are capable of taking care of their own workforce, even with the revenues taking a large hit. In a study based in the Middle East and Turkey, more than 50% of SMEs owners reported a negative impact of the pandemic on the company

Table 10.1 Contributions by Indian companies to battle COVID-19

Name of the company	*Contributions made (in INR)*
Tata Sons and Trusts	5,000 Crore
Reliance Industries	5 Crore and a 100-bed hospital
JSW Group	100 Crore
Kotak Mahindra Bank	35 Crore
ITC Ltd	150 Crore
Mahindra and Mahindra	Production of ventilators at its manufacturing units, resorts to be used as makeshift care units
Hero Cycles	100 Crore contingency fund
Paytm	500 Crore
Bajaj Group	100 Crore dedicated to rural areas
Axis Bank	100 Crore
HUL	100 Crore

which had to be combatted with the measures of cutting back on the owners' salary, reducing the scale of services, temporarily suspending the workforce and curtailing wages for the employees (RAND Corporation, 2020). On similar lines, a recent survey by Goldman Sachs (CNBC, 2020) revealed that around 1500 small businesses believe that they are not in a position to sustain their operations for more than a quarter amid the prevailing situation of pandemic.

A business cannot function in isolation from the political forces in action. With a pandemic of this tune, it is imperative that businesses and government function hand-in-hand. Measures such as collateral-free loans for MSMEs would aid small businesses to thrive during these challenging times (KPMG, 2020; Subagyo et al., 2020). Implementation of sustainability in a top-down approach leads to a central focus on government in managing and regulating for corporate sustainability (Oberoi, 2014). A popular food brand, Epigamia, has joined hands with Danone Manifesto Ventures for the second phase of the social initiative called "Step-Up Initiative". The initiative has aimed to reach out to rural communities affected by the pandemic and has distributed over 7.5 lakhs bottles of yoghurts to many homeless children in Mumbai (The Logical Indian, 2021).

Future Strategies

The new normal calls for a change in the overall strategy and having a different outlook. For instance, India's spending on healthcare as a proportion of GDP stands at the lowest in the world at around 5%, which is questionable in a nation of such a huge population (Livemint, 2015). To add, the government contribution stands at a mere 1.4%. The CSR funding from corporates is not enough to solve the issue because the root cause lies in the inadequate infrastructural facilities. However, companies could earmark a certain percentage of their CSR funds toward innovation in healthcare processes and medical equipment and can also collaborate with firms operating in the healthcare sector so as to develop better in-house R&D facilities to foster speedy manufacture of products. The key to long-term growth would remain sustainability. Looking at the massive level of bio-medical waste generated during the pandemic (Express Healthcare, 2020), the corporates in any arena of business must emphasize reducing their carbon footprints and manufacturing products in a way such that the ecological balance remains intact. As observed, few companies have a contingency fund already in place to meet uncertainty. This practice should be followed by all the companies, whether small or big, so that profit doesn't dip significantly or is converted into losses in times of uncertainty like COVID-19. Moreover, companies should provide time-to-time training for the employees to make them more adaptive toward handling technology so that a smooth transition can be made from the traditional brick-and-mortar model of operation to work-from-home.

MSMEs and other small businesses can focus on building a more robust and reliable technological infrastructure to handle any immediate shifts in the working environment.

Conclusion

In times of emergency, it seems inappropriate to think of long-run sustainability for businesses. Rather, urgent action is a requisite for the business leaders and government at an aggregate level. It is an apt time for companies to exhibit their commitment to safety, health and prosperity of all stakeholders by addressing the existing inequalities in their business models (World Resources Institute, 2020). The 3Ps of the Triple Bottom Line are closely knit and interrelated, which means that one factor impacts the other and so on. The key lesson learnt from the entire crisis situation is that people should be kept in the forefront, ahead of any other objective, as without human resource there is no way to efficiently and profitably run a business. Even sustenance would be a challenge if the workforce's well-being is not taken care of by the corporations. However, this objective in itself cannot be fulfilled if the company uses all of its previously generated profits for expansion and growth, without retaining any proportion of it for such unforeseen contingencies. Therefore, previously preserved profits can take care of the future well-being of the workforce of any organization.

References

Aguinis, H. (2011). Organizational responsibility: Doing good and doing well. In S. Zedeck (Ed.), *APA handbook of industrial and organizational psychology*, Vol. 3 (pp. 855–879). Washington DC: American Psychological Association.

Bloomberg Quint. (2020). www.bloombergquint.com/business/hit-by-covid-19-arcelormittal-resorting-to-cost-reduction-measures-to-protect-profitability (Last accessed on 15 September 2020).

BusinessLine. (2020). www.thehindubusinessline.com/companies/ramky-enviro-engineers-partners-ah-investment-for-medical-hazardous-waste-treatment-plant-in-abu-dhabi/article33394321.ece (Last accessed on 17 January, 2021).

Business Standard. (2020a). www.business-standard.com/article/companies/covid-19-hindustan-coca-cola-beverages-to-allow-permanent-work-from-home-120100701326_1.html (Last accessed on 17 January, 2021).

Business Standard. (2020b). www.business-standard.com/podcast/current-affairs/how-indian-companies-are-contributing-to-the-war-against-coronavirus-120033001663_1.html (Last accessed on 26 August 2020).

CNBC. (2020). www.cnbc.com/2020/03/23/how-small-businesses-across-us-are-coping-with-covid-19-pandemic.html (Last accessed on 10 January 2021).

Deodhar, S.Y. (2016). Trapping India's CSR in a legal net: will the mandatory trusteeship contribute to triple bottom line? *Vikalpa, 41*(4), 267–274.

Economic Times. (2020a). https://economictimes.indiatimes.com/industry/services/advertising/how-brands-are-endorsing-social-distancing/nike/slideshow/74927377.cms.

Economic Times. (2020b). https://economictimes.indiatimes.com/small-biz/hr-leadership/leadership/survival-strategies-for-businesses-during-covid-19-lockdown/articleshow/75371157.cms (Last accessed on 27 August 2020).

Economic Times. (2020c). https://economictimes.indiatimes.com/small-biz/startups/newsbuzz/25-of-indian-startups-in-serious-trouble-if-covid-19-persists-for-long-expert/articleshow/75658341.cms (Last accessed on 30 September 2020).

Elkington, J. (1998a). Accounting for the triple bottom line. *Measuring Business Excellence, 2*(3), 18–22.

Elkington, J. (1998b). Partnerships from cannibals with forks: The triple bottom line of 21st-century business. *Environmental Quality Management, 8*(1), 37–51.

Elkington, J. (2018). 25 years ago I coined the phrase "triple bottom line." Here's why it's time to rethink it. *Harvard Business Review, (25)*, 2–5.

Entrepreneur. (2020). www.entrepreneur.com/article/362162 (Last accessed on 9 January 2021).

ERM. (2020) www.erm.com/insights/covid-19-and-people-planet-and-profit-where-to-from-here.

Express Healthcare. (2020). www.expresshealthcare.in/covid19-updates/handling-covid-biomedical-waste-critical-to-prevent-future-epidemics/425554/ (Last accessed on 17 January, 2021).

EY. (2020). www.ey.com/en_gl/covid-19/covid-19-and-pandemic-planning--how-companies-should-respond (Last accessed on 30 August 2020).

Financial Express. (2020). www.financialexpress.com/brandwagon/covid-19-ads-raising-awareness-continues-to-be-a-top-priority-for-brands-and-agencies/1961536/ (Last accessed on 17 January, 2021).

Freight Week. (2020). www.freightweek.org/index.php/en/latest-news/5288-covid-fails-to-impede-dhl-growth (Last accessed on 1 October 2020).

Gimenez, C., Sierra, V., & Rodon, J. (2012). Sustainable operations: Their impact on the triple bottom line. *International Journal of Production Economics, 140*(1), 149–159.

GlobeNewswire. (2020). www.globenewswire.com/news-release/2020/12/17/2147174/0/en/Nature-s-Path-Becomes-the-First-Food-Manufacturing-Company-to-Install-Far-UVC-Light-Technology-in-its-North-American-Facilities.html (Last accessed on 8 January 2021).

Gupta, A., & Kumar, A. (2010). Composites materials: Addressing the climate change. *Asia Pacific Business Review, 6*(1), 78–89.

Harvard Business Review. (2016). https://hbr.org/2016/06/why-companies-are-becoming-b-corporations (Last accessed on 27 August 2020).

ilo.org. (2020). www.ilo.org/empent/whatsnew/WCMS_749275/lang--en/index.htm (Last accessed on 15 September 2020).

Invest India. (2020). www.investindia.gov.in/siru/changing-landscape-csr-india-during-covid-19#:~:text=On%2023%20March%202020%2C%20the,treated%20as%20eligible%20CSR%20activity2.&text=Companies'%20CSR%20funds%20can%20now,healthcare%20infrastructure%20and%20disaster%20management (Last accessed on 9 January 2021).

KPMG. (2020). https://home.kpmg/xx/en/home/insights/2020/04/india-government-and-institution-measures-in-response-to-covid.html (Last accessed on 10 December 2020).

Kumar, V., & Vidhyalakshmi, P. (2012). Cloud computing for business sustainability. *Asia-Pacific Journal of Management Research and Innovation, 8*(4), 461–474.

Leyens, P.C. (2018). Corporate social responsibility in European Union Law: Foundations, developments, enforcement. In *Globalisation of corporate social responsibility and its impact on corporate governance* (pp. 157–176). Springer.

Lata, M., & Gupta, A. (2020). Role of social media in environmental democracy. In *Examining the roles of IT and social media in democratic development and social change* (pp. 275–293). IGI Global.

Littleton, A.C. (1928). What is profit? *Accounting Review*, 278–288.

Livemint. (2015). www.livemint.com/Companies/boSuroFjWnoZq4yvly0itO/Can-CSR-funds-make-a-difference-in-healthcare.html (Last accessed on 17 January, 2021).

Livemint. (2020a). www.livemint.com/industry/advertising/netflix-amul-lifebuoy-create-topical-awareness-campaigns-around-covid-19-11583399363527.html (Last accessed on 17 January, 2021).

Livemint. (2020b). www.livemint.com/companies/news/byju-s-acquires-code-training-app-whitehat-jr-for-300-million-11596647959030.html (Last accessed on 13 September 2020).

Lokhandwala, S., & Gautam, P. (2020). Indirect impact of COVID-19 on environment: A brief study in Indian context. *Environmental Research, 188*, 109807.

McKinsey (2020). www.mckinsey.com/business-functions/marketing-and-sales/our-insights/revenue-growth-management-in-the-covid-19-crisis (Last accessed on 30 August 2020).

McWilliams, A., Parhankangas, A., Coupet, J., Welch, E., & Barnum, D.T. (2016). Strategic decision making for the triple bottom line. *Business Strategy and the Environment, 25*(3), 193–204.

Moravcikova, K., Stefanikova, Ľ., & Rypakova, M. (2015). CSR reporting as an important tool of CSR communication. *Procedia Economics and Finance, 26*, 332–338.

Norman, W., & MacDonald, C. (2004). Getting to the bottom of triple bottom line. *Business Ethics Quarterly*, 243–262.

Oberoi, R. (2014). Benchmarking sustainability: Study of initiatives towards Triple Bottom Line by Indian public sector enterprises. *Asia-Pacific Journal of Management Research and Innovation, 10*(1), 27–37.

Painter-Morland, M. (2006). Triple bottom-line reporting as social grammar: Integrating corporate social responsibility and corporate codes of conduct. Business *Ethics: A European Review, 15*(4), 352–364.

RAND Corporation. (2020). www.rand.org/pubs/research_reports/RRA607-1.html (Last accessed on 11 January 2021).

Reuters Events. (2020). www.reutersevents.com/sustainability/heres-how-companies-can-show-they-put-people-profit (Last accessed on 10 January 2021).

Subagyo, Kumar, V., & Ernestivita, G. (2020). Entrepreneurial parameters and performance of MSMEs in East Java Province of Indonesia. *International Journal of Business Innovation and Research (IJBIR), 23*(2), 267–282.

Tate, W.L., Ellram, L.M., & Kirchoff, J.F. (2010). Corporate social responsibility reports: a thematic analysis related to supply chain management. *Journal of Supply Chain Management, 46*(1), 19–44.

The Environmental Magazine. (2020). https://emagazine.com/the-environ mentally-friendly-companies-leading-the-way/ (Last accessed on 10 January 2021).

The Hindu. (2020). www.thehindu.com/news/national/companies-spending-to-tackle-covid-19-to-be-considered-csr-government/article31143327.ece#:~:text=Companies'%20expenditure%20to%20deal%20with,activities%2C%20according%20to%20the%20government.&text=%E2%80%9CIt%20is%20hereby%20clarified%20that,ministry%20said%20in%20a%20circular. (Last accessed on 8 January 2021).

The Logical Indian. (2021). https://thelogicalindian.com/responsiblebusiness/covid-19-epigamias-step-up-initiative-helps-migrant-workers-rural-communities-get-food-water-26192 (Last accessed on 17 January, 2021).

Van Marrewijk, M. (2003). Concepts and definitions of CSR and corporate sustainability: Between agency and communion. *Journal of Business Ethics, 44*(2–3), 95–105.

We Forum. (2020). www.weforum.org/agenda/2020/04/on-earth-day-heres-what-covid-19-can-teach-us-about-improving-our-planetary-health/ (Last accessed on 13 September 2020).

World Resources Institute. (2020). www.wri.org/blog/2020/04/coronavirus-pandemic-could-give-business-leaders-broader-mandate-sustainability (Last accessed on 28 August 2020).

Zambrano-Monserrate, M.A., Ruano, M.A., & Sanchez-Alcalde, L. (2020). Indirect effects of COVID-19 on the environment. *Science of the Total Environment, 728*, 138813.

11 Online Learning Trends During the Pandemic

Case of Service Sector Professionals

Arunava Dalal, Ajay Kumar Ganguly and Subrata Chattopadhyay

Introduction

Learning is an ongoing process and it continues throughout one's professional career (Kumar & Nanda, 2019). Industry professionals during their corporate careers remain extremely engaged with their performance-related activity. Learning increases the competitive edge and allows one to put the same into practice and enhances growth in one's professional career. Organizations identify the gaps of their employees and try to plug the gaps through training but some gaps continue to exist which is detrimental for the organization (Drysdale, 2012). Also with the advancement in technologies, high-skills jobs call for experts and so online certifications are considered as a feasible solution by the educated professionals to upgrade their knowledge (Balaraman & Kamalakannan, 2016).

As per a report by KPMG and Google (2017), online learning related to "test preparation" and "re-skilling and online certification" is very popular, thus moving this segment from "rapid growth" to the "maturity" stage. But very little research has been done specifically on online learning by professionals who are working at different organizational levels. This realization has encouraged the authors to evaluate if the pandemic has changed the way the working professionals looked at enhancing their knowledge and skills. During the COVID pandemic with the employees in the different sectors working from home, there was perceptually spare time for self-development and enhancement of knowledge. The objective was thus to understand whether the same was perceived as an opportunity by the corporate and professionals and utilized fruitfully.

The research paper is a study on the professionals from the service sector to understand their inclination toward enhancement of their learning during the COVID pandemic. It investigates the areas of learning as carried out by them and the reasons for doing the same. The intention of pursuing the same is also carried out. Services professionals in the middle management category were taken in as the sample for study to understand their preferences, the reason for increasing knowledge in their pursuits, and how far they were satisfied in carrying out the same;

DOI: 10.4324/9781003125648-11

also, how organizations can take advantage of the new technological developments by reskilling and upskilling their employees through a well-designed learning and development framework.

A structured questionnaire was administered to the respondents on the factors of investigation and was analyzed to arrive at the outcomes. The study brings out the perspectives considered effective by the corporates and the decision-making strategies to enhance their growth and employees' learning initiatives.

The next part of the paper is dedicated to the reviews of earlier literature on online learning and knowledge management. After this, the hypothesis of the study is stated followed by a discussion on the research methodology. Next, data analysis and the findings are discussed followed by a proposed framework and conclusions.

Literature Review

Need for Upskilling by Employees

In this world, technological advances are changing the way organizations will work in the future. A report by World Economic Forum (2018) has identified four specific technological developments, namely the ever-increasing presence of "high-speed mobile internet", "artificial intelligence (AI)", "big data analytics" and "cloud technology" as the drivers for growth during 2018 and 2022.

Automation will make many present job functions redundant and so there is a requirement for upskilling the existing workforce. The increased demand for big data, Internet of Things (IoT) and machine learning has created a void in the technology market, due to which companies are looking at upskilling and reskilling activities for their at-risk workforce to reduce the skill gap (Iyer, 2020).

As per a report by Deloitte (2020), AI adoption had been instrumental in the automation of several business processes leading to an increase in efficiency and allowing the workforce to concentrate on more value-added productive work. But due to this transformation, it is estimated that 37% of UK jobs, 47% of US jobs, and 77% of Chinese jobs are susceptible to loss.

So, it's imperative that employees understand the changing technological landscapes and look at ways to remain relevant to their organizations. The expected loss of existing jobs will be taken over by the new job functions inline with the new technological advances. So, upskilling can be considered by present employees to continue with their professional life and be part of the new industrial revolution.

Organization and Employee Upskilling

Traditionally organizations used to recruit university graduates and postgraduates to fill up their vacancies and to bring new skills, capabilities and knowledge and groom them for future leaders. With the reduction in the average lifespan of a skill, the above approach is being seen as insufficient to close the skill gaps (Deloitte (2020). This fact can be corroborated from the suggestion made by the United Kingdom's Career and Employability service that their schools need to come out with ten times the present production of computer science graduates to meet the market demand for data scientists (Boyd, 2017).

As per a survey conducted by LinkedIn for their third annual report on Workplace Learning (2019), there has been an increase in budget and executive support for proactively working on ways to identify the skill gaps as the decreasing shelf life of skills is posing a major challenge for organizations.

As per a report by the World Economic Forum (2018), 54% of all employees need to be reskilled or upskilled by 2022 due to changes in ways of doing business. The scenario leads to employees being apprehensive of losing their jobs and the organizations finding a dearth of suitable manpower to take advantage of the new industrial wave. The cost of replacing an existing employee is high and can be 150% of the annual salary of the person (Lucas, 2013). Under such a situation, organizations are looking at upgrading the skillsets and knowledge of their existing workforces to overcome the potential skill gap.

Use of Knowledge Management in Organizations

Knowledge management (KM) gets formulated in an organization when it builds a process in a systematic, deliberate and explicit way to manage knowledge, with the objective to maximize its value through effective usage of knowledge (Bixler, 2005). KM is used by organizations to drive agility in their operations (Kumar & Vidhyalakshmi, 2012). Mittal and Kumar (2019) have suggested that a good KM project needs to be aligned with the corporate strategy, identify the existing knowledge prevailing in the organization, and put the correct processes in place along with garnering the support and consent of both the internal and external stakeholders.

The knowledge management framework can be broadly grouped into different steps, starting with recognition of the need and identifying the knowledge resources. After the identification stage is the step for gaining, generating or eliminating knowledge-related resources. This is followed by accessing, applying, sharing of the knowledge, and finally storage of the knowledge. All the steps are interrelated and dependent on various factors in any organization so they need to identify the KM model to be implemented by them depending on their existing needs and organizational structure (Mittal & Kumar, 2019).

Different KM frameworks have been put forward during the past years. Table 11.1 provides some noteworthy knowledge management models considering the dynamic and fast-evolving technological advances in today's world.

Table 11.1 Knowledge management models

Knowledge management model	*Key elements of the model*
Bukowitz and Williams (1999)	1. Knowledge used to respond to the dynamic requirements of the marketplace 2. Available knowledge and strategic framework of the organization complement each other
Gamble and Blackwell (2001)	1. Organization accesses its strengths and weaknesses and the knowledge is disseminated and used as per requirement using different techniques
Selamat et al. (2006)	1. Systems Thinking 2. Knowledge generation and usability through iterative processes 3. Requirement of robust technological infrastructure
Birkinshaw and Sheehan (2002)	1. Creation of Knowledge 2. Mobilization 3. Distribution 4. Commoditization

The Present State of Employee Upskilling Activities

The indicators in the above discussions point toward a complete change in ways of doing business where more than 50% of all employees will find their job being declared as redundant. Though the existing jobs may get outmoded, many new jobs will get created in line with the new technological developments. So, to remain relevant and employed, employees need to upskill or look at reskilling themselves.

The upskilling and reskilling activities can be employee-driven or employer-driven because businesses will be looking at meeting their skillset gaps through upskilling their existing workforces. The upskilling could be through online courses, instructor-led training or a hybrid mode of training.

Amazon announced in a press release (2019) their pledge to upskill 1 lac US employees for in-demand jobs by 2025. They claimed to be spending $700 million on different programs for upskilling employees so that they be conversant with the new technologies like machine learning and software engineering. IBM in 2016 announced its commitment to invest $1 billion in training and upskilling employees (Oesch, 2016). These are examples of some organizations that have already started to upskill their employees for the future.

Udemy is an online learning platform for different types of skills and catering to a wide variety of people segments. Research conducted by them highlighted the fact that 95% of their respondents agreed to the point that lifelong learning was essential for their professional growth and about 50% of the respondents were willing to upskill themselves by spending their own time and money (Shinkus, 2017).

The above instances highlight that the employees are aware that upskilling is the only way for them to remain productive for their organizations. So, to remain relevant and in tune with the technological developments, they are willing to invest their time and money to upskill themselves.

Online Courses for Upskilling

In the 22nd Global CEO Survey report published by PricewaterhouseCoopers (PwC) (2019), 55% of the CEOs interviewed expressed their inability to innovate effectively due to skill gaps. The major constraints for organizations to upskill their workforce are organizing, time management, training capabilities and skill development (Probst & Scharff, 2019). A few of these constraints can be mitigated through Massive Online Open Courses (MOOCs) as these courses are easily accessible over the web and can be accessed by everyone.

The main benefits of MOOCs for employees are that these courses from reputed universities and institutions can be accessed by them from anywhere, at their own time, and are self-paced (Sharma & Kumar, 2017). Employees can be proactive in taking up courses depending on their requirements and intention. Professionally, these courses will be beneficial for them as they will be able to showcase their newly acquired skills and knowledge to their organization. These courses allow the employees to be responsible for their development and excel in the rapidly changing business scenarios.

For companies, the advantages of including MOOCs in their training programs are help in reskilling and upskilling their employees and increasing their flexibility. It also works as an incentive for retaining existing employees and attracting new people as it sends a message to their workforce that the organization cares for their development so that they can perform better and is a learning organization (Villepin & Cook, 2020).

Besides online courses can be made interactive by adding elements of gamification and customization. So, these translate into advantages like greater flexibility, increased level of convenience and lesser cost (Mitra, 2020)

Along with the advantages MOOCs have for both the employers and employees, there are a few disadvantages too and that is the comparatively low completion rate for online courses (Kumar & Sharma, 2016). The completion rate ranges from 0.7% to 52.1%, with the median at 12.6% (Jordan, 2015), where completion rate is the percentage of students enrolled for a course and among them who have completed it. The other drawbacks include lack of interactivity between the facilitator and the learner, different levels of comprehension of a subject matter by the participants, and difficulty to measure learners' involvement during the learning process.

Upskilling During the COVID-19 Pandemic

The COVID-19 pandemic has forced organizations toward faster digital transformation. The Organization for Economic Cooperation and Development (OECD) on 10 June 2020 had projected the global economic growth to drop by 6% under a single-wave scenario and 7.6% for a second-wave scenario in 2020.

Under such global economic distress, many organizations are expected to face difficult situations and it's expected that they will be relooking at their way of doing business. This will include continuing, at least for a certain percentage of the workforce, with a virtual office setup and remote working along with upskilling of their employees "work from home" (WFH) culture, which during the COVID-19 pandemic has left people with enough time to themselves as they are saving on commuting, socializing and running errands (Ghosh, 2020).

For organizations, this is an opportune time to upskill their employees while they are working from home to safeguard themselves from the future market turmoil by building an agile and knowledgeable workforce. On the part of the employees, looking at the uncertain market conditions, they might also like to upskill themselves to equip themselves for the future workplace post-COVID-19 pandemic.

The work-from-home concept can lead to a drop in hiring costs and developing cross-function teams for organizations (Sytch & Greer, 2020). If the job can be done from remote locations, it opens up alternatives for organizations to hire from any location as distance would not be a constraint. Employees with the required skills and proficiency will be able to work for organizations offering remote working facilities. So, for employees, it will be beneficial to hone their knowledge and develop new skills as per the current and future industry requirements so that their employability factor increases. This situation has arisen due to the present pandemic situation and was not explored by businesses during pre-COVID times.

So, the COVID-19 pandemic has opened up opportunities for businesses and employees to operate differently and more efficiently. "Upskilling" and "reskilling" of the workforce have gained paramount importance to overcome the difficult and uncertain future that this pandemic has pushed the world into.

Objectives

- To understand the self-motivation for taking online courses and its effect on career development
- To investigate the effectiveness of learning in virtual vis-à-vis physical form

- To understand the significance of digital proficiency on adaptation to online learning
- To understand the impact of pedagogical and technical competency enhancement through online learning

Formulation of the Hypotheses

The importance of the upskilling of the working professionals has been accepted and established through different literature. The pandemic times may have accelerated the process but understanding how it is perceived by people who are at the center of this whole action is the object of this study. The authors, in this study, have tried to identify the importance that the professionals, mainly from the service sector, are putting into learning during the COVID-19 period and the benefits that they expect from this exercise in their professional career during the pandemic times.

Self-motivation for Taking Online Courses

The COVID-19 scenario has put the world economy in a downslide and it will have its impact on different sectors across the world. There is a projection of huge job losses due to the pandemic. The International Labour Organization (ILO) in its June 2020 report has estimated 400 million full-time job losses in the second quarter of 2020. Another report titled "Tackling the COVID-19 youth employment crisis in Asia and the Pacific", by Asian Development Bank (ADB) and ILO, published in August 2020, has estimated job loss for 4.1 million youth in India due to the pandemic (Economic Times, 2020)

Under such a situation it can be expected that the professionals will be self-directed toward upskilling themselves to remain employable and significant for the industry. As the study was considered among professionals from the service sector so the hypothesis has been formulated as:

> *Ha1: There is a significant relationship between self-motivated online courses and the career development of professionals engaged in the service industry.*

The Physical Form of Learning Versus Virtual Learning

With the advance in technologies, a learner need not have to physically visit any place to get trained or educated on a skillset (Kumar & Nanda, 2020). Using the Internet one can communicate and collaborate and this helps in having interactions between the learners and the teachers, thus creating an irreplaceable learning environment (Burbules & Callister, 2000, p. 277).

Even with the deluge of online portals offering different courses that can be accessed by all and explored at their convenience by the learners, the learning experience is different from that of a face-to-face classroom. This has been because the involvement of the faculties and their acceptance has been moderate for online courses along with limited modifications in online pedagogies (Natriello, 2005).

Previous studies have indicated that students initially feel that they learn less through virtual courses as compared to the classroom or physical form of courses (Zeng & Perris, 2004).

It may be safely considered that all the professionals would have undergone a formal education system before embarking on their professional life. During the pandemic, the level of digitization has accelerated so that physical interactions can be avoided and professionals have taken virtual platforms for fulfilling their learning needs. While taking the online courses, the learners would have compared the output with that of the physical form of learning which everyone has experienced. The medium and environment also play a major role in the effective learning process, for which the second hypothesis for the study was:

> *Ha2: The professionals are very much more inclined toward the physical form of learning than virtual learning.*

Digital Proficiency and Online Learning

With online learning for upskilling being the "new normal" during the COVID-19 days, it is imperative to consider that professionals would be accessing these courses, online lectures, training, or workshops on digital platforms.

For this reason, the level of digital adeptness of the learners could be a major element for them in successfully completing, comprehending and internalizing the learnings from the online courses. So the third hypothesis considered by the authors was:

> *Ha3: There is a significant relationship between the digital proficiency of professionals and online learning.*

Online Pedagogy and Technical Competency Enhancement

Previous studies have identified that for having effective online courses, there needs to be well-developed forums and communities for online learning, the instructors need to be available for the students and the learners must possess the correct device and the right technology. Also, quality and timely interactions between the students and the instructors, consistent and relevant course design, technical knowhow of the instructors, and technical support were the other factors which the students considered essential for having a satisfying experience of their online learning (Lao & Gonzales, 2005; Northrup, 2002).

One of the major differences between face-to-face and online learning environments is that the teachers are required to be attentive to the individual learners more in the virtual mode than in face-to-face for effective online pedagogy. This happens because, in a physical setup, learners have the opportunity to interact and learn from each other and the instructor, whereas in virtual classes, learning is more from the instructors than from other students (Park et al., 2013).

Thus, online pedagogy is an important aspect for enhancement of the technical competency of the learners, thus leading to the next hypothesis as:

> *Ha4: There is a significant relationship between online pedagogy and technical enhancement of the learners.*

Research Methodology

This study is restricted to the state of West Bengal, a state in the eastern part of India.

Data Collection

In this study, data were collected from primary sources. A structured questionnaire was designed to collect primary data. This questionnaire was prepared in Google forms so that it can be circulated digitally to the respondents The questionnaire was shared with people working at the middle management level in different organizations and practicing professionals. The authors approached their acquaintances for their responses with the objective that there was representation from different industries. Respondents were from 12 different industries, thus having representation from all major service sectors. To collect the secondary data, different related books, research papers, journals and online sources were referred to.

Sampling Design

Convenience Sampling is the sampling method of this study: 128 responses were received during the data collection period which was from 14 August 2020 to 2 September 2020, out of which 120 samples were finally considered, which had all the required details for further analysis.

Tools of Analysis

The data were collected through a proper questionnaire and the data were sorted out, ordered, and analyzed deliberately utilizing some significant measurable statistical tools.

Statistical Tools for Data Analysis

The responses were validated and filtered, and then analyzed using SPSS 25 packages with chi-square with p-values and Factor Analysis.

Profile of the Respondents

Among the total respondents, 62.5% were male (Table 11.2).

The professionals were mainly from two age brackets – 25 years to 40 years (34%) and 41 years to 60 years consisting of the remaining bracket (Table 11.3). The industry-wise distribution is given in Table 11.4

Analysis and Findings

From among the total responses received, 14 questionnaire forms received by the method of primary data assortment were loaded into the SPSS package for the preliminary analysis. It was observed that some criteria had a bearing on online learning. But, to arrive at a Discriminant Analysis output, having all the standards would result in an extended model. To overcome this issue, the correlational analysis was used for data reduction. Also, inputs of these professionals from the service industry were taken for the method of data reduction.

Cronbach's test was conducted to check the data reliability, and the value was revealed as 0.859 – that is considered fair to proceed (Table 11.5). Here the authors conjointly tried to spot the comment or comments that if omitted would enhance the value of Cronbach's alpha and it was identified that if the Likert scale comment "My organization

Table 11.2 Gender-wise distribution

Gender	*Frequency*	*Percent*	*Cumulative Percent*
Male	75	63%	63%
Female	45	38%	100%
Total	**120**		

Source: Primary data

Table 11.3 Age group-wise distribution

Age group	*Frequency*	*Percent*	*Cumulative percent*
25 to 40	41	34%	34%
41 to 60	79	66%	100%
Total	**120**		

Source. Primary data

Table 11.4 Industry-wise distribution

Industry	*Frequency*	*Percent*	*Cumulative percent*
Banking	8	6.7%	6.7%
Supply chain / logistics	9	7.5%	14.2%
Education	14	11.7%	25.8%
Healthcare	12	10.0%	35.8%
Hospitality	10	8.3%	44.2%
E-commerce	11	9.2%	53.3%
Consultancy	12	10.0%	63.3%
Information technology	11	9.2%	72.5%
Media & entertainment	8	6.7%	79.2%
Insurance	8	6.7%	85.8%
Professional services	9	7.5%	93.3%
Retail	8	6.7%	100.0%
Total	**120**		

Source: Primary data

Table 11.5 Reliability statistics

Reliability statistics		
Cronbach's alpha	*Cronbach's alpha based on standardized items*	*N of items*
0.859	0.880	9

Source: Primary data

supports me to take the courses Financially and Officially" was omitted then the value would be increased to 0.906 (Table 11.6)

Next, the inter-item correlation matrix (Table 11.7) was measured, which delineated that every of the queries is considerably correlative with one another except the following Likert scale comment, "My organization supports me to take the courses Financially and Officially".

To measure the sampling adequacy KMO analysis through SPSS software was done. The result arrived was at 0.845, which is fair enough to proceed with the correlational analysis. During this case, Bartlett's test was done and a desirable result was obtained to proceed for further steps.

The Kaiser-Meyer-Olkin (KMO) is used to measure the sampling adequacy, which ranges from 0 and 1. The values which are nearer to 1 are considered better, with the suggested minimum value being 0.6.

The test for the null hypothesis is done through Bartlett's Test of Sphericity. In this, the correlation matrix has a scalar matrix. Considering the above discussion points, these tests present the minimum standard to go ahead for conducting the correlational analysis.

Table 11.6 Item – total statistics

	Scale mean if item deleted	*Scale variance if item deleted*	*Corrected item – total correlation*	*Squared multiple correlation*	*Cronbach's alpha if item deleted*
Skill augmentation and bridging knowledge gap through online courses	29.90	30.410	.796	.762	.825
Utilize spare time attending webinar in professional domain	29.97	31.024	.683	.718	.835
Online certification program will give me an extra competitive professional edge	30.03	28.688	.811	.748	.820
Online conferences and online idea-sharing platforms sharpen ideas and knowledge domain	29.90	30.242	.777	.750	.826
The pedagogical and technical competency of the instructor and organizing platform	29.68	31.398	.678	.613	.836
Faculty interaction and easy to grab their concentration on my doubts	30.43	30.769	.661	.565	.836
The organization supports me to take the courses financially and officially	31.34	35.151	.119	.301	.906
I do believe that e- certification and certification is very important along with course content for personal uplift	30.08	32.809	.461	.394	.856
Very much satisfied with these online courses, webinars and management development programs	30.34	32.697	.604	.514	.843

Source: Primary data

Table 11.7 Inter-item correlation matrix

	Q6	*Q7*	*Q8*	*Q9*	*Q10*	*Q11*	*Q12*	*Q13*	*Q14*
Q6	1.00	.748	.702	.792	.677	.598	.137	.332	.535
Q7	.748	1.00	.769	.681	.656	.428	-.040	.360	.401
Q8	.702	.769	1.00	.733	.678	.545	.120	.530	.515
Q9	.792	.681	.733	1.000	.690	.521	.004	.462	.611
Q10	.677	.656	.678	.690	1.000	.351	.151	.294	.400
Q11	.598	.428	.545	.521	.351	1.000	.363	.352	.555
Q12	.137	.040	.120	.004	.151	.363	1.000	–.032	.024
Q13	.332	.360	.530	.462	.294	.352	–.032	1.000	.509
Q14	.535	.401	.515	.611	.400	.555	.024	.509	1.00

Source: Primary data

The correlational analysis was executed to understand the core factors for online learning and career enhancement of the professionals engaged within the service sectors. This method was considered suitable as it does not require any preexistence of functional relationships. It is used commonly for the process of data reduction. Its application is to reduce a huge count of variables to a smaller count of core factors.

Test of Hypothesis Regarding Interrelationship between the Variables

- **Null Hypothesis H_0:** There is no statistically significant interrelationship between variables affecting the Online Learning of Professionals in the spare time of this pandemic situation and their satisfaction level.
- **Alternate Hypothesis H_1:** There may be a statistically significant interrelationship between variables affecting the Online Learning of Professionals in the spare time of this pandemic situation and their satisfaction level.

Bartlett's Test of Sphericity

Considering a 95% degree of Significance, Alpha = 0.05.

The p-value (Sig.) of .000 < 0.05 is indicative of the validity of the Factor Analysis.

As p < alpha, the Null Hypothesis (H_0) is rejected and acknowledges the substitute or alternative Hypothesis (H_1) that there might be a factually huge interrelationship between factors.

The Kaiser-Meyer Olkin (KMO) and Bartlett's Test which are used for measuring the sampling adequacy were utilized to analyze the fittingness of Factor Analysis (Table 11.8). The estimated value of chi-square is 673.114 with 36 degrees of freedom. At a 0.05 level of significance, it is significant. The KMO measurement of 0.845 is likewise noteworthy as it is more than 0.50. Thus Factor Analysis has been considered as a suitable procedure for additional investigation of the information.

Table 11.8 KMO and Bartlett's test

Kaiser-Meyer-Olkin measure of sampling adequacy		*.845*
Bartlett's Test of Sphericity	Approx. chi-square	673.114
	Df	36
	Sig.	.000

Source: Primary data

Generally, 0 < KMO < 1, if KMO > 0.5, the sample is adequate. Here, KMO = 0.845.This shows that the sample is adequate and Factor Analysis can be executed.

Eigenvalues (Selection of the components with Eigenvalues >= 1)

The underlying components are the quantities of the factors utilized in the Factor Analysis. In any case, not each of the nina factors will be held. In the current examination, just the two components will be extracted by joining the pertinent factors. The eigenvalues are the differences between the components and the column indicates the eigenvalue. The primary factor will consistently represent the most difference and consequently have the most elevated eigenvalues. The following element will represent the leftover difference as far as possible and a similar procedure will be continued till the last factor. The level of change indicates the percentage of overall change that is responsible due to each factor and the total percentage indicates the total level of fluctuation accounted for by the present and the former elements.

In the current study, the initial two components clarify 68.166% of the fluctuation (Table 11.9). The rotation totals of the squared stacking speak of the distribution of the change after running the varimax rotation with Kaiser normalization. The varimax turn attempts to maximize the difference of every one of the factors.

Commonality means the regular variance and it varies from 0 to 1. Quantities nearer to 1 propose that extracted variables clarify a greater amount of the variation of a single item. Details are given in Table 11.10.

Finding the Core Factors

The Rotated Factor Matrix speaks to the turned factor loadings, which are the relationships between the factors and the elements. The factor segment speaks to the turned elements that have been extricated out of the complete factors. These are the center elements, which have been utilized as the last factor after information decrease. As per the gathering of the components, each gathering of variables is named which will speak to the assembled factor and speak to the elements as is represented in Table 11.11.

Table 11.9 Total variance explained

Component	*Initial eigenvalues*			*Extraction sums of squared loadings*		
	Total	*% of variance*	*Cumulative %*	*Total*	*% of variance*	*Cumulative %*
1	**4.947**	54.971	54.971	4.947	54.971	54.971
2	**1.188**	13.195	68.166	1.188	13.195	68.166
3	.960	10.666	78.831			
4	.592	6.578	85.409			
5	.448	4.973	90.383			
6	.275	3.060	93.443			
7	.243	2.703	96.145			
8	.208	2.307	98.452			
9	.139	1.548	100.000			
Extraction method: principal component analysis.						

Source: Primary data

Table 11.10 Communalities

Communalities (h^2)		
	Initial	*Extraction*
Augment my skill and knowledge gap through online courses	1.000	.772
Utilize my spare time by attending a webinar in my professional domain	1.000	.713
Utilization of time in different online certification program will give me an extra competitive edge in my professional domain	1.000	.783
Online conferences and online idea-sharing platforms sharpen my ideas and knowledge domain	1.000	.804
The pedagogical and technical competency of the instructor and organizing platform for my interest as a professional	1.000	.602
Online learning mode, satisfaction in faculty interaction and easy to grab their concentration on my doubts	1.000	.687
My organization supports me to take the courses financially and officially	1.000	.895
e-Certification and certification is very important along with course content for personal uplift	1.000	.379
Satisfaction with these online courses, webinars and management development programs	1.000	.500
Extraction method: principal component analysis.		

Source: Primary data

Table 11.11 Related component matrix

	Component	
	1	*2*
Online conferences and online idea-sharing platforms sharpen my ideas and knowledge domain	.894	
Utilization of time in different online certification programs will give a competitive edge in my professional domain	.871	
Augment my skill and knowledge gap through online courses	.846	
Utilize my spare time by attending a webinar in my professional domain	.844	
The pedagogical and technical competency of the instructor and organizing platform bearing as a professional	.760	
Satisfaction in online courses, webinars and Management Development Programmes	.695	
e-Certification and certification is very important along with course content for personal uplift	.612	
My organization supports me to take the courses financially and officially		.943
Online learning mode, satisfaction in faculty interaction, and easy to grab their concentration on my doubts	.575	.597
Extraction method: principal component analysis.		
Rotation method: varimax with Kaiser normalization.[a]		

Source: Primary data
a Rotation converged in three iterations.

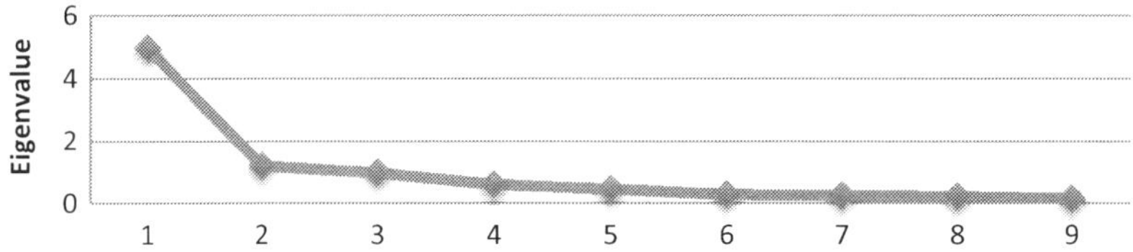

Figure 11.1 Scree plot.
Source: Primary data

Scree Plot

The Scree plot diagrams the eigenvalue against each factor. The diagram (Figure 11.1) represents the sudden change in the slope of the line after factor 2 of the Scree plot. This indicates that after factor 2 the complete change represents very little variation as the line is almost parallel to the x-axis. Table 11.12 gives the name of the two key variables.

Table 11.12 Name of the two key factors

Factor	*Variables included*	*Name of the factors*
1	Online conferences and online idea-sharing platforms sharpen my ideas and knowledge domain in my spare time An online certification program will give me an extra competitive edge in my professional domain Augment skill and knowledge gap through online courses Utilize my spare time by attending a webinar in my professional domain The pedagogical and technical competency of the instructor and organizing platform Satisfaction in online courses, webinars and management development programs e-Certification and certification is very important along with course content for personal uplift	**Utilizing spare time & career advancement**
2	My organization supports me to take the courses financially and officially Online learning mode aids faculty interaction, and easy to grab their concentration on my doubts	**Individual Satisfaction**

Source: Primary data

Hypothesis Testing

Hypothesis 1

Ha0: There is no significant relationship between self-motivated online courses and career development of professionals engaged in the service industry.

Ha1: There is a significant relationship between self-motivated online courses and the career development of professionals engaged in the service industry.

Remarks: Since the p-value in the case of the chi-square test and Phi and Crammer-V test is less than 0.05 (Table 11.13), it can be said that the Null Hypothesis is rejected and the Alternate Hypothesis has been accepted.

Hypothesis 2

Ha0: The professionals are very much indifferent toward the physical form of learning versus virtual learning.

Table 11.13 Testing of Hypothesis 1

Pearson chi-square test value	*Df*	*Asymptotic significance (2-sided) or p-value*	*Likelihood ratio*	*Df*	*Asymptotic significance (2-sided) or p-value*	*Symmetric measures*		
						Phi -Test	*Cramer's V*	*Approximate significance*
13.209	5	.021	15.325	5	.009	.332	.332	.021

Source: Primary data

Table 11.14 Testing of Hypothesis 2

Pearson chi-square test value	*df*	*Asymptotic significance (2-sided) or p-value*	*Likelihood ratio*	*Df*	*Asymptotic significance (2-sided) or p-value*	*Symmetric measures*		
						Phi -Test	*Cramer's V*	*Approximate significance*
33.939	5	.000	37.103	5	.000	.532	.532	.000

Source: Primary data

Ha2: The professionals are very much inclined toward the physical form of learning rather than virtual learning.

Remarks: Since the p-value in the case of the chi-square test and Phi and Crammer-V Test is less than 0.05 and even 0.00 (Table 11.14), so it can be said that the Null Hypothesis is rejected and the Alternate Hypothesis has been accepted.

Hypothesis 3

Ha0: There is no significant relationship between the digital proficiency of professionals and online learning.

Ha3: There is a significant relationship between the digital proficiency of professionals and online learning.

Remarks: Since the p value in the case of the chi-square test and Phi and Crammer-V test is greater than 0.05 (Table 11.15), it can be said that the Null Hypothesis is accepted and Alternate Hypothesis has been rejected. Thus, there is no significant relationship between the digital proficiency of professionals and online learning.

This seems to be at variance to earlier literature, but this may have happened due to the specific nature of the respondents. The respondents being all professionals, and in today's world must have been using digital

Table 11.15 Testing of Hypothesis 3

Pearson chi-square test value	*Df*	*Asymptotic significance (2-sided) or p-value*	*Likelihood ratio*	*Df*	*Asymptotic significance (2-sided) or p-value*	*Symmetric measures*		
						Phi -Test	*Cramer's V*	*Approximate significance*
8.834	5	.116	8.346	5	.138	.271	.271	.116

Source: Primary data

Table 11.16 Testing of Hypothesis 4

Pearson chi-square test value	*df*	*Asymptotic significance (2-sided) or p-value*	*Likelihood ratio*	*Df*	*Asymptotic significance (2-sided) or p-value*	*Symmetric measures*		
						Phi -Test	*Cramer's V*	*Approximate significance*
81.091	16	.000	55.396	16	.000	.822	.411	.000

Source: Primary data

devices for their office work, one might have thought that no further digital proficiency is required for undergoing the online learning sessions than what they already possessed. Hence this result was arrived at.

Hypothesis 4

Ha0: There is no significant relationship between online pedagogy and technical enhancement of online learners.
Ha4: There is a significant relationship between online pedagogy and technical enhancement of online learners

Remarks: Since the p-value in the case of the chi-square test and Phi and Crammer-V test is less than 0.05 and even 0.00 (Table 11.16), thus it can be said that the Null Hypothesis is rejected and Alternate Hypothesis has been accepted.

Proposed Model for Organizations' Learning and Development Project Post-COVID

The findings indicate the willingness and acceptance by the professionals that the utilization of the COVID times for upskilling and reskilling is an appropriate thing to do. Organizations should ensure that the efforts and intentions of their employees should also be channeled in the right direction in line with the business goals through the correct usage of

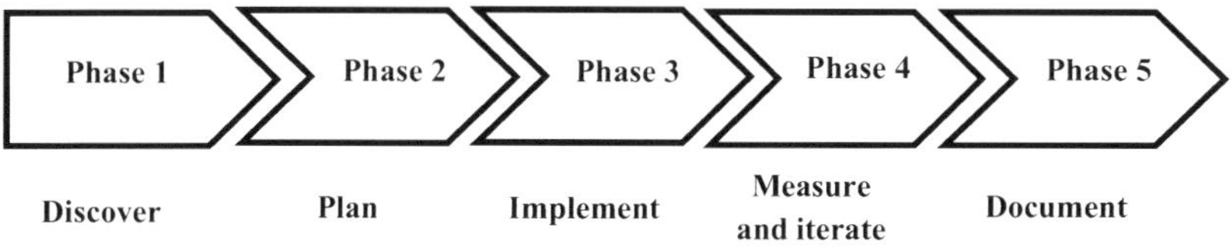

Figure 11.2 Different phases of the proposed model.

online teaching-learning tools and the implementation of effective online pedagogy.

The pandemic situation has led to the "new normal" for businesses across the world where "digital transformation" has happened in an accelerated mode. The movement to digital learning "Work From Home" working positions leading to a dispersed workforce are a few of the challenges that organizations need to address while framing their learning and development

Based on the "new normal" situation, a framework through which organizations can reskill and upskill their employees to remain relevant in the post-pandemic times is proposed here. The model is broken down into five key phases as in Figure 11.2, namely Discovery Phase, Plan Phase, Implementation Phase, Measure and Iterate, Documentation Phase.

Discovery Phase

a During this stage, the organization needs to identify the skills that are required by it as per their business strategy in the post-COVID period.
b The organization also needs to evaluate its present available knowledge and skills.
c Gap analysis is to be done to identify the skills that need to be acquired by the employees or knowledge that needs to be reinforced.

Planning Phase

a The organization needs to identify sources for the acquisition of the required knowledge and develop the skill sets of its employees, considering the "new normal" situation. This will include moving to a technology-enabled digital model, where collaboration with external institutions can also be an option.
b Expand the capabilities of the employees so that they are comfortable operating in a digital environment.
c Besides developing or enhancing the technical skills of the workforce, the social and emotional skills of the employees need to be worked upon so that they remain motivated and inclined toward

their upskilling exercises by the organization. This is important considering that WFH and remote working for employees are a possibility in the "new normal".

d A few other skills like adaptability and resilience are a focus area to ensure the sustainability of the organization along with its employees in the post-COVID era. So, this also needs to be looked at in this phase.

Implementation Phase

a After the planning, it is the execution stage where reskilling and upskilling programs for the respective employees are to be rolled out.
b Customized training programs in the virtual platform are to be launched to close the identified knowledge gaps.

Measure and Iterate

a The effectiveness of the learning and development strategy of the organization need to be evaluated periodically to ensure that the learning exercises are going on as planned and results obtained as desired.
b This will enhance the organization's knowledge base and by understanding what works and what doesn't, the learnings could be applied during the planning phase in the future.
c This is an iterative process to reach the desired result and building on the organization's knowledge base.

Documentation Phase

a Though this is mentioned as the last phase, ideally, this can be executed after the completion of each phase for convenience and ensuring no loss of data due to the time gap.
b This will ensure formalizing and refining the process in the future, thus saving on valuable resources like time and money.
c Documentation will support training, communication and reuse of the program.

Conclusions

The research paper mainly envisages the professionals from the service sector to understand the effectiveness of learning in the virtual mode in the pandemic situation and to investigate the self-motivation for taking the online courses, and its effect on career advancement. The COVID-19 pandemic has opened up opportunities for service professionals to operate differently – upskilling themselves with different virtual opportunities. The paper emphasizes the need to understand the career advancement of professionals from service industries by utilizing the spare time in this pandemic situation, and how organizations can utilize the learning attitude of their employees for advancing their business objectives in the post-COVID period.

From this statistical analysis, it has been inferred that irrespective of age and gender difference most of the professionals from the service industries are inclined toward upskilling by taking online courses through different modes and want to fully utilize the spare time which arises in this pandemic situation. From the organizations' perspective, this is a good sign as upskilled and reskilled employees will be able to help the organizations to take full advantage of the new technologies for better value creation for the businesses. A framework has been proposed by the authors using which companies can guide their workforce in their journey of upskilling, by creating customized learning and development plans for their employees where WFH and a distributed workforce are expected to the "new normal". It will be symbiotically beneficial for the employees and the employers as both will be complementing each other for a better business process after the pandemic and overcoming the uncertain future which COVID-19 has caused.

Research Limitations/Future Scope of Research

The study has been conducted in one state of India and covering only the service sector. This can be extended to other sectors and other geographical areas to make it more generalized. There is ample scope of the study of the practical implications of online learning of the professionals and the nature of the application of this acquired knowledge in different sectors.

References

Amazon. (2019). Amazon Pledges to Upskill 100,000 U.S. Employees for In-Demand Jobs by 2025. Retrieved September 14, 2020, from https://press.aboutamazon.com/news-releases/news-release-details/amazon-pledges-upskill-100000-us-employees-demand-jobs-2025.

Balaraman, P., & Kamalakannan, P. (2016). Skill gap analysis and training needs in Indian aerospace industry. *Journal of Airline and Airport Management, 6*(2), 115–132.

Birkinshaw, J., & Sheehan, T. (2002). Managing the knowledge life cycle. *MIT Sloan Management Review, 44*(1), 75.

Bixler, C.H. (2005). Developing a foundation for a successful knowledge management system. In M. Stankoshy (Ed.), *Creating the discipline of knowledge management: The latest in university research* (pp.51–65). Amsterdam, Boston: Elsevier Butterworth-Heinemann

Boyd, C. (2017). AI scientists: How can companies deal with the shortage of talent? Retrieved September 12, 2020, from https://towardsdatascience.com/ai-scientists-how-can-companies-deal-with-the-shortage-of-talent-11ab48566677.

Bukowitz, W.R., & Williams, R.L. (1999). *The Knowledge Management Field Book*, Knowledge management process framework: 9–12.

Burbules, N., & Callister, T. (2000). Universities in transition: The promise and the challenge of new technologies. *The Teachers College Record, 102*(2), 271–293.

Deloitte. (2020). The upskilling imperative – Building a future-ready workforce for the AI age. Retrieved September 16, 2020, from www2.deloitte.com/content/dam/Deloitte/ca/Documents/deloitte-analytics/ca-covid19-upskilling-EN-AODA.pdf.

Drysdale, S. (2012). Addressing the skills gap. *Power Engineering, 116*(12), 13–15.

Economic Times. (2020, August 18). 41 lakh youth lose jobs in India due to COVID-19 pandemic: ILO-ADB Report. Retrieved September 16, 2020, from https://economictimes.indiatimes.com/news/economy/indicators/41-lakh-youth-lose-jobs-in-india-due-to-covid-19-pandemic-ilo-adb-report/articleshow/77613218.cms?from=mdr.

Gamble, P.R., & Blackwell, J. (2001). *Knowledge management: A state of the art guide* (pp. 118–134). Kogan Page.

Ghosh, S. (2020). Upskilling and work from home are key aspects during Covid-19 crisis. Retrieved September 14, 2020, from https://hr.economictimes.indiatimes.com/news/trends/upskilling-and-work-from-home-are-key-aspects-during-covid-19/76793144.

International Labour Organization. (2020, June). ILO Monitor: COVID-19 and the world of work. Fifth edition. Retrieved September 15, 2020, from www.ilo.org/wcmsp5/groups/public/@dgreports/@dcomm/documents/briefingnote/wcms_749399.pdf.

Iyer, R.K. (2020). Upskilling and reskilling for workforce of the future. Retrieved September 17, 2020, from www.lntinfotech.com/wp-content/uploads/2020/04/Upskilling-and-Reskilling-for-Workforce-of-the-Future.pdf.

Jordan, K. (2015). Massive open online course completion rates revisited: Assessment, length and attrition. *International Review of Research in Open and Distributed Learning, 16*(3), 341–358.

KPMG and Google. (2017). Online education in India: 2021. Retrieved September 12, 2020, from https://assets.kpmg/content/dam/kpmg/in/pdf/2017/05/Online-Education-in-India-2021.pdf.

Kumar, V., & Nanda, P. (2019). Social media in higher education: A framework for continuous engagement. *International Journal of Information and Communication Technology Education (IJICTE), 15*(1), 109–120.

Kumar, V., & Nanda, P. (2020). Social media as a tool in higher education: A pedagogical perspective. In *Handbook of research on diverse teaching strategies for the technology-rich classroom* (pp. 239–253). IGI Global.

Kumar, V., & Sharma, D. (2016). Creating collaborative and convenient learning environment using cloud-based moodle LMS. *International Journal of Web-Based Learning and Teaching Technologies, 11*(1), 35–49.

Kumar, V., & Vidhyalakshmi, P. (2012). Cloud computing for business sustainability. *Asia- Pacific Journal of Management Research and Innovation, 8*(4), 461–474.

Lao, T., & Gonzales, C. (2005). Understanding online learning through a qualitative description of professors and students' experiences. *Journal of Technology and Teacher Education, 133*, 459–474.

LinkedIn. (2019). 2019 Workplace learning report. Retrieved September 15, 2020, from https://learning.linkedin.com/content/dam/me/business/en-us/amp/learning-solutions/images/workplace-learning-report-2019/pdf/workplace-learning-report-2019.pdf.

Lucas, S. (2013). How much employee turnover really costs you. Retrieved September 13, 2020, from www.inc.com/suzanne-lucas/why-employee-turnover-is-so-costly.html.

Mitra, G. (2020). How important are digital skills in the current scenario? Retrieved September 16, 2020, from www.expresscomputer.in/features/how-important-are-digital-skills-in-the-current-scenario/58618/.

Mittal, S., & Kumar, V. (2019). Study of knowledge management models and their relevance in organisations. *International Journal of Knowledge Management Studies, 10*(3), 322–335.

Natriello, G. (2005). Modest changes, revolutionary possibilities: Distance learning and the future of education. *Teachers College Record, 107*(8), 1885–1904.

Northrup, P.T. (2002). Online learners' preferences for interaction. *Quarterly Review of Distance Education, 32*, 219–226.

Oesch, T. (2016). IBM's $1 Billion Training Investment. Retrieved September 12, 2020, from https://trainingindustry.com/articles/it-and-technical-training/ibms-1-billion-training-investment/.

Organization for Economic Cooperation and Development. (2020). OECD Economic outlook, June 2020. Retrieved September 15, 2020, from www.oecd.org/economic-outlook/june-2020/.

Park, G., Johnson, H., Vath, R., Kubitskey, B., & Fishman, B. (2013). Examining the roles of the facilitator in online and face-to-face professional development contexts. *Journal of Technology and Teacher Education, 21*(2), 225–245

PricewaterhouseCoopers. (2019). 22nd annual global CEO survey. Retrieved September 14, 2020, from www.pwc.com/gx/en/ceo-survey/2019/report/pwc-22nd-annual-global-ceo-survey.pdf.

Probst, L., & Scharff, C. (2019). A roadmap for strategically upskilling staff. Retrieved September 16, 2020, from www.digitalpulse.pwc.com.au/strategic-upskilling-staff/.

Selamat, M.H., Abdullah, R., & Paul, C.J. (2006). Knowledge management framework in a technology support environment. *International Journal of Computer Science and Network Security, 6*(8A), 101–109.

Sharma, D., & Kumar, V. (2017). A framework for collaborative and convenient learning on cloud computing platforms. *International Journal of Web-Based Learning and Teaching Technologies (IJWLTT), 12*(2), 1–20.

Shinkus, D. (2017). Your top employees are learning new skills on their own time. Here's what you should do. Retrieved September 15, 2020, from www.entrepreneur.com/article/296636.

Sytch, M., & Greer, L. (2020). Is your organization ready for permanent WFH? *Harvard Business Review.* Retrieved September 16, 2020, from https://hbr.org/2020/08/is-your-organization-ready-for-permanent-wfh.

Villepin, B., & Cook, T. (2020). Making the most out of MOOCs for business. Retrieved September 13, 2020, from www.digitalpulse.pwc.com.au/moocs-upskilling-motivating-employees/.

World Economic Forum. (2018). The future of jobs report 2018. Retrieved September 12, 2020, from www3.weforum.org/docs/WEF_Future_of_Jobs_2018.pdf.

Zeng, W.Y., & Perris, K. (2004). Researching the efficacy of online learning: A collaborative effort amongst scholars in Asian open universities. *Open Learning, 193*, 247–264.

12 Global Impact of COVID-19 on the Manufacturing Industry and Supply Chain Management

An Indian Perspective

Pravin Kumar and Anu Gupta

Introduction

In December 2019, an unknown pneumonia case was detected in Wuhan, China, and the possibility of influenza and other coronaviruses were ruled out by laboratory testing. But, on 7 January 2020, the Chinese authorities announced it as a new type of coronavirus, i.e. novel coronavirus (nCOV). Later, this virus was called COVID-19 by the Word Health Organization (WHO) (Sahin et al., 2020). Initially, it was communicated on social media that the coronavirus was developed in animals, as the Huanan is a big seafood market, where livestock animals are traded on a large scale. But the real facts about the growth and spread of the virus could not be identified. An increasing number of positive cases were caused by cross-infection, i.e. human-to-human transmission (Munster et al. 2020).

The nCOV outbreak spread all over the world, travel was banned, flights were stopped, general demand reduced, and the travel industry experienced a complete shutdown. Dahl et al. (2020) observed a decline in the market from 15 to 25% during the first quarter of the year 2020. Many countries imposed restrictions on travel, closing their borders or prohibiting travelers from select countries (Antonia, 2020). Initially, India banned entry from the European Union, Turkey and the United Kingdom. All the international and domestic flights were canceled till 15 April 2020.

Haren and Simchi-Levi (2020) examined the current situation very closely and they opined that the supply chain disruption was due to COVID-19 and that the present disruption of supply chains may exist for a longer time. It may be characterized as the propagation of the nCOV virus in the huge world population, unpredictable scaling and simultaneous disruptions in supply, demand and logistics infrastructure.

Most of the global manufacturing industries are interlinked with China in terms of the supply of raw materials, component manufacturing and marketing of the finished goods. The entire supply chains in the

DOI: 10.4324/9781003125648-12

world were disrupted. The failure of the global supply chains adversely affected the production and supply of the required products like face masks, medical kits, ventilators etc. (Ahani and Nilashi, 2020). The risks in supply chains were multifaceted and can be explained as operational and disruption risks (Xu et al., 2020; Choi et al., 2019; Ivanov, 2018; Govindan et al., 2017). Operational risks are concerned with the daily operations of the supply chain such as lead time variations and demand fluctuations. Similarly, the disruption risks are concerned with the events which occur less frequently but with high impact (Kinra et al., 2019; Hosseini et al., 2019).

We have not only lost the lives of a huge number of people but we are also facing an economic slowdown which had been continuing for the last 2–3 years before the pandemic outbreak of COVID-19. It is suspected that the COVID-19 virus was developed in the laboratory of Wuhan Institute of Virology, China. Regardless of the effort, the exact source and causes of outbreaks of the infections are not obvious yet (Wu et al., 2020). Total coronavirus cases had increased to 62,573,188 and deaths to 1,458,305 up to 29 November 2020. The United States is the worst sufferer of coronavirus, with the total number of positive cases 13,610,357 and total deaths 272,254 (Worldometer, 2020). The president of the United States demanded the WHO to allow an American team into Wuhan to investigate the origins of the novel coronavirus. China refused the investigation and said that "the virus is a common enemy of mankind. It may appear at any time anywhere in the world. China is a victim instead of the culprit" (Livemint, 2020).

At the same time, China not only refused the investigation demanded by the US president but also started to divert attention from COVID-19 by creating border issues with neighboring countries in the South China sea and in Ladakh, India, on the line of actual control (LAC). However, the border conflict of India with China has been going on since 1962 but for the last 40–45 years no casualty has been reported except in the Galwan valley clash on the night of 15/16 June 2020. In the past few months, China not only clashed with India in one of the worst border flare-ups in decades, but also escalated standoffs with Vietnam and Malaysia in the South China Sea, pressured Taiwan with nighttime drills in the Taiwan Strait, and threatened Australia with boycotts of wine, beef, barley and Chinese students. Many countries like India, Japan, Malaysia and Australia came closer and decided to reduce their economic ties with Beijing. Many companies started to explore new locations and shift their manufacturing facilities from the Chinese mainland (Ford and Gewirtz 2020). The excessive ambitions of China to become the world's super economic and political power triggered new geopolitical equations in Asia. An informal strategic forum named QSD (Quadrilateral Security Dialogue) has been formed whose aim it to conduct semi-regular summits, exchange information and conduct military drills between the member countries. They can use each other's military bases to counter the threats from China. Thus, the COVID-19 crisis is likely to be remaking the geopolitics of the Indo-Pacific region (CNN, 2020).

We are also facing supply chain disruption due to the pandemic outbreaks of nCOV. The present disruption of supply chains can be characterized as the existence of disruptions for a longer time, pandemic outbreak propagation of the virus in the huge world population and long-term existence of disruption and its unpredictable scaling, and simultaneous disruptions in supply, demand and logistics infrastructure. Unlike other disruption risks, the epidemic/pandemic outbreaks start from a small area, but scale fast and disperse over many geographic regions or throughout the world. We are observing the increasing disrupting of supply and manufacturing due to outbreaks of nCOV in more than 200 countries of the world.

The crisis is very similar to SARS, MERS, Ebola and swine flu, but nCOV outbreaks have affected most of the countries severely. The COVID-19 outbreak started in Wuhan, China, and disrupted the Chinese exports and global supply chains. Linton and Vakil (2020) reported the disruption of most of the large supply chains and shutdown of the industries in the COVID-19 quarantine areas. COVID -19 disrupted both the demand and supply of the goods. In the field of manufacturing, many countries are dependent on China for a large number of products, supplies of which were completely disrupted.

The pandemic outbreak of COVID-19 became the triggering point to reshape the geopolitics in the Indo-pacific region. China had been considered as the global supplier of medical equipment and medicine. Due to the disruption of the global supply chain and cross-border movements, China could not supply the necessary items during the time of crisis. Besides, China started border conflicts with all the neighboring countries like India, Taiwan, Malaysia, Indonesia, Vietnam, Japan, South Korea, etc. The rival countries of China came closer. The old trade war between China and the United States leads to the shifting of manufacturing companies from China to other South-Asian countries. The Japanese government has provided $2.2 billion to its companies shifting from China. Thus COVID-19 became a blessing in disguise for all the South-Asian countries willing to become manufacturing hubs. The main objectives of the study are:

- a To analyze the impact of COVID-19 on Make in India initiatives and Atam Nirbhar Bharat of the Indian government.
- b To compare the business environment in India with other peer countries like Thailand, Vietnam, Malaysia and Taiwan.
- c To explore the opportunity of foreign investment in Indian manufacturing and the pharmaceutical sector.
- d To highlight the change in trade policy to make it more flexible and favorable to the foreign investors.
- e To find the impact of COVID-19 on supply chain management.

The rest of the chapter has been arranged as follows: the second section explores the SWOT (Strength, Weakness, Opportunity and Threats) analysis of the Indian manufacturing sector. The third section presents the geopolitical scenario post-COVID-19. The fourth section compares India with its peer countries. The fifth section represents the impact of COVID-19 on global supply chains. The sixth section discusses the initiative taken by the government of India and the seventh section presents the suggestions made to make the supply chains more resilient. The eighth section concludes the study and makes some recommendations.

SWOT Analysis of the Indian Manufacturing Sector

The Indian economy is continuously growing and it has become the fifth-largest economy of the world. The infrastructure has been developing in terms of logistics facilities, land availability, electricity production and providing a favorable business environment for foreign investment. The contribution of the manufacturing sector to the Indian GDP is 20% and 50% of this contribution is from the automobile sector. The growth of electronics manufacturing has increased from 1.3% in 2012 to 3% in 2018. The export of electronic goods has increased from Rs. 38,263 crores in 2014–15 to Rs. 61,908 crores in 2018–19 (The Economic Times, 2020). The micro, small and medium enterprises (MSME) in India are the second-largest employment sector after agriculture. Approximately 80 million people are employed in MSMEs and their contribution is 8% of the country's GDP. India has emerged as the second-largest mobile phone manufacturer (11% in 2018) in the world (Mittal & Kumar, 2020). The Indian pharmaceutical sector produces 20% of the world's drug production by volume. The size of the Indian pharma sector is approx. Rs. 3.5 lakh crores and exports are 1.2 lakh crores. The above information shows that the Indian manufacturing sector is continuously growing and is a great investment opportunity. The overall business environment in India has been presented in the form of SWOT analysis in the following subsection.

Strength

- India has a population of 1.3 billion, which leads to a large domestic market. It is estimated that if a company sells its product to only 5% of the population of India, it will be more than the total population of many single countries in Europe.
- India has a large pool of more skilled and cheaper laborers than China as it is the second most highly populated country in the world and availability of the workers is more than the demand.
- The Indian government has implemented GST (Goods and Services Tax) in place of many taxes. It becomes easier for companies to pay their taxes as a single tax.

- India has a democratic political structure and it is one of the largest democracies in the world. The democratic structure leads to ease of adoption for many Western companies.
- India is the fifth largest economy in the world.
- India's manufacturing industries are continuously growing at a rate of 8% per year.
- The Indian government has lifted 217 million people out of poverty in the last 10 years (UNDP 2019) and is continuously making efforts for a better life for the people.

Weakness

- India has relatively poor infrastructure and slow growth.
- It has complex business procedures (to start manufacturing in India, companies have to go through 12 procedures and it takes approx. 27 days) compared to Vietnam (only eight procedures to start a new business and it requires less time).
- The Indian currency is more volatile because it is free-floating, compared to Vietnamese currency which is pegged to the US dollar.
- In India, land acquisition becomes a political issue for the opposition. Now the government has identified 460,000 acres for the companies shifting from China.
- Corruption, red tape and labor laws are some major issues. The Indian government is continuously reforming the laws in favor of companies.

Opportunity

- The US-China trade war has accelerated the shifting of foreign production out of China and it is a great opportunity for India to attract these companies for investment in India.
- The "where will they go index" shows Thailand, Malaysia, Vietnam, Taiwan and India are likely to benefit from the production relocation activities.
- Decline in the working-age population in China and increasing labor cost in China. The increasing labor cost in China and the approx. half wage rate of a laborer in India is an attraction for foreign companies (India: average $70 to $200 labor/month; China: average $140 to $340 labor/month).
- India has declared a very low corporate tax (cut down from 30% to 22% for the old and existing companies and new manufacturers 15% from 25%).
- Recently, Japan has provided $2.2 billion to its companies to move out of China. India may be the new location for many companies.

Threats

- India faces tough competition from peers like Thailand, Vietnam, Malaysia, Indonesia and Taiwan as these countries have a better "where will they go" index position than India.
- Vietnam and Thailand are major threats for India in terms of attracting Chinese companies. These countries are geographically very close to China and shifting of the entire supply chain is not required. If a company shifts to India, they will have to develop the complete supply chain in India due to geographical as well as political reasons.
- South-East Asian countries and Japan are the first preference for most Japanese companies.
- The imposition of tax by the Trump administration on the American companies shifting elsewhere other than the USA is a major threat for the American companies willing to shift to India.
- Mexico is one of the important choices of American companies and is very close to the USA.

Geopolitical Scenario

China has been known as the manufacturing house of the world. Most countries are dependent on China for most goods and services. The Chinese economy is growing continuously at a fast rate. The United States used to import goods from China to a value of $500 billion whereas China imports goods of only $100 billion from the United States. Thus, due to the unbalanced trade policy of China, the US president imposed a 10% tariff on Chinese goods (Giesbergen et al., 2019) and recently it has been increased to 25%. China's foreign policy is very aggressive as it has border issues with all the 14 countries touching the Chinese border. The expansion policy of China has brought many South-Asian countries closer to each other. The Chinese president tried to take advantage of the pandemic crisis. China's Belt and Road Initiatives (BRI) is one of their over-ambitious projects to control the entire world through its trade and expansion policy.

After the end of the cold war between the United States and the Soviet Union, the United States had been enjoying a unipolar world. Now, China has become a big threat to the United States. It has also been said that the coronavirus was developed in the laboratory of the Wuhan Institute of Virology and intentionally spread in Wuhan city where most of the foreign companies have business operations.

China wants to capture the entire South China Sea as it holds about 190 trillion cubic feet of natural gas and 11 billion barrels of oil in proved and probable reserves (as per the estimates of the US Energy Information Agency.) China wants to restrict movements for most of the countries in the South China Sea and capture the islands and regions of the other

South-Asian countries. This is a major reason for the dispute (Asiatimes, 2020). Also, due to this rivalry between China and the US, it has been suspected that some Chinese companies are illegally involved in spy-related activities. Recently, the US banned Huawei for spying on the American network and India banned 59 mobile applications including TikTok. India has reformed its foreign investment policy and made a provision of Government permission as mandatory for the neighboring countries for investment in Indian companies. China does not obey the IPR (Intellectual Property Right) rigorously. China is one of the countries that have been heavily criticized by Western countries, especially the United States, for failing to enforce intellectual property protection (Li, 2003). This is another reason that many companies are planning to shift their manufacturing plant to other locations. China has been claiming the territory of many countries including Russia. Some of the countries have already imposed a ban on many Chinese products, including India, USA, Japan, etc.

Comparative Analysis of India with other Asian Countries

Many indexing techniques are available in the literature that have been used for comparing the performance regarding the business activities of the different countries in the world. Some indexing techniques are used for comparing the suitability indices for investment. Table 12.1 shows the ease of doing business ranking of the top 10 countries of the world including some peers of India. This ranking is provided by Macrobond, World Bank (Rabobank, 2019). In 2019, India had 63rd rank regarding the ease of doing business. It has improved from 2018 (77th rank) to 2019 (63rd rank). New Zealand is at the top of the ranking. In this ranking, Vietnam lies below India in 70th rank.

Similarly, the World Economic Forum (2019) has provided a Global Competitive Index 4.0, 2019 which is shown in Table12.2. The Global Competitive Index (GCI) is based on 12 pillars: these are Institutions; Infrastructure; ICT adoption; Macroeconomic stability; Health; Skills;

Table 12.1 Ease of doing business ranking

As of May	*2019*	*2018*	*As of May*	*2019*	*2018*
New Zealand	1	1	Norway	9	7
Singapore	2	2	Sweden	10	12
Hong Kong	3	4	China	31	46
Denmark	4	3	India	63	77
S. Korea	5	5	Russia	28	31
United States	6	8	Brazil	124	109
Georgia	7	6	Vietnam	70	69
U.K	8	9	Philippines	95	124

Table 12.2 The Global Competitiveness Index 4.0 2019 rankings

Top 10 countries	*GCI (score)*	*Country (South-Asian region)*	*GCI (score)*
Singapore	1 (84.8)	Taiwan	12 (80.2)
United States	2 (83.7)	Malaysia	27 (74.6)
Hong Kong SAR	3 (83.1)	China	28 (73.9)
Netherlands	4 (82.4)	Thailand	40 (68.1)
Switzerland	5 (82.3)	Indonesia	50 (64.6)
Japan	6 (82.3)	Mauritius	52 (64.3)
Germany	7 (81.8)	Vietnam	67 (61.5)
Sweden	8 (81.2)	**India**	**68 (61.4)**
United Kingdom	9 (81.2)	Sri Lanka	84 (57.1)
Denmark	10 (81.2)	Bangladesh	106 (52.1)
		Pakistan	110 (51.4)

Table 12.3 Production capacity in China might move to the country preference list

Country	*Where will they go (index)*
Thailand	0.62
Malaysia	0.61
Vietnam	0.60
Taiwan	0.55
India	0.31
Singapore	0.30
Philippines	0.18
South Korea	0.17
Indonesia	0.17

Product market; Labor market; Financial system; Market size; Business dynamism; and Innovation capability. In this indexing system, Singapore is at the top with a score of 84.8 and India is in 68th rank with a score of 61.4. Taiwan, Malaysia, China, Thailand, Indonesia, Mauritius and Vietnam lie above India.

Table 12.3 shows the option for the companies shifting from China, with the "where will they go" (WWTG) index (Rabobank 2019). This ranking shows the suitability of the countries for investment or shifting of the production facility to South-Asian countries. The WWTG index is prepared from the four parameters: export similarity, institutional quality, wages, and ease of doing business, as shown in Table 12.4. In this table, all the four parameters are shown with standard normal distribution with individual z-scores (Rabobank, 2019). Regarding the export similarity, Indonesia has a zero z-value and India has a 0.4 z-score but regarding institutional quality, India has a negative z-score of –0.1 whereas South Korea, Taiwan, Japan and Singapore have positive

Table 12.4 Z-score of WWTG index

Country	*Export similarity*	*Institutional quality*	*Wages*	*Ease of doing business*
Vietnam	1.5	−0.3	0.5	0.4
Thailand	1.3	−0.3	0.2	1.2
South Korea	0.9	0.8	−2	1.6
Taiwan	0.8	1.1	−0.7	1.4
Japan	0.7	1.4	−2.4	1
Malaysia	0.7	0.3	0.2	1.3
Philippines	0.6	−0.3	0.5	−0.4
India	0.4	−0.1	0.5	0.3
Singapore	0.3	1.6	−1.5	1.7
Indonesia	0	−0.2	0.4	0.4
Sri Lanka	−0.7	−0.1	0.6	−0.1
Laos	−0.8	−0.7	0.6	−0.9
Cambodia	−0.8	−0.7	0.6	−0.6
Pakistan	−0.9	−1	0.5	−0.6
Myanmar	−1.1	−0.9	0.6	−1.4
Bangladesh	−1.2	−0.8	0.6	−1.6
Mongolia	−1.9	0	0.8	0.4

z-scores of 0.8, 1.1, 1.4, 1.6 respectively. Regarding wages, India has a positive z-score of 0.5. Regarding ease of doing business, India has a 0.3 z-score whereas Taiwan, Japan, Vietnam, Malaysia, Indonesia, South Korea and Singapore have better z-scores than India.

The Rabobank (2019) report presented the similarity of export items (in percentage) of different countries with China. India has only 36% similarity with Chinese export items whereas Vietnam, Thailand, South Korea, Taiwan, Japan, Malaysia and Philippines have 50%, 48%, 42%, 41%, 40%, 39% and 38% similarity respectively.

Based on the various indexing, it is observed that it is very difficult to attract companies in India. India has tough competition with Taiwan, Vietnam, Thailand, Malaysia, Indonesia, Singapore, South Korea and Japan. India will have to make more effort to improve the business environment, administration, labor laws, trade rules and regulations so that the companies can do business easily. But India has one of the strong points of a huge domestic market which is not available to most of the countries. The government of India is continuously making efforts to attract companies to invest in India and they have already started the movement for "Make in India" and "Atama Nirbhar Bharat".

Impact of COVID-19 on Supply Chain Management

The impact of the spread of the COVID-19 on demand and supply of relief materials for the people working in different sectors in India can be explained through Figure 12.1. Due to supply chain disruption and

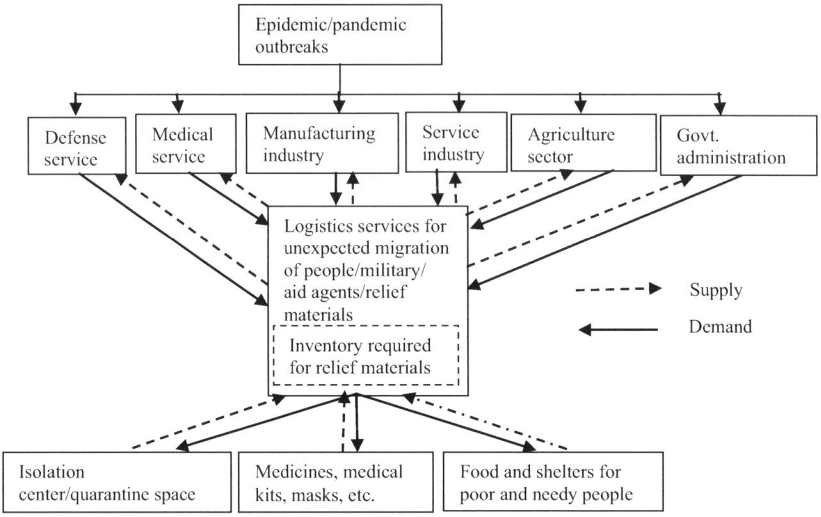

Figure 12.1 A framework for linkage of supply of relief materials to the people engaged in different sectors.

complete lockdown, the logistics services were also disturbed, which connects the various organizations with the suppliers, distributors and producers.

A large section of the Indian workers work in the unorganized sectors and the main challenge was to send the relief materials, shelters and medical facilities to these people. Also, all the doctors, nurses and hospitals were devoted to COVID-19 treatment and most of the regular patients were suffering and not getting proper treatment. Many security forces were deployed for searching for positive cases and sending them to isolation centers for treatment. The doctors, nurses and security forces were not equipped with effective safety gear, medical kits or coveralls in all the hospitals. Most of the people engaged in the agriculture sector live in rural areas where poor logistics and medical infrastructure became the major challenge. Most of the government offices were closed due to the lockdown. The volunteers were afraid of the infectious disease. Besides these challenges, the government of India has taken many appreciable initiatives to face the crisis.

It has also been observed that due to the infectious nature of the COVID-19, a smaller number of aid agents and NGOs were willing to work in the relief operation. In another type of disaster like earthquake, flood or terrorist attack, a large number of NGOs and social agents start to help the needy people immediately. But in the case of this pandemic outbreak, very few people were interested in working due to the lack of personal protective equipment during the initial stage of COVID-19. No private transporters, except some airline companies, were ready to send laborers to the nearest places of respective native places. However, there was another complication in the migration of a huge number of workers from one state to another and the government stopped the movement. Supply chains were completely disrupted. No delivery man was available to deliver the items door-to-door due to lack of sanitization of the vehicles and PPEs. Some of the common observations in disruption in supply chains are discussed below.

***High production and distribution cost*:** Lockdown during the COVID-19 period affected most of the supply chain activities. Due to transport restrictions, migration of workers and maintaining the social distancing, the production and distribution of the necessary items became very difficult and both production and distribution time and cost increased. Extending the "key workers" designation to workers involved in all aspects of food supply chains can help mitigate disruptions due to movement and travel restrictions (Hobbs, 2020).

***Lack of trust in international trade*:** To ensure the availability of food products in the domestic markets, countries impose export restriction for the short term, which may result in a price drop and hence a major loss to the manufacturers. The second major loss is the loss of reputation of the exporters in the international markets due to disruption in export-import activities, thereby reducing trust in the international trade and a negative impact on the future business opportunities for the exporters (Espitia et al., 2020).

***Lack of response*:** During the first phase of the lockdown, it has been observed that there was lack of response at various points in the supply chain. Also, there was some mismatch between the state and central government in India regarding the policy related to the lockdown and its preparation. The central government was reactive whereas the state government was observing the situation and unable to take any initiatives regarding the prevention of pandemic spread, arrangement of food for poor people, shelter for the laborers and arrangement of transport facilities for the workers to return to their native places. Due to the lack of response and the flow of information, people started to store food items unnecessarily. A major crowd was observed in the market. The measure of the responsiveness concerned with the effectiveness of product management includes customer response time, fill rate, shipping errors, product lateness and consumer complaints (Persson & Olhager, 2002).

***Poor accessibility and availability*:** The accuracy, availability and accessibility of information and degree of information sharing are stressed in the literature as the dimensions to measure the degree of transparency within supply chains (Forslund & Jonsson, 2009).

***Transport restriction*:** Restrictions to control the spread of COVID-19 are causing delays and disruptions to logistics services. Border closures and additional procedures and checks have led to congestion and delays. Social distancing requirements have reduced the numbers of import and export inspectors at borders, increasing the time needed for customs clearance.

Import disruption: Port closures pose a problem too when product has to be diverted from one port to another or to a different importing country altogether. At the time the virus struck, large numbers of shipping containers were in Chinese ports, and restrictions on their movement have led to a shortage that has seen the price of containers rise in some cases considerably (OECD, 2020).

Migration of workers: Limits on the mobility of people and lockdowns are contributing to labor shortages for industrial as well as agricultural activities in many countries, particularly those characterized by periods of peak seasonal labor demand. A shortage of labor could lead to production losses and shortages in the market. In many countries, this comes on top of existing difficulties in sourcing seasonal labor (OECD, 2020).

Shift in consumer demands/behavior: A major shift in the structure of demand with a collapse in demand from restaurants, hotels and catering, the closure of open markets, and a surge in demand from supermarkets has been observed during the lockdown period. There are signs that businesses along the food chain are already adapting to shifts in demand, for example by switching production lines and increasing their capacity to manage larger inventories, moving to on-line platforms and direct delivery to households, and hiring temporary staff (OECD, 2020).

Government Initiatives for Make in India and Atam Nirbhar Bharat

The Indian government has declared a package of Rs. 20 lakh crores to boost the economy during the crisis. A package of Rs. 3 lakh crores is allocated for MSMEs. The package of 1 lakh crore is specially allocated for the salary of workers in MSMEs. A package of Rs. 2,500 crores is allocated for EPF for those companies with less than 100 workers and with 90% of their workers on a salary of less than Rs. 15,000/month. Small projects of Rs. 200 crores have been decided to be given only to Indian companies (i.e. the companies doing business in India). Beyond the above investment in MSMEs, the government of India has taken the following initiatives:

- Rs. 1 lakh crore for the agriculture sector for infrastructure development.
- Investment of Rs. 50,000 crores in the coal industry to increase the production (having 7% coal reserve of the world).
- Approved the investment of Rs. 130 billion in pharma sector to cut down the dependency on China for medical equipment and medicines.
- Prioritizing its focus on medical equipment, food processing units, textiles, automobile parts and electronics among 550 other products.

- Plan to develop complete supply chains and self-dependency and Atam Nirbhar Bharat.
- Identified nearly 460,000 acres of land across the country for the facilities of manufacturing companies.
- Changing the labor rule in favor of the companies.
- India is in contact with 1,000 companies moving out of China. Reserve Bank of India has reduced the interest rate so that start-up companies can do the business easily.
- Lowering the corporate tax for the new companies.
- India may amend and review its other policies in future in favor of the companies.

Recommendation for Effective Supply Chains

Considering all the observations as mentioned in the previous sections, we can analyze that even with great success in preventing the fast spread of COVID-19 in India, many things are to be improved in future. This may be concerned with the medical research and production of medical equipment, humanitarian supply chain management, multiple sourcing, and make to stock strategy. Some of the major learnings are discussed below:

Balancing the local and global sourcing: During the complete lockdown period, most of the global supply chains were disrupted. Nowadays, most of the global manufacturing and service organizations are integrated with Chinese organizations. For example, there were acute shortages of masks, PPEs and ventilators. In this situation, alternative local suppliers could be used for supply of these items. Local suppliers are to be preferred and developed for such items. In the USA, the hospital workers in Washington State had no option other than producing the protective medical gear themselves due to a severe shortage of equipment needed to care for COVID-19 patients.

Preference for multiple sourcing: To meet the market competition in the global market, a strategic relationship with the single supplier is given more importance. But, from the COVID-19 crisis, we observed the importance of multiple sourcing to continue the supply of the required items uninterrupted. We must have the alternate source of supply of at least a few necessary items like medicines, medical equipment, food items, etc.

Preference to make to stock for relief items: The sufficient inventory must be maintained for some necessary relief items. During the crisis all the production activities were stopped. Labor was not available. Thus, a make to order policy for these items is not successful. We can observe that most of the state health workers and hospitals had not sufficient amount of PPEs, medicines, face masks, etc. If inventory of these items is maintained, the shortage can be avoided.

Use of information and communication technology: Use of information and communication technology, digitization of the business activities may reduce the burden of the service providers during the crisis (Saurabh & Kumar, 2017). The people can get the same facility online and can work from home. Industry 4.0 may be used for the supply chains, humanitarian organizations, industries, etc. There should be connectivity between all the rural and urban people through the Internet facility.

***Addressing safety and labor constraints*:** Industry must be directed to provide the shelter, food, and medical facilities to the daily wage/contract workers during the health crisis. Also, there should be a quarantine facility for the workers infected by the viral disease. Using the PPEs, face masks and maintaining the social distancing the production can be continued despite the health emergency situation. This will help in reducing the financial as well as production losses. To avoid the shut down some actions may be recommended such as keeping all large meetings virtual, restricting outside and third parties visitors, flexibility to work from home, enabling the virtual communication and collaboration tool, frequent sanitization of offices and workplaces, quarantine the employee who visited the affected area, distributing the care packages to all employees, thermal scanning of the employees at the entrance of the building/premises, and temporary closing the production sites in highly affected areas.

To minimize the supply chain disruption, searching the supplies from unaffected areas and use of the alternate routes, digitization of the process and tools for resource planning including demand and supply, collaboration with all parties to jointly leverage freight capacity etc. may be used. According to Bellini (2020), resilience should be the inherent property of a supply chain so that the collaborative networks can enact as a team when there is disruption.

Conclusion

In this study, we have observed the series of effects of COVID-19 on the geopolitics in the Asia Pacific region and the impact of the change in geopolitics and pandemic outbreak of COVID-19 on the manufacturing industry and global supply chain. Most of the countries have already faced the scarcity of life-saving items such as face masks, PPE kit, ventilators, medicine during the pandemic and lost the lives of their people due to the dependency on a single country like China and disruption of the global supply chain. The major learning from the crisis is that we should not be dependent on a single source for the life-saving items. We must develop some alternate source of supply including local sourcing. A large number of countries with low labor cost and ease of doing business are there. The company should invest in a distributed manner as learning from the global political and pandemic crisis in China. Due to sourcing from a single country, the labor cost and infrastructure cost start to increase during the time. Also, in the global supply chain, multiple sourcing is proved to be a better option in place of single sourcing. Due to the conflict with China, all the South-Asian countries have the opportunity to get foreign companies for the investment. Now, it is very difficult to attract all the shifting companies from China to only one location. As per the index developed for ease of doing business many countries may be considered as a new location. Including the USA many countries are facing the unemployment problem and are willing to get investment.

References

Ahani, A., & Nilashi, M. (2020). Coronavirus outbreak and its impacts on global economy: the role of social network sites. *Journal of Soft Computing and Decision Support Systems*, 7(2), 19–22.

Antonia, W. (2020). Coronavirus travel updates: Which countries have restrictions and FCO warningsin place? www.theguardian.com/travel/2020/mar/24/coronavirus-travel-updates-which- countries-have-restrictions-and-fco-warnings-in-place (accessed 19 March 2020).

Asiatimes. (July 22, 2020). Oil and gas fueling South China Sea tensions. https://asiatimes.com/2020/07/oil-and-gas-fueling-south-china-sea-tensions/. Retrieved on 24/8/2020.

Bellini, J. (2020). Global disruption due to covid-19 removes decades of supply chain inertia –now what? https://supplychainbeyond.com/coronavirus-covid-19-disrupts-global-supply-chains/ (accessed 6 March 2020).

Choi, T.M., Wen, X., Sun, X., & Chung, S.H. (2019). The mean-variance approach for global supply chain risk analysis with air logistics in the blockchain technology era. *Transportation Research Part E: Logistics and Transportation Review*, *127*, 178–191.

CNN. (2020). A border dispute with China may push India closer to some of Beijing's top rivals. https://edition.cnn.com/2020/06/18/asia/china-india-border-dispute-quad-us-intl-hnk/index.html. Retrieved on 28/8/2020.

Dahl, J., Dhar, S., Katsuki, F., & Kaushik, V. (2020). Wealth management in Asia: Navigating the impact of coronavirus. www.mckinsey.com/industries/financial-services/our-insights/wealth-management-in-asia-navigating-the-impact-of-coronavirus. Retrieved on 15/03/2020.

Espitia, A., Rocha, N., & Ruta, M. (2020). Covid-19 and food protectionism: The impact of the pandemic and export restrictions on world food markets. Policy Research Working Paper No. 9253. Washington DC: World Bank.

Ford, W.L., & and Gewirtz, J. (2020). China's post-Coronavirus aggression is reshaping Asia. https://foreignpolicy.com/2020/06/18/china-india-aggression-asia-alliances/. Retrieved on 24/08/2020.

Forslund, H., & Jonsson, P. (2009). Obstacles to supply chain integration of the performance management process in buyer-supplier dyads. *International Journal of Operations & Production Management*, *29*(1), 77–95.

Giesbergen, B.J.C., de Groot, E., & Every, M. (2019). US-China trade war update: No turning back. Rabobank.

Govindan, K., Fattahi, M., & Keyvanshokooh, E. (2017). Supply chain network design under uncertainty: A comprehensive review and future research directions. *European Journal of Operational Research*, *263*(1), 108–141.

Haren, P., & Simchi-Levi, D. (2020). How coronavirus could impact the global supply chain by mid-March. https://hbr.org/2020/02/how-coronavirus-could-impact-the-global-supply-chain-by-mid-march (accessed 28 March 2020).

Hobbs, J.E. (2020). Food supply chains during the COVID-19 pandemic. *Canadian Journal of Agricultural Economics/Revue canadienne d'agroeconomie*. DOI: 10.1111/cjag.12237.

Hosseini, S., Ivanov, D., & Dolgui, A. (2019). Review of quantitative methods for supply chain resilience analysis. *Transportation Research Part E: Logistics and Transportation Review, 125*, 285–307.

Ivanov, D. (2018). Revealing interfaces of supply chain resilience and sustainability: a simulation study. *International Journal of Production Research, 56*(10), 3507–3523.

Kinra, A., Ivanov, D., Das, A., & Dolgui, A. (2019). Ripple effect quantification by supplier risk exposure assessment. *International Journal of Production Research, 58*(18), 5559–5578.

Li, L. (2003). The sky is high and the emperor is far way: The enforcement of intellectual property law in China. www.scielo.org.mx/scielo.php?script=sci_arttext&pid=S0041-86332003000300007. Retrieved on 26/08/2020.

Linton, T., & Vakil, B. (2020). Coronavirus is proving we need more resilient supply chains. Harward business review, March 5, 2020. https://hbr.org/2020/03/coronavirus-is-proving-that-we-need-more-resilient-supply-chains (accessed 10 March 2020).

Livemint. (20 April, 2020). China rejects Donald Trump's demand to allow US team to Wuhan to probe coronavirus. www.livemint.com/news/world/china-rejects-donald-trump-s-demand-to-allow-us-team-to-wuhan-to-probe-coronavirus-11587383543120.html. Retrieved on 28/08/2020.

Mittal, S., & Kumar, V. (2020). A framework for ethical mobile marketing. *International Journal of Technoethics (IJT), 11*(1), 28–42.

Munster, V.J., Koopmans, M., van Doremalen, N., van Riel, D., & de Wit, E. (2020). A novel coronavirus emerging in China—key questions for impact assessment. *New England Journal of Medicine, 382*(8), 692–694.

OECD. (April 29, 2020). COVID-19 and the food and agriculture sector: Issues and policy responses. www.oecd.org/coronavirus/policy-responses/covid-19-and-the-food-and-agriculture-sector-issues-and-policy-responses-a23f764b/.

Persson, F., & Olhager, J. (2002). Performance simulation of supply chain designs. *International Journal of Production Economics, 77*(3), 231–245.

Rabobank. (August 8, 2019). Leaving China: Which countries might benefit from a relocation of production? https://economics.rabobank.com/publications/2019/august/leaving-china-countries-might-benefit-from-relocation-production/. Retrieved on 10/05/2020.

Sahin, A.R., Erdogan, A., Agaoglu, P.M., Dineri, Y., Cakirci, A.Y., Senel, M.E., ... Tasdogan, A.M. (2020). 2019 novel coronavirus (COVID-19) outbreak: a review of the current literature. *EJMO, 4*(1), 1–7.

Saurabh & Kumar, V. (2017). Technology integration for the success of B2C M-commerce in India: Opportunities and challenges. *IUP Journal of Information Technology, 13*(1), 24–35

The Economic Times. (June 3, 2020). India unveils Rs 50,000 crore schemes to attract electronics makers. https://economictimes.indiatimes.com/tech/hardware/govt-starts-inviting-application-for-rs-50000-cr-electronic-incentive-schemes/articleshow/76153644.cms?from=mdr.. Retrieved on 04/06/2020.

UNDP. (2019). Report: India lifted 271 million people out of poverty in a decade. www.forbes.com/sites/niallmccarthy/2019/07/12/report-india-lifted-271-million-people-out-of-poverty-in-a-decade-infographic/#65437c662284. Retrieved on 30/08/2020.

World Economic Forum. (2019). The global competitiveness report. www3.weforum.org/docs/WEF_TheGlobalCompetitivenessReport2019.pdf. Retrieved on 30/8/2020.

Worldometer. (November 29, 2020). Covid-19 Corona virus pandemic. www.worldometers.info/coronavirus/.

Wu, F., Zhao, S., Yu, B., Chen, Y.M., Wang, W., Song, Z.G., ... Yuan, M.L. (2020). A new coronavirus associated with human respiratory disease in China. *Nature, 579*(7798), 265–269.

Xu, S., Zhang, X., Feng, L., & Yang, W. (2020). Disruption risks in supply chain management: a literature review based on bibliometric analysis. *International Journal of Production Research, 58*(11), 3508–3526.

Index

Made in the USA
Las Vegas, NV
24 October 2024

1fd50374-4fba-4c8d-8909-84e73cbe1ae8R01